© Tao Ruspuli

ANDREW COCKBURN is the Washington editor of *Harper's* magazine and the author of many articles and books on national security, including the *New York Times* Editor's Choice *Rumsfeld* and *The Threat,* which destroyed the myth of Soviet military superiority underpinning the Cold War. He is a regular opinion contributor to the *Los Angeles Times* and has written for, among others, *The New York Times, National Geographic,* and the *London Review of Books.*

## ALSO BY ANDREW COCKBURN

*Rumsfeld: His Rise, Fall, and Catastrophic Legacy*
*The Threat: Inside the Soviet Military Machine*

Additional Praise for *Kill Chain*

"A thorough and fascinating look at American targeted killing."
—Alex de Waal, *Boston Review*

"*Kill Chain: The Rise of the High-Tech Assassins*, by *Harper's* journalist Andrew Cockburn, should be required reading. . . . captivating, terrifying . . . Cockburn expertly describes the era we've made, the one we're stuck with until we change our ways, the era of high-tech, self-defeating assassins."
—David Axe, *War is Boring*

"Cockburn is a crackerjack writer. . . . He draws a high-resolution picture of vested interests (kickbacks, egos, along with Raytheon, Lockheed, Northrop, Hughes, General Dynamics, Booz Allen, and company), leading us down the garden path to the seventy-two virgins. The tools don't work—on many levels, drones cut 'a wide and indiscriminate swath through local society'—and the military's strategy is a failure."
—Peter Lewis, *The Christian Science Monitor*

"Sharp-eyed and disturbing, especially Cockburn's concluding assessment that, nourished by an unending flow of money, 'the assassination machine is here to stay.'"
—*Kirkus Reviews*

"Cockburn, Washington editor for *Harper's,* delivers an unflattering critique of the U.S. military's reliance on advanced technology—from remote-controlled drones to databases to complex fighter planes—rather than on boots-on-the-ground presence and simpler, less expensive, often more manageable hardware. . . . A report that is both enlivening and terribly troubling."
—Alan Moores, *Booklist*

"[Describes] a program rooted in emotional button-pushing over the war on terror that was riddled with egos, overzealous commanders, dead civilians, and lucrative government contracts for a weapon whose performance was often less accurate than promised . . . The program and its effects—both intended and not—are ripe for a takedown, and Cockburn admirably explains the strategies, intentions, and emotions that continue to surround the program."

—*Publishers Weekly*

"Drones, or unmanned aerial vehicles (UAVs), have actually been around for several decades, but have gained notoriety in the past ten years for their use in attacking hard-to-reach, high-priority human targets. While this form of warfare undoubtedly saves some American lives and is easier to stage than sending in the troops, the civilian toll from the strikes seems to drive more people to oppose the United States. . . . An informative and easy-to-read book for those interested in this hot topic. Perhaps a drone will drop it off at your front door."

—*Library Journal* (starred review)

"Cockburn pulls back the camera to provide a wider historical perspective, setting the policy of targeted killing via drones within the larger context of the American military-industrial complex. From the repeated failures of the stealth bombing campaigns in the Kosovo and Vietnam wars, to the way in which the drug wars stepped in to perpetuate the security bureaucracy of the Cold War, Cockburn sees America's killer drone policy as the culmination of a historical pattern of lies, deception, and greed in the deployment of lethal military force around the world. . . . [In *Kill Chain*] Cockburn, the righteous political leftist, [carries] the torch of the antiwar crusade into current debates."

—*The Washington Post*

"Time will tell whether drones will finally meet the conditions that match their strengths (though that's to say nothing of the moral quandary that death delivered from a distance presents). Until then, Cockburn makes a strong case that drones have never done so in the past, despite great costs measured in foreign blood and American treasure."

—*Cicero Magazine*

"I was literally blown away by this book. . . . What makes Cockburn's book so powerful, in my opinion, is not only his sourcing and detail (which are amazing), but the fact that he has written a book that is at once overwhelming in terms of information, yet so well-written, it is accessible to the general reader. It is a page-turner."

—Chuck Spinney, *CounterPunch*

"*Kill Chain* is a fascinating book, its arguments filed to slice the fingers and shred the arguments of many who appear within it. This is rhetoric effectively weaponized to do the most damage to a little-debated policy consensus forged with little input from voters.... A revelatory, must-read account of drones and killing from the air."

—Joel Whitney, *San Francisco Chronicle*

"[An] exceedingly useful book ... makes a strong case that the results [of targeted assassination], whether achieved by relying on missile-firing drones or by employing commando raids, have been politically counterproductive and morally disastrous ... [Cockburn] possess[es] a Waugh-like aptitude for the English language."

—Andrew Bacevich, *Commonweal*

"In this first-rate history, Andrew Cockburn takes readers from the Pentagon's mainframe-driven dreams of the Vietnam War era through today's visions of stealth super-drones, exposing the dark realities of twenty-first-century robotic warfare. Richly informative, superbly researched, and utterly illuminating, *Kill Chain* shines much-needed light on the shadowy theories and theorists, secret military and intelligence programs, and classified technologies that spawned our current age of remote-controlled assassination."

—Nick Turse, author of
*Kill Anything That Moves*

"In this riveting book, Cockburn puts the reader in the pilot's seat as kill teams go on their deadly hunts before dashing home for their children's soccer games. Wrapped in enormous secrecy, the only way past the armed guards and cipher-locks and into this new world of Hellfire diplomacy is Cockburn's great new read. Rather than voter

IDs, people should prove they have read this book before being allowed to vote in the next election." —James Bamford, author of *The Shadow Factory: The NSA from 9/11 to the Eavesdropping on America*

"A compellingly readable book that not only tells us why drones cannot live up to the overblown expectation of politicians but lucidly explains the vulnerability of intelligence, either robotic or human, better than any book I have ever read." —Edward Jay Epstein, author of *Deception: The Invisible War Between the KGB and the CIA*

"This brilliant book tells us how computers kill soldiers and civilians and explains with bone-chilling clarity how generalship gave way to microchips from Vietnam to Afghanistan. A blood-curdling account of the rise of robot warfare, a great story, and a prophecy to be read and heeded." —Tim Weiner, author of *Legacy of Ashes: The History of the CIA*

# KILL CHAIN

# KILL CHAIN

---

### THE RISE OF

### THE HIGH-TECH

### ASSASSINS

---

## ANDREW COCKBURN

## WITH ILLUSTRATIONS BY DANIJEL ZEZELJ

Picador   Henry Holt and Company   New York

picadorusa.com • picadorbookroom.tumblr.com
twitter.com/picadorusa • facebook.com/picadorusa

Picador® is a U.S. registered trademark and is used by Henry Holt and Company under license from Pan Books Limited.

For book club information, please visit facebook.com/picadorbookclub or e-mail marketing@picadorusa.com.

Excerpt from "Damn, I'm a Gook" by Vincent Okamoto from *Patriots: The Vietnam War Remembered from All Sides* by Christian Appy, copyright © 2003 by Christian G. Appy. Used by permission of Viking Penguin, a division of Penguin Group (USA) LLC. Excerpt from *My Share of the Task: A Memoir* by General Stanley McChrystal, copyright © 2013 by Stanley McChrystal. Used by permission of Portfolio, an imprint of Penguin Group (USA) LLC.

Illustrations by Danijel Zezelj
Designed by Meryl Sussman Levavi

The Library of Congress has cataloged the Henry Holt edition as follows:

Cockburn, Andrew, 1947–
  Kill chain : the rise of the high-tech assassins / Andrew Cockburn.—First edition.
    p. cm.
  Includes bibliographical references and index.
  ISBN 978-0-8050-9926-3 (hardcover)
  ISBN 978-0-8050-9927-0 (e-book)
1. Drone aircraft—History.   2. Targeted killing—United States—History.   3. Drone aircraft—Moral and ethical aspects—United States.   4. History—Military—Weapons.
5. Political science—Political freedom & security—General.   6. Political science—Political freedom & security—international security.   7. History—Military—United States.   I. Title.
  UG1242.D7 C63 2015
  623.7469'0973dc23                                                    2014029340

Picador Paperback ISBN 978-1-250-08163-6

Our books may be purchased in bulk for promotional, educational, or business use. Please contact your local bookseller or the Macmillan Corporate and Premium Sales Department at 1-800-221-7945, extension 5442, or by e-mail at MacmillanSpecialMarkets@macmillan.com.

First published by Henry Holt and Company, LLC

First Picador Edition: March 2016

10  9  8  7  6  5  4  3  2  1

For Declan and Otis

# CONTENTS

# KILL CHAIN

# 1

# REMEMBER, KILL CHAIN

I n a cold February dawn in 2010, two small SUVs and a four-door
pickup truck headed down a dirt road in the mountains of southern Afghanistan. They had set out soon after midnight, traveling
cross-country to reach Highway 1, the country's principal paved road,
which would lead them to Kandahar and north to Kabul. Crammed
inside were more than thirty men, women, and children, four of them
younger than six. Everyone knew one another, for they all came from
the same cluster of mountain villages roughly two hundred miles south-
west of Kabul. Many of the men, unemployed and destitute, were on
their way to Iran in hopes of work. Others were shopkeepers heading
to the capital to buy supplies, or students returning to school. The
women carried turkeys, gifts for the relatives they would stay with in
Kabul. A number were Hazaras, an ethnic minority of Shia Muslims
whom the Taliban treated with unremitting cruelty whenever they had
the opportunity. Now they were in western Uruzgan Province, Taliban
country and therefore very dangerous for them, but they risked the
shortcut because they were short on gas.

They met no other cars and little foot traffic; the world around them must have seemed empty. But it was not. Unbeknownst to them, they were being watched and their every movement—even the warmth from their bodies—transmitted across the globe. As the ramshackle vehicles—one of them kept breaking down and another blew a tire—clattered along, people they would never meet conferred across oceans and continents as to who they were, where they were going, what they were carrying, and whether they should live or die.

Unwittingly, the little group was driving toward an Operational Detachment Alpha, a U.S. Special Forces patrol dropped in with a supporting force of Afghan soldiers soon after midnight to attack the nearby village of Khod. Such raids were routine in Afghanistan, planned and executed by the semimythic Special Operations Command that specializes in the pursuit and elimination of "high-value targets." Someone thought this operation important enough to give it the code name Operation Noble Justice.

**Sunday, February 21, 4:12 a.m.**

*Pilot of MQ-1 Predator, call sign Kirk 97: We are eyes on the first vehicle; observing to try and PID on the pax in the open; stand by for movement on the second.*

The 27-foot-long Predator drone was circling at 14,000 feet. Below its belly protruded a "sensor" ball carrying a variety of cameras, including an infrared video that picked up the warmth thrown off by the vehicles and passengers 2.5 miles below. Almost in an instant—but not quite—the images flashed across the world to twin screens inside a metal box roughly the size of a shipping container at Creech Air Force Base in the Nevada desert. Facing the screens sat "Kirk 97," a pilot guiding the drone by remote control. Beside him sat a sensor operator who guided the cameras and weapons-targeting laser. In another room nearby a third member of the crew, the mission intelligence coordinator, was watching the same video images.

The pictures had audiences elsewhere. Hurlburt Air Force Base in the Florida Panhandle is headquarters of Air Force Special Operations

Command and home to one station of the vast but little-known global network referred to as the Distributed Common Ground System (DCGS). This is the central nervous system funneling, collating, and sharing the unimaginable quantities of imagery and electronic information collected by air force drones and reconnaissance planes (ISR for Intelligence, Surveillance, and Reconnaissance) around the globe. In theory, anyone in any part of DCGS has access to any information that has been fed into the system, wherever they are.

Thus it was that the images captured by the Predator were being watched at Hurlburt by a dedicated team, a minibureaucracy of young men and women, each with specialized tasks. In overall charge was an intelligence tactical coordinator (ITC) supervising two "screeners." The chief screener, a civilian on contract from SAIC, a major defense corporation heavily involved in drone operations, outranked the second screener, a junior air force officer who happened to be her husband. Also present were two full-motion video analysts (FMVs). While one FMV watched the screen, the other typed "products," conclusions drawn from the imagery, which were then passed to the screeners for onward transmission via a system known as Internet Relay Chat to the mission intelligence coordinator sitting in his trailer in Nevada. A geospatial analyst tasked with generating relevant geographical information for the other analysts made up the complement.

The video had still more destinations. Special Operations, born in World War II as a term for agents sent behind enemy lines to train and lead friendly guerrillas, had by the twenty-first century ballooned into a 66,000-strong branch of the U.S. military, with an inevitably complex command arrangement. The little raiding party in Uruzgan that night was under the supervision of a Special Operations Task Force headquartered in Kandahar, which was naturally in receipt of the ubiquitous video, along with the written messages streaming back and forth between Nevada and Florida. Kandahar in turn answered to Combined Special Operations Task Force headquarters at Bagram, outside Kabul, where the video was also screening.

The ultimate beneficiary of all these complex arrangements was a sergeant attached to the raiding party. Known as a "joint terminal attack controller," he was responsible for communicating via radio with any and all air support, including the Predator, and relaying orders and intelligence to and from the young captain commanding the party. Calling himself Jaguar 25, the sergeant was the force's only link with the team in Nevada, which in turn was the sole link with the screeners in Florida.

Almost as soon as the raiding party disembarked from their helicopters shortly after midnight, someone out in the darkness had switched on a handheld radio and broadcast a general call to arms. "They are here," he said, "let us get all the Mujaheddin together and defend this place." It was a simple, uncomplicated exhortation addressed to no one in particular and audible to anyone with a radio, utterly unlike the assorted esoteric systems employed by the U.S. forces. Americans listening in were bemused by their enemy's unconcern for eavesdropping, and indeed the Taliban summons—if that was what it was—was overheard by a host of U.S. military intelligence posts on the ground and in the air. Accordingly the word was passed to look out for enemy reinforcements. Two vehicles in tandem, the pickup and one SUV, lumbering into the area easily fit that picture, and suspicions hardened when they and another SUV flashed lights at each other before continuing on together in the direction of the patrol as it waited for daylight.

**4:15 a.m.**

> *Mission intelligence coordinator: See if you can zoom in on that guy, 'cos he's like . . .*
>
> *Pilot: What did he just leave there? Is that a fucking rifle?*
>
> *Sensor: Maybe just a warm spot from where he's been sitting.*
>
> *Pilot: I was hoping we could make a rifle out. Never mind.*
>
> *Sensor: The only way I've ever been able to see a rifle is if they move them around, when they're holding them, with muzzle flashes out or slinging them across their shoulders.*

Drone operators are not in immediate contact with the real world, literally, thanks to the phenomenon known as latency, a reference to the time it takes for information to make its way from the drone to a satellite twenty-two thousand miles up in space, down again to a ground station in Ramstein, Germany, switching to a fiber-optic cable through which it travels across western Europe, the Atlantic Ocean, and the continental United States, before reaching Nevada and the screen in the pilot's trailer. As the electronic pulses are split, reunited, and buffered for assembly into packages pending their dispatch to the next way station, microsecond delays steadily accumulate. It means that the scene on a pilot's screen is out of date, usually two seconds but sometimes as much as five seconds. As the crew reacts to what they are seeing, moving their controls to send an instruction to the aircraft they are "flying," that signal in turn takes two to five seconds to deliver. This time lapse is why drone takeoffs and landings must be handled by a separate team of pilots stationed close to the runway so that they can see the planes they are flying in real time. Potential targets on the ground are aware of the delay: Yemeni members of al-Qaeda reported in 2011 that when they hear a drone overhead, they move around as much as possible.

Nor do the pictures themselves necessarily always bear close resemblance to the world as the rest of us see it and sometimes are "no better than looking at Google Earth through a straw," as one veteran remarked of the plane's "spotter TV" feature. Thus for most of the time the convoy was under watch, the sensor could only focus on two of the three vehicles at a time. If the operator zoomed out even slightly, the already imperfect resolution was lost. Imagery became even less precise if there was dust in the air, if the drone was too high, at dusk or dawn (when both infrared and daylight-use electro-optical cameras lose efficiency), or when the sensor operator could not focus properly. The video as received by troops on the ground that night in Uruzgan was even poorer, described by one as "crap, full of static and crackling."

**4:24 a.m.**

> *Jaguar 25 (call sign of the JTAC, a Special Forces sergeant on the ground liaising with the Predator): What we're looking for is a QRF (Quick Reaction Force); we believe we may have a high level Taliban commander.*

*Pilot: Wouldn't surprise me if this was one of their important guys, just watching from a distance, you know what I mean?*

Then came an unwelcome message from Florida.

**4:37 a.m.**

*Mission intelligence coordinator: Screener said at least one child near SUV.*

*Sensor: Bullshit . . . where? Send me a fucking still [picture]. I don't think they have kids at this hour, I know they're shady, but come on.*

*Pilot: At least one child . . . Really? Listing [him as a] MAM [military-aged male]—that means he's guilty.*

*Sensor: Well maybe a teenager, but I haven't seen anything that looks that short, granted they're all grouped up here, but.*

*Mission intelligence coordinator: They're reviewing.*

*Pilot: Yeah, review that shit . . . Why didn't he say possible child, why are they so quick to call fucking kids but not to call shit a rifle.*

Just as the sun rose above the mountains, the convoy halted on a riverbank, and many of the passengers got out. To the watchers, the pictures revealed something ominous.

**5:18 a.m.**

*Pilot: They're praying.*

*Sensor: This is definitely it. This is their force. Praying? I mean, seriously, that's what they do.*

*Mission intelligence coordinator: They're going to do something nefarious.*

All the adults in the party, including the six or seven women, got out when the convoy stopped at the river. But to the infrared camera high above—and so, too, to the watchers far away—the men and women were merely indistinguishable blobs. Since the party was presumptively one of Taliban reinforcements, no one thought to ponder their gender.

An hour later the vehicles, which had been heading south toward the American ground unit, turned off in a different direction. This led them ultimately twelve miles away from the Americans on the ground, an indication that, whoever they were, they most likely had no hostile intent. Nevertheless the Predator pilot assessed this as merely a "flanking" maneuver to get behind the troops and cut off their escape route.

Low on fuel, the AC-130 Specter gunship that had been on the scene earlier had by now departed. However, the Predator was about to be joined by two OH-58 Kiowas, light, two-man Special Forces helicopter gunships armed with Hellfire missiles and 2.75" rockets. Back in Nevada, the crew was getting impatient.

**6:59 a.m.**

> Pilot: *Can't wait till this actually happens, with all this coordination and shit.*
>
> Sensor operator and mission intelligence coordinator: *(Murmuring) Yeah.*

Down on the ground, the travelers in the pickup heard the drumming of helicopter rotor blades. Several urged the driver to slow down in hopes they would look less suspicious. It was just beginning to get light.

Though far removed from the scene of the action, drone crews see themselves in the same martial tradition as the fighter pilots of an earlier age, down to the flight suits they wear to work, the combat stress they report experiencing, not to mention the combat pay and awards they have successfully demanded. Their trailer chatter that night echoed that of combat crews who are flying through a battle zone for real. Only once in a while does the record reveal that they were in fact firmly on the ground, seven and a half thousand miles away.

**7:11 a.m.**

> Sensor Operator: *Well, sir, would you mind if I took a bathroom break real quick?*
>
> Pilot: *No, not at all, dude.*

This particular pilot, a major who had formerly flown C-130 transport planes, was a veteran of a thousand "missions" and deemed experienced enough to train other pilots. The sensor operator, an enlisted man, was also highly experienced, and they were used to working as a team. As their commander later explained, "These two guys for the last couple of years have been together on shift, they have the same weekends together, they cycle through the schedule over and over."

The crews spoke a language almost incomprehensible to outsiders, so laden with acronyms that plain English was often supplanted. But that night's conversations show that the military jargon, like the two-second video delay, imposed another layer between them and the reality on the ground. Any MAM (military-aged male) became by definition an enemy fighter, irrespective of age, and therefore a legitimate target. *Positive identification* (PID) is an official U.S. military term for someone positively identified as an immediate hostile threat and therefore a legitimate target. As investigators subsequently discovered, the term meant entirely different things to different people.

**7:38 a.m.**

> Pilot: *Our screeners are currently calling 21 MAMs, no females, and two possible children. How copy?*
>
> Jaguar 25: *Roger, and when we say children, are we talking teenagers or toddlers?*
>
> Sensor: *I would say about twelve. Not toddlers; something more towards adolescents or teens.*
>
> Pilot: *Yeah, adolescents.*

▸▸▸

On paper, the system was fail-safe. The pilot and sensor operator could check each other's assessments, and if that was not sufficient they had the mission intelligence coordinator and the safety observer right there beside them. Beyond that, the team in Florida had the full-motion video analysts and the screeners and the intelligence tactical coordinator reviewing the pictures, joined later by two immediate superiors. There were in addition the two separate Special Forces headquarters in Afghanistan itself, each with an assigned "battle captain" supervising ongoing operations.

**7:40 a.m.**

> *Pilot: Our screener identified only one adolescent, so that's one double-digit age range. How copy?*
>
> *Jaguar 25: We'll pass that along to the ground force commander. But like I said, 12 to 13 years old with a weapon is just as dangerous.*
>
> *Sensor: Oh, we agree, yeah.*
>
> *Pilot: Hey, good copy on that. We understand and agree.*

Matters were moving toward a climax. Reliant on bulletins from the Predator crew, the captain commanding the raiding party on the ground had interpreted the news that the convoy was now heading away from the Americans on the ground as confirmation not only that the enemy was "maneuvering" but that it contained an HVI (high-value individual), always a priority target for U.S. forces in this war. He gave the order to strike. The helicopters would take the first shot. The helicopter crews, who had come on the scene late, were simply informed that there had been positive identification of three weapons, at a minimum, along with twenty-one MAMs, and that they were "clear to engage." No one had told them about adolescents, still less children. Two continents and an ocean away, the Predator crew in Nevada made their own final preparations for action.

**8:35 a.m.**

> *Pilot: Alright, so the plan is, man, uh, we're going to watch this thing go down and when they Winchester [run out of ammunition] we can play cleanup.*
>
> *Sensor: Initial plan: without seeing how they break up, follow the largest group.*
>
> *Pilot: Yeah, sounds good. When it all comes down, if everybody is running in their separate direction, I don't care if you just follow one guy, you know like whatever you decide to do, I'm with you on it . . . as long as you keep somebody that we can shoot in the field of view I'm happy.*

The crew was now making final preparations for the attack, arming the missile and going through the final checklist. The sensor operator reminded his intelligence colleague to focus on the business at hand.

8:45 a.m.

Sensor: Hey, MC.

Mission intelligence coordinator: Yes?

Sensor: Remember, Kill Chain!

MIC: Will do.

The first missile from the lead helicopter scored a direct hit on the pickup, instantly killing eleven passengers. The two following SUVs jerked to a halt, and the passengers began frantically to scramble out. The second missile hit the rearmost vehicle, but in the engine block, which absorbed enough of the blast to allow some of the passengers to escape. Four died immediately. The third missile missed the middle SUV, barely, with the blast blowing out the rear window as passengers bailed out. As a matter of routine, the attackers pursued these *squirters*, their word for people fleeing a strike, with 2.75" rockets, though all of these missed.

Then someone noticed something strange. The people who had escaped were not running.

8:52 a.m.

Sensor: That's weird.

Pilot: Can't tell what the fuck they're doing.

Safety observer: Are they wearing burqas?

Sensor: That's what it looks like.

Pilot: They were all PIDed as males. No females in the group.

Sensor: That guy looks like he's wearing jewelry and stuff like a girl, but he ain't . . . if he's a girl, he's a big one.

Despite the sensor operator's hopeful theory, these were not Taliban in drag but women who had scrambled out and were waving their brightly colored scarves at the circling helicopters, which eventually ceased fire. Twenty-three people had been killed, including two boys,

Daoud, three years old, and Murtaza, four. Eight men, one woman, and three children aged between five and fourteen were wounded, many of them severely.

**9:10 a.m.**

> *Mission intelligence coordinator: Screener said there weren't any women earlier.*
>
> *Sensor: What are those? They were in the middle vehicle.*
>
> *Mission intelligence coordinator: Women and children.*

The conversation in the Nevada trailer was losing its previously jaunty tone, as MAMs became mothers, and adolescents turned back into children.

**9:15 a.m.**

> *Pilot: It looks like, uh, one of those in the, uh, bright garb may be carrying a child as well.*
>
> *Sensor: Younger than an adolescent to me.*
>
> *Safety observer: Well . . .*
>
> *Safety observer: No way to tell, man.*
>
> *Sensor: No way to tell from here.*

Soon afterward the Predator turned and flew away ahead of bad weather that was moving in from the west.

Even as the wreckage burned and shell-shocked survivors stumbled about, news was beginning to spread. Local villagers were soon on the scene, and within an hour Taliban radios were broadcasting word that "forty to fifty civilians" had been killed by an American air strike. By early afternoon, the reports had reached the Palace, the crenellated nineteenth-century fortress in the middle of Kabul that housed President Hamid Karzai. Meanwhile, U.S. military communications were proving rather less efficient.

The sudden, silent, flash of the first missile that incinerated the pickup and passengers on their screens caught most of the spectators in Afghanistan and the United States entirely by surprise. The

intricate network of observation, control, and communication linking the myriad headquarters and intelligence centers stretching
between Nevada and Kabul had somehow failed to alert participants—
other than the crews actually pulling or preparing to pull the
triggers—that events had reached their natural conclusion, and people
were about to die. Then, even when it was almost immediately clear
that things had not gone according to plan, the news moved at glacial
speed through the U.S. command system. Messages rumbled back and
forth between different headquarters regarding BOG (boots on the
ground), meaning sending someone to have a close-up look at the
scene for BDA (battle damage assessment).

Eventually helicopters were sent to bring the raiding party itself to
the site where the dead bodies, or at least those that were intact, had
been laid out by villagers who had flocked to the scene. The captain,
according to a brother officer, was in a state of panic, searching fruit-
lessly for a weapon, anything, that would justify this as a legitimate
target. "He wasn't finding anything. I think it overwhelmed him." Special Operations Task Force headquarters meanwhile told him "not to
second-guess yourself; we'll figure it out later."

The captain was not the only officer to panic. Despite the services
of a multibillion-dollar system of intelligence and communication, it
took twelve hours for news that the U.S. had killed twenty-three civilians to make its way up the chain. Despite confirmation from the helicopter crews, the Predator team, and the troops that arrived on the
scene, successive layers of Special Operations commanders refused to
report CIVCAS (civilian casualties). Bizarrely, the technology was less
efficient than the Taliban's. With the inflated volume of traffic, emails
were taking four and a half hours to move through the classified system
from Kandahar to Kabul.

Only when surgeons at a Dutch military hospital talked to their
U.S. counterparts about the wounded civilians that had just been admitted was the truth officially disclosed, but by that time, anyone in
Afghanistan with a radio already knew. At the time, Stanley McChrystal, the U.S. and allied commander, was laboring to garner support
among Afghans by restricting airstrikes in an effort to reduce civilian

casualties. He was not pleased to hear the belated reports from Uruzgan, and raced over to President Karzai's palace to tender his apologies. "I express my deepest, heartfelt condolences to the victims and their families. We all share in their grief," he declared on Afghan television two days later. "I have made it clear to our forces that we are here to protect the Afghan people. I pledge to strengthen our efforts to regain your trust to build a brighter future for all Afghans."

Families of the dead ultimately received $5,000 each, plus one goat.

McChrystal meanwhile appointed a senior officer who was also an old friend, army Major General Timothy McHale, to lead an investigation to determine exactly what had happened and why. McHale's first act was to fly to the remote hospital where the wounded were being treated and meet the victims, among them a six-year-old boy, the same age as his own son, Riley, whose leg had just been amputated. "That really shook me up," he told me later.

McHale, a logistics specialist appointed to command the entire supply effort for the U.S. expeditionary force, had only been in Afghanistan a matter of weeks., Now he quickly recruited a small but well-connected team of officers to help him explore the strange and, to him, unknown worlds of ISR (intelligence, surveillance, and reconnaissance) and DCGS (distributed common ground systems), not to mention Special Operations. Untrammeled by institutional connections to these organizations, he was unafraid to ask hard questions, an attitude that clearly upset some of the interviewees. The Predator squadron commander at Creech, for example, objected to McHale's apparent impression that his crew "were out to employ weapons no matter what." McHale tartly responded that according to the transcript of their chatter, the crew had stated exactly that intention "about fourteen times." Furthermore, he pointed out, "You have a sensor operator whose response to a call out of children is 'bullshit.' Do you think he is likely to be focusing on potential for children or is he only looking for weapons or trying to confirm that this is a target?"

Within six weeks McHale and his staff had interviewed over fifty witnesses in Afghanistan, Nevada, and Florida, creating in the process a hand-drawn time line of the events that ultimately stretched

for sixty-six feet around the four walls of the hangar he had comman-
deered for his office. He delivered a withering report that described the
Special Operations headquarters responsible for Operation Noble Justice as "ineffective," while reserving his deepest scorn for the Predator
crew, characterizing them as "almost juvenile in their desire to engage
the targets," and recommended that the air force conduct its own
investigation of the crew's "unprofessional conduct."

The investigation's interviews, transcribed and included in the
report, track McHale's exploration of the tangled links in the kill chain,
much of which came as a revelation to the general, despite a lifetime
in the service. Thus he was astonished to learn from the Florida team
in their $750 million station that they had no means of communicating
with the men on the ground in Afghanistan, relying on the mission
intelligence coordinator in Nevada to pass on their information. "We
cannot hear what he is saying," one of the Florida staff told McHale, "so
we hope that he is providing the best information possible." The chief
screener, an intelligence professional who supposedly had been
trained to make lethal judgments on the basis of her observations,
provided insight into her training in cultural awareness when she
recalled how the vehicles had "stopped and a large group of MAMs
began to get water, wash, and pray. To us that is very suspicious because
we are taught that they do this before an attack." Several hundred million non-Taliban Muslims also wash and pray every morning, but the
little party's ablutions had fed into the pattern already established by
the flashing headlights and anonymous radio summons to the "Mujaheddin."

The general eagerness in Nevada to "go kinetic" had done the rest.
A safety officer, present to advise the Predator crew when the attack
seemed imminent, summed up the prevailing attitude at Creech in a
candid admission: "Well, to be honest sir, everyone around here, it's
like 'Top Gun': everyone has the desire to do our job, employ weapons
against the enemy."

McHale's voyage of discovery as chronicled in the interviews, tran-
scripts, and conclusions of his 2010 report not only retraced what he
saw as a saga of bloody-minded incompetence and confusion but also

revealed something more profound. The technological architecture in which the assorted participants operated was a tribute to the notion that if it is possible to see everything, it is possible to know everything and therefore automate the process of empirical deduction. Technology had supposedly made it possible to see down through the dark from almost three miles up and count the passengers inside a moving vehicle as well as any weapons they might be carrying. Technology enabled these images to move around the world for multiple viewers to assess and draw their own conclusions. Finally, it could be taken for granted that each target required only a single shot. In sequence, it was a very efficient kill chain.

But however miraculous the technology, the information it delivered was inevitably ambiguous ("Was that a fucking rifle?") partly because, contrary to popular belief, the imagery delivered by ISR (the overworked acronym for intelligence, surveillance, reconnaissance) pictures tends to be fuzzy. Quizzing one Special Forces major as to why he had been slow to report the casualties despite the pictures coming from the drone, McHale remarked, "Your ISR knows there are civilians there . . ." To which the officer responded exasperatedly: "The ISR? Literally, look at this rug right here sir, that's what an ISR looks like."

Inevitably, everyone involved tried to clarify the ambiguity by shaping the information to fit a predetermined pattern, in this case that of hostile Taliban. Figures gathered on a riverbank at dawn to pray? "That's what [the Taliban] do," ergo they're going to do something nefarious. For what other reason would three cars be driving away from the friendly force? Given the pervasive concentration throughout the U.S. war effort on the importance of HVI (high-value individuals), the ground force commander was quick to assume that this was an "exfill"—an assisted escape—of a high-ranking Taliban commander. Subsequently he accepted the alternative explanation of the "flanking maneuver," equally well fit to the cast-iron assumption that the little convoy fitted the pattern of a threat. The complexity of this system, especially given its widely dispersed components (Nevada, Florida, Afghanistan), made it even harder for the people involved to adapt to changing reality. Instead, reality was adjusted to fit the predetermined pattern. This, in other words, was a "signature strike" in which the victims were targeted solely on the basis of their behavior.

Nor did it help that the system came with its own language—MAM (military-age male) for *man*, PID (positive identification) for *see*, TIC (troops in contact) for *coming under fire*—imposing its own framework. A military-age male, after all, is almost self-evidently a legitimate target, whereas a man might well be an innocent civilian. Officially fostered as a means of succinct, precise communication, the language adapted and divided, with different meanings for different people. So PID, for example, had a different definition depending on whether someone was in Florida, Nevada, or Afghanistan. Everyone had different notions of what *adolescent* meant and whether it was OK to kill one.

As recommended by McHale, the air force did indeed hold an investigation. Conducted by a major general, it concluded that the Predator crew had perhaps "clouded the picture on adolescents" but laid much of the blame on the special operations command for failing to supervise the operation. Neither of the reports highlighted the statement of a Special Forces sergeant from the ground force, a veteran of seven tours in Afghanistan, including three in Uruzgan, who lodged a protest against the system of complex technology embodied in the kill chain:

> Looking at the video afterwards, someone was saying when the vehicles stopped, the (passengers) were praying. Someone said there might be people pulling security. When I looked at the video they could also have been taking a piss. Whoever was viewing the video real-time, maybe they needed a little more tactical experience. It needs to be someone that knows the culture of the people. If I can say anything, they just need to be familiar with what they are looking at.

But the system had not been built to work that way, not in a long time.

# 2
# WIRING THE JUNGLE

Twenty years after the last bombs had fallen, the So Tri, an indigenous group who had lived in the remote wilderness of southeastern Laos for centuries, still didn't know who had bombed them. For nine years, high explosives of all shapes and sizes had rained down out of the sky, killing men, women, and children and obliterating their homes and much of the old forest. The survivors had retreated deep into the mountains, hiding in underground shelters to stay alive. When the bombing finally stopped they came back and rebuilt their villages along the muddy trail they called the war road. Cluster-bomb casings dug from under the bushy bamboo that had replaced the forest were ideal as stilts to support their houses. The yellow bomblets could be turned into oil lamps, though some of them would still occasionally explode. Asked by a visitor in 1994 who it was that had bombed them over and over for all those years, the Tri laughed and shrugged: "The enemy." Asked who the enemy was, they laughed louder and replied, "We don't know." When told that the bombs had come from the United States, they expressed thanks for the information, grateful to have the mystery solved at last.

It would have been harder to explain that at its heart the enemy had been a machine. A massive computer hundreds of miles away, prompted by devices hidden in the forest that were designed to detect the sound, movement, and even smell of humans and their vehicles, had directed when and where the bombs should land. Unwittingly, the So Tri had hosted the world's first automated battlefield. Grounded on an unswerving faith that the vagaries of conflict can be overcome by technology, this half-forgotten project was the precursor of the drone wars that America would fight in the twenty-first century.

The scheme had been conceived far away on the east coast of the United States, in a leafy suburb of Boston, Massachusetts. Here, in 1966, Dana Hall, a prep school for girls, had been selected as the venue for the annual summer get-together of an elite and very secret group. Known as the Jasons, they were eminent scientists and scholars, most of whom were graduates of the Manhattan Project that designed and built the first atomic bomb. These men were accustomed to deploying their intellects to assist the U.S. government with the most fundamental and secret issues of national security, especially with regard to nuclear warfare. George Kistiakowski, an acerbic Russian-born physicist, had helped develop the atom bomb and gone on to be President Eisenhower's science adviser. Carl Kaysen, who had helped plan bombing targets in World War II, held high rank in the Kennedy White House and at one point had urged a preemptive nuclear attack on the Soviets, providing precise calculations on likely casualties. The hyperactive Richard Garwin had worked on the design of the very first hydrogen bomb, tested in 1952, and now enjoyed a lofty position as senior scientist with the IBM Corporation. Many among the group were or would become Nobel Prize winners, and their ideas were assured of respectful attention at the highest levels.

Given their background in nuclear weapons, it was natural that the initial topics to which the Jasons were asked to address their intellects would involve nuclear warfare, specifically the problems of defense against intercontinental ballistic missiles as they came over the North

Pole from the Soviet Union. It was assumed that with the right radars, enough computing power, and suitable interceptors, it would be possible to track and shoot down the missiles before they reached the United States. Possible solutions—the Jasons at one point suggested interceptor lasers—could never be realistically tested, so the problem remained pleasingly abstract, a rich field for abstruse technological speculation and, not least, a lucrative source of contracts for corporations such as IBM.

However, in 1966, the group was asked to turn its attention to a real and ongoing war. The principal topic of discussion at Dana Hall that June was "technical possibilities relating to our military operations in Vietnam." The war was going badly; although the Johnson administration had been pouring troops into South Vietnam, the North Vietnamese had apparently matched this escalation, sending ever more troops and supplies down the jungle routes through Laos known as the Ho Chi Minh Trail. "Rolling Thunder," a sustained bombing campaign against North Vietnam's infrastructure, appeared to have had little effect on these supplies while drawing worldwide condemnation. It was a problem that had plagued the air force throughout its history. Deep in the service's DNA was the traumatic memory of its early life as the "army air corps," a mere branch of the army no different in status and with a budget lower than that of the artillery. In those days the air corps had nurtured dreams and schemes of revolt and independence that were based on a dogma that strategic bombing of an enemy heartland can win a war without any need for armies or navies. In-house theoreticians took as their gospel the writings of an Italian artillery officer, Giulio Douhet, who argued in the aftermath of World War I that since modern technology favored the defense on land and at sea, airpower alone could bring an enemy to his knees.

On the eve of World War II, these crusaders had convinced themselves that the destruction of no more than 154 key targets identified as critical to the German economy, such as power-generation plants, would bring the enemy war machine to its knees after six months. As it turned out, this ambitious assumption, based on the most assiduous analysis of the enemy economy, turned out to be wholly wrong.

The 154 targets, even when they could be located and hit, either turned out not to be so vital to the enemy war effort as supposed, or the Germans adapted by replacing them or using substitutes. The attackers suffered heavy losses, and the enemy had to be defeated the old-fashioned way, by massive armies slogging across Europe. Nevertheless, the bomber generals' campaign for independence ultimately bore fruit in 1947, without their having to shed any of their core beliefs in the utility of strategic precision bombing, which they accordingly proceeded to apply in Vietnam once unleashed by President Johnson.

Early in 1966 air force planners believed they had identified the "critical node" underpinning the North Vietnamese war economy: storage tanks in Hanoi and Haiphong allegedly holding most of the country's supply of oil. Furious raids on the tank farms produced gratifyingly fierce fires and towering columns of smoke, but it soon emerged that the Vietnamese stored most of their oil in hidden sites elsewhere, and that these were not the magic targets after all. As had been and would be the recurring pattern in such affairs, the targeting committees set about expanding the target list, always in hopes of finding the crucial node whose elimination would prove mortal to the enemy. Meanwhile however, Defense Secretary Robert McNamara, a determined technocrat, was eager for an alternative approach and thus sought counsel from the Jasons.

After a series of highly classified intelligence briefings on the war, especially the results of the bombing campaign, the group moved west from Massachusetts to the University of California at Santa Barbara. Delving into the reams of classified reports and briefings at their disposal, they concluded that the ultimate critical node in the enemy war effort was the route from North Vietnam by which men and supplies reached the communist insurgents fighting in South Vietnam, the legendary Ho Chi Minh Trail that led though the jungles and rugged terrain of southeastern Laos. They were confident that if the trail could be blocked, thereby preventing any further communist reinforcements and resupply, the war would slowly but inevitably come to an end. Over the next two months they crafted the blueprint of a fence to straddle the trail across thousands of square miles. This would not be a physical barrier but something never seen before in the world: an invisible electronic network that would detect, identify, and destroy any enemy seeking to cross it.

The first stage consisted of arrays of sensors distributed across the jungle. Some were acoustic, microphones listening for the sound of trucks or footfalls or voices. Others were seismic, ready to detect movements of these same trucks or people. Yet more "sniffed" the air for telltale traces of ammonia, denoting urine and therefore people. Another variety was on the alert for the ignition spark of an engine. If and when a sensor picked up an indicator of enemy presence, it would transmit the signal to planes circling constantly overhead, which would in turn relay the message to distant computers programmed to sift through the necessarily ambiguous information—a column of troops or a herd of elephants?—and match up the apparent source of the signals with the map of enemy trails implanted in the computer memory. To process the data Garwin, the IBM scientist, recommended the IBM-360 computer to analyze the signals, he explained, and "try to characterize the sounds so you wouldn't be bombing birds or peasants but convoys, trucks, or whatever." Once birds and peasants had been eliminated, promised Garwin, the computer would order "response, immediate response" from attack aircraft. (Even though they were dealing with the movements of humans and trucks, the scheme echoed their solutions for detecting and intercepting incoming Soviet missiles.)

This was no casual back-of-the-envelope scheme. Ensconced in Santa Barbara, the scientists, with occasional breaks for surfing or walks on the beach, delved deep into finer details, such as the necessary camouflage for sensors impaled on spikes in the ground (disguised to look like weeds native to the area) and munitions suitable for use against enemy formations once they were located. Their preferred choices were SADEYE/BLU-26B cluster bombs, which blew open after release to disburse 600 yellow shrapnel bomblets over a radius of 800 feet. For sensors, they recommended acoustic devices adapted from the traditional microphone-equipped buoys used by the navy when searching for submarines. Since these might fail to pick up the sound of sandal-clad Vietnamese or their trucks, the area would also be seeded with 300 million tiny firecrackers the size of aspirins. When detonated by a rolling tire, or a stealthy footfall, they would make a sharp bang and so trigger the sensors. The cost of the entire effort was estimated at about $800 million a year (roughly $10 billion in 2015 dollars), which they deemed a bargain because the war would consequently "taper off." In any case this initiative was positively humane, in the scientists' view, compared to the wholesale bombing of North Vietnam then underway.

In September, leading Jasons returned east to brief Defense Secretary Robert McNamara on the carefully thought-out scheme. The secretary, who was very fond of neat technical solutions to human problems, was highly enthusiastic and ordered the air force to get to work immediately. Though initially irked at having an operation dreamed up by civilian eggheads foisted on them, the service chiefs soon reconciled themselves to the limitless funds available, and by mid-1967 the system was largely in place.

F-4 fighter-bombers and other aircraft strewed hundreds and then thousands of sensors across the jungle. Fleets of assorted aircraft were deployed to circle day and night and relay radio signals from the sensors back to Nakhon Phanom, a military base on the west bank of the Mekong River in northeast Thailand that was so secret it officially did not exist. The base hosted a whole variety of unacknowledged "black" activities, but at its heart, behind additional layers of razor wire and guard posts, sat an enormous air-conditioned building, the largest in Southeast Asia, that was home to Task Force Alpha, the "brain" of the automated battlefield. Behind air locks pressurized to keep the omnipresent red dust of northeast Thailand away from the delicate machines, technicians monitored incoming sensor signals as they were fed to two IBM 360/65 mainframe computers, the very fastest and most powerful in existence at that time. Teams of programmers on contract from IBM labored to rewrite software that would make sense of the data. Not coincidentally, the layout of the darkened, aseptic "war room" resembled that of the command centers of the air force ballistic missile early warning system back in the U.S. waiting for signs of a Soviet nuclear attack.

In the view of the military command, the highly classified project represented the first step into a world in which human beings, with all their messy, unpredictable traits, would be eliminated, except as targets. By the time Task Force Alpha began operating Igloo White, the secret code name for the overall electronic barrier (the military likes to preserve the illusion of security with a proliferation of code names), this approach was already failing against the Vietnamese "people's war," but there was little inclination for a change of heart.

General William Westmoreland, the army chief of staff and former commander in Vietnam, expressed the vision most concisely in October, 1969: "On the battlefield of the future," he declared in a lunchtime speech to the Association of the U.S. Army, a powerful pressure group, "enemy forces will be located, tracked and targeted almost instantaneously through the use of data links, computer assisted intelligence evaluation, and automated fire control. With first round kill probabilities approaching certainty, and with surveillance devices that can continually track the enemy, the need for large forces to fix the opposition will be less important."

As it so happened, other components of the air force were fighting a very different kind of war. Marshall Harrison, a former high school teacher, spent 1969 piloting a slow-flying air force plane with excellent visibility called an OV-10 Bronco over South Vietnam as a forward air controller tasked with tracking and fixing the enemy for bombing by jet fighter-bombers. Equipped with no surveillance device more sophisticated than his own eyes, he learned to look for signs that no sensor would ever catch: "fresh tracks along a trail, smoke coming from areas where there should be no smoke, too many farmers toiling in the paddy fields . . . small vegetable patches where they shouldn't be." No computer would calculate, as he learned to do, that footprints on a muddy trail early in the morning if it had rained only during the night probably belonged to the enemy, since civilians were wary of moving at night and being killed if caught breaking curfew.

Needless to say, Harrison did not encounter senior officers at the barebones strips where he was usually based. The futuristic complex at Nakhon Phanom, on the other hand, could move privileged visitors to awe. "Just as it is almost impossible to be an agnostic in the

Cathedral of Notre Dame," reported Leonard Sullivan, a high-ranking Pentagon official who visited in 1968, "so it is difficult to keep from being swept up in the beauty and majesty of the Task Force Alpha temple."

Sullivan's boss, Dr. John S. Foster, was even more unbridled in his enthusiasm, telling a congressional committee in 1969 that "this system has been so effective . . . that there has been no case where the enemy has successfully come through the sensor field . . . It is a very, very successful system." Foster's support was potent. His title, director of defense research and engineering, a post he occupied from 1965 to 1973, belied the immense power of his office, since the research projects he authorized and paid for could turn into multibillion-dollar production programs. The suave, smooth-talking physicist-bureaucrat was an ardent proponent of high-technology weapons programs, the more esoteric the better, dispensing billions of dollars for weapons development without excessive concern for cost or practical results.

Among the aspects of the electronic fence that most excited Foster, an avid model plane hobbyist, was the plan to deploy unmanned planes—drones—not only to relay sensor signals back to Thailand but also ultimately to attack targets. Remotely piloted aircraft had been a topic of military interest ever since World War I, when a prototype radio-controlled biplane designed to attack enemy trenches had been tested and discarded for lack of accuracy and reliability, not to mention frequent crashes. Further radio-control experiments in the interwar years led to the actual coining of the term *drone* by a pair of naval scientists in 1936, according to an official history, "after analyzing various names of insects and birds." In World War II the U.S. Navy had brought about the death of the heir to the Kennedy fortune by enlisting him in Operation Aphrodite, a scheme to fly remote-controlled B-17 and B-24 bombers packed with explosives into German submarine pens. Human pilots were required to handle takeoff and to switch on the radio controls. When Joseph Kennedy Jr. flipped the switch prior to bailing out, the plane promptly blew up. None of Aphrodite's other eleven attempts were successful. By the 1960s drones had carved out a useful niche mission as semirealistic targets for aerial gunnery training. Come the Vietnam War, they were adapted for reconnaissance, though without much success, being easy targets for enemy gunners. Foster, however, cherished the notion that they could soon begin replacing manned attack planes in various roles, and so money poured into a variety of drone programs under development by corporations such as Boeing, Vought, and Teledyne Ryan.

None of them worked very well. Most were canceled after a suitable interval, including those assigned to the electronic fence. Yet the desire for aircraft that could be controlled from some remote location was already deeply ingrained at high levels, perhaps because their missions could be more easily kept secret. In 1969, for example, President Nixon and Henry Kissinger decided to begin bombing Cambodia without any notice to Congress or the public. The raids were therefore conducted in deepest secrecy. The flight paths of the B-52 bombers assigned to Operation Menu were under the direct control of a ground station that also precisely controlled the release of their huge bomb loads. Most of the crews thought they were bombing Vietnam, as usual, with only pilots and navigators briefed on the true target. As we shall see, this attribute of remotely piloted aircraft would become even more attractive to higher authority in the following century.

Drones were not the only elements of the electronic fence that failed to perform as advertised. The plan that appeared so complete and elegant on the beach at Santa Barbara or in a congressional hearing did not prosper in contact with the real world, a world that shifted and adapted even as the mighty computers struggled to make it fit the maps and patterns programmed into their memories. The network of trails, totaling 12,000 miles, radically changed in each rainy season. The ingenious notion of having the enemy announce his presence by stepping on the pill-sized firecrackers had not taken into account the moist Laotian climate, which almost immediately rendered the explosives as dangerous as a wet match.

Further complicating matters was the inaccuracy of the high-tech LORAN (long-range navigation) radio-navigation system used to drop the sensors, so no one knew for sure where they, and consequently any targets they might detect, actually were. "If we got within four or five miles of the aim point we were doing pretty good," remembers Rex Rivolo, an F-4 pilot who dropped "hundreds" of sensors into the darkness. LORAN, which was also used to guide bombing runs, once led Rivolo inadvertently to bomb the huge American base at Da Nang.

Most important of all, Task Force Alpha was not confronting a fixed target that would faithfully behave as predicted but a living enemy skilled in camouflage and deception that could watch, think, and adapt. Even before the arrival of Task Force Alpha, large sections of the trails system led nowhere, decoys that were purposely put in place to confuse American reconnaissance planes. Fake bridges were erected to draw attack, while real ones, resting on inflated inner tubes, lay invisibly submerged during the day. Back in Santa Barbara, the Jasons had entertained the possibility that the enemy might eventually adopt countermeasures of some kind against the sensors, though they were confident that this would take "some period of time."

It took the Vietnamese a week.

General Dong Si Nguyen, a veteran revolutionary and transportation genius who commanded the entire Ho Chi Minh Trail for most of the war, later reminisced how "the devices were dropped over an area as large as 100 kilometers covering our transportation network. We spent seven days trying to arrive at a solution. We brought vehicles to the area and ran them back and forth throughout the day (to make listeners believe the area was active) . . . While we distracted the Americans in this manner, the actual convoys were then able to safely move by means of a different route."

Specialized teams were meanwhile set up in every section of the trail to hunt for sensors. "They were hard to find," one hunter said later. "Sometimes they were in an area that was not really important to us, so we deliberately triggered them." Otherwise, the Vietnamese ran herds of cattle down the trail to simulate troop columns to fool infrared cameras or bottles of human and animal urine to confuse the sniffer-sensors.

The electronic barrier cost almost $2 billion to set up and roughly $1 billion a year to operate. The funds for the secret operation were so artfully hidden in the defense budget that for years Congress had almost no knowledge or oversight of the operation for which it was voting huge sums of money. There was therefore little official incentive to under-count the amount of damage being inflicted on the enemy. To calcu-late enemy losses without sending men to look for themselves, deemed an impossibly dangerous task, the air force simply multiplied the num-ber of bombs dropped by the number of people who could in theory be killed by varying types of bomb, such as the SADEYE. The tally produced by this arithmetic—20,723 for Igloo White's first season—conveyed an air of precision that had little basis in reality. "This process," an official U.S. Air Force historian tartly noted some years later, was "based on so many assumptions that the end product represented an exercise in metaphysics rather than mathematics."

Truck kills were assessed by similarly esoteric methods, even though year after year the Vietnamese still seemed to have the necessary num-ber of trucks on hand to supply their armies in the South. Partisans of the electronic fence explained this away by suggesting that North Vietnam simply replaced lost trucks with imports from Russia and other communist allies. As the same air force historian pointed out, "estimates of North Vietnamese truck imports tended to keep pace with the claims of trucks killed and disabled."

Finally, in April 1972, the North Vietnamese launched a devastat-ing offensive using hundreds of tanks and thousands of trucks that had passed down the trail completely unnoticed. When General Lucius Clay, commander of the Pacific Air Force, asked how this mass of vehi-cles and weapons had totally escaped Igloo White scrutiny, he was told that the matériel must have come by routes "we don't know about." In fact, for much of the war, the North Vietnamese had moved a consid-erable portion of their supplies by sea via the Cambodian port of Sihanoukeville, thus avoiding the Ho Chi Minh Trail altogether. A CIA analyst's suggestion that people be recruited simply to watch comings and goings at the port was rejected in accordance with the officially accepted understanding that the enemy was entirely depen-dent on the trail.

Ironically, although the project had proved less than effective in defeating the communist enemy, it came to serve as a global symbol of the soulless but deadly American war machine. The Pentagon Papers, the secret history of the war leaked by Daniel Ellsberg in 1971, contained a detailed account of the original Jason deliberations, including those cerebral ruminations on the relative lethal merits of cluster bombs and other munitions. Amid the general horrors of the war, the specter of an automated battlefield, in which targets were selected and struck by remote control, touched a sensitive public nerve, just as drone attacks unleashed by the Obama administration forty years later ignited similar debate. At scientific conferences in Europe, venerable Nobel Prize winners confronted by angry demonstrators had to be rescued by riot police. Other Jasons received death threats at home. An antiwar tract published by dissident scientists at Berkeley in 1972 cited the electronic battlefield as "an especially clear instance of Jason's intervention contributing decisively to the prolongation of the Indochina war." At a public meeting in Boston of the antiwar Winter Soldier movement, an embittered veteran, Eric Herter, testified eloquently and presciently about "the new forms of war that are to replace the unpopular struggle of infantry and patrol against guerrilla bands . . . This new war will not produce My Lais. It will be a war not of men at arms, but of computers and weapons systems against whole populations. Even the tortured bond of humanity between enemies at war will be eliminated. Under its auspices, the people of the villages have gone from being 'gooks' and 'dinks' to being grid-coordinates, blips on scan screens, dots of light on infrared film. They are never seen, never known, never even hated . . . It is hard to feel responsible for this type of war, even for those who were close to it. There is little personal involvement. The atrocity is the result of a chain of events in which no man plays a single decisive part."

Less emotional but more formidable opposition to Task Force Alpha was building up elsewhere. By 1972, a faction at the highest levels of the U.S. Air Force was becoming increasingly disenchanted at having to shell out a billion dollars a year for no appreciable return on a system that had not really been their idea in the first place. But even though the dissidents, including General Clay, were powerful four-star generals, there were also potent forces maneuvering to keep the system operating, even if peace broke out. These latter included John Foster's directorate of defense research and engineering, along with other interested military and corporate parties, including IBM. Clearly the generals had to tread carefully in disposing of the unwanted project. Fortunately, they had someone on hand they were confident could accomplish the mission. "Someone very senior was fed up with the idiocy [of Task Force Alpha]," remembers Tom Christie, a former high-ranking Pentagon official. "They knew what they were doing when they sent John."

"John" was Colonel John Boyd, a legendary fighter pilot known as Forty-Second Boyd, thanks to his standing $40 bet that he could beat any pilot in a mock dogfight in forty seconds. He never lost. As fearless and skillful in bureaucratic combat as he was at the controls of a jet fighter, with no inhibitions about speaking truth to power (once, gesturing emphatically with his habitual cigar during an argument with a general, he burned a hole in the latter's tie), Boyd could be counted on to cut through the technological pretensions of the electronic barrier. His superiors had already used him to shoot down a project foisted on them by civilian overseers in the Pentagon, in this case a joint fighter development project with the Germans. Boyd had accomplished this by touring Luftwaffe bases and explaining how they would be shot down in droves if the proposed fighter ever saw action.

In April 1972, just after fleets of enemy tanks and artillery had unexpectedly emerged from the trail for that year's devastating spring offensive, Boyd arrived at Nakhon Phanom, assigned as the new base commander. By that time the huge base displayed many features emblematic of the disintegrating American war effort in Southeast Asia. Packs of wild dogs roamed unmolested across the secret base. Racial tension was so high that black and white servicemen dared not venture near each other's quarters. Behind the double razor-wire fence and the armed guards surrounding the Infiltration Surveillance Center, the heart of Task Force Alpha, the mess hall provided metal forks and knives but only plastic spoons; all the metal spoons had been stolen by heroin-addicted personnel to use in cooking up their fix.

After giving orders to shoot the dogs, Boyd set to work researching the truth behind the system's reported successes. One suggestion actively touted by an air force research base, the Rome Air Development Center, closely linked to IBM, had been to use the system to pinpoint enemy artillery in South Vietnam from the sound of its guns. Seven hundred sensors were accordingly dropped around the battlefield in a precise pattern decreed by the technologists. Boyd made an on-the-spot inspection and immediately saw that the idea could never work because the sound of enemy guns was inevitably drowned by the noise of friendly artillery. Bypassing intervening layers of command, he sent word to his sponsors in Washington that the scheme had been an utter failure. Other initiatives by barrier partisans, such as an attempt to locate antiaircraft missile batteries, or to monitor possible peace accords, proved no more successful. "They sent me to close it down," Boyd told me before he died in 1997, "and I closed it down."

The war that had begun with such promise for American technology was ending in futile retreat, but not before the air force's mightiest bombers, the B-52s, were sent out on one last campaign of destruction into the heart of Hanoi itself, the enemy capital previously off-limits. Rex Rivolo, the fighter pilot whose high-tech navigation aid had led him to bomb the American base at Da Nang, was assigned to fly escort on the first raid, December 18, 1972.

"I wasn't worried," he told me years later. "We were briefed that the B-52s would be using their most secret 'war mode' electronic countermeasures, previously reserved for World War III with the Soviets, that would easily blind the Vietnamese SAM missiles. I knew the countermeasures in my plane didn't work, but I believed the B-52s had secret, magic stuff that would make them invulnerable. So I thought everything would be OK. That was until three SAMs flew right by me and then hit a B-52 high above. The magic boxes didn't work." Rivolo watched in amazement as the giant plane cracked open "like an egg" and slowly turned over. Burning jet fuel streamed out in a wave that split into two and then four in vast cascading sheets of flame. "The sky," he told me, recalling the vivid scene in every detail after forty years, "was raining fire." Fourteen more B-52s were to go down before the raids were called off eleven days later. By that time, Rivolo's previously unquestioning faith in the promises of the technologists had disappeared forever. "I had really believed all that hype," he told me. "And then I realized it was all bullshit. None of it worked." That searing moment of truth would cause a lot of trouble in Washington later on.

Task Force Alpha was finally switched off on December 31, 1972. Out in the jungle, the last sensors went on faithfully broadcasting sounds, movements, and smells that no one would hear, until their batteries ran down. Once the last raid on Laos had flown home—an average of one planeload of bombs had landed on that country every eight minutes, twenty-four hours a day, for nine years—the surviving So Tri emerged from the hidden dugouts where they had waited out the cataclysm and returned to rebuild their ruined villages amid the countless craters. They did not teach their children about the war.

Among the items shipped home from the giant base on the banks of the Mekong was a tape recording. For years afterward it was a highlight at Christmas parties on air force fighter bases across the country, featuring as it did the unmistakable sound of someone out on the Ho Chi Minh Trail standing over an acoustic sensor and subjecting it to a long and leisurely piss.

Given that the roughly $6 billion spent on the barrier overall (no one could ever agree on the exact total) had failed to achieve its purpose, that tape might have served as the final epitaph for the dream of war by remote control. But such was not the case. Its best days were yet to come.

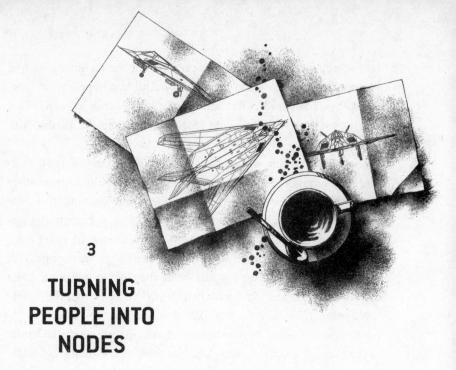

3

# TURNING
# PEOPLE INTO
# NODES

"Don't knock the war that feeds you" read a sign on the wall of a Lockheed plant in California in the late 1960s. The bitter struggle in Southeast Asia may have killed millions of people, including 58,000 Americans, but it had been very good for business. It therefore stood to reason that with the outbreak of peace and the withdrawal of the huge U.S. expeditionary force from Vietnam, Pentagon weapons spending would inevitably decline. But that was not what happened. Money authorized for buying weapons and developing new ones ballooned from $26 billion in 1975, as the last shots were fired in Indochina, to $40 billion three years later. Defense-industry profits marched in tandem. In 1976, McDonnell Douglas, then the largest contractor, announced that its profits had grown 75 percent in a year.

The inspiration for the rearmament drive no longer came from third world peasants lurking under the jungle canopy but from something more ominous: the enormous forces of the mighty Soviet Union, supposedly ready, able, and eager to confront the United States across the globe. Intelligence reappraisals of Soviet intentions and capabilities smoothed the way for a readjustment of U.S. defense priorities. In this scenario, the specter of a Soviet blitzkrieg smashing into outnumbered NATO forces in central Europe occupied a central role. The Fulda Gap in the mountains of central Germany, the presumed route of a Soviet invasion, may have been a long way from the Ho Chi Minh Trail, but the dream of remote-controlled warfare, which inevitably led to the drone strikes of the twenty-first century, never died. Five years after closing Task Force Alpha, the Pentagon began planning another electronic barrier.

The project was publicly justified by the assumption that Soviet forces vastly outnumbered NATO defenders, whose only hope supposedly lay in "force-multiplier" high-technology weapons. The military bookkeeping was in truth highly suspect: readily available evidence showed that the numbers were almost even, while Soviet troop and weapons quality was far inferior. Nevertheless the defense lobby effortlessly ignored such discordant notes right up until the day that the USSR finally crumbled, laying bare the sorry state of its vaunted military.

The new barrier fostered by the Pentagon's DARPA (Defense Advanced Research Projects Agency) in conjunction with the air force and army, was called Assault Breaker. There were no carpets of sensors strewn among the trees this time, but the basic idea was faithful to General Westmoreland's promise in 1969 of "surveillance devices that can continually track the enemy" and "first round kill probabilities approaching certainty." Instead of the sensors, airborne radar would peer far behind enemy lines and detect suspicious movements of Soviet "second-echelon" reinforcements moving up behind the front line. An on-board computer would process the information and sort out which signals revealed a genuine target. On the basis of this information, missiles would be launched in the general direction of the enemy. At ten thousand feet above the targeted armored formations, the missiles would burst open and dispense a carpet of self-guiding bombs equipped with heat seekers and tiny radars that would drop down and then search out their armored targets. A variant added a further layer of complexity with "skeet" projectiles that would fly off from the bomb canisters at speed to impact on the tanks. Proponents claimed Assault Breaker could destroy "in a few hours" sufficient vehicles in (Soviet) reinforcement divisions "to prevent their exploiting a breakthrough of NATO defenses," without—and this was an important selling point—anyone having to resort to nuclear weapons, all for a bargain price of $5.3 billion.

Task Force Alpha had used powerful software programs to try and distinguish trucks from elephants, soldiers from peasants. Assault Breaker followed the same concept: ambiguous sensor signals were processed into coherence by massive computing power, thereby discriminating a tank army from traffic on the autobahn, tanks from East German tractors, and armored personnel carriers from Volkswagens. Even the bombs homing in on the final targets had to be able to decide if a hot spot was really a tank or a smoking bomb crater or some other distraction. Everything depended on recognizing preset patterns. A tank, for example, would be expected to have a distinctive pattern of hot spots to distinguish it from some other heat-emitting object, such as a bus. To disorient the weapon, an enemy merely needed to rearrange the pattern, just as General Nguyen had hung buckets of urine on the Ho Chi Minh Trail.

Presiding over the entire operation was a man destined to exert a potent influence on U.S. defense for decades to come. In 1977 President Carter appointed William J. Perry, an affable Californian defense contractor, to John Foster's old job overseeing all Pentagon research and development. (Foster had moved to defense contractor TRW Inc. in 1973.) Like Foster before him, Perry loved esoteric weapons projects, and he outmatched his predecessor in his ability to charm all comers. He was soon a popular figure in Washington, conveying an air of deeply considered expertise in the mysteries of defense technology that served him well in selling his agenda while dispensing billions of dollars on development programs that might, if actually put into production, yield contracts worth multiples of the development money. Politicians appreciated his gentlemanly and patient explanations of technological mysteries. The military, though occasionally irritated by his interference in their prerogatives, appreciated his ability to extract money from the politicians. Liberals warmed to his unmilitaristic demeanor, not least his support for strategic nuclear arms limitation agreements.

Before entering government, Perry had spent his career exclusively in the defense-electronics industry, initially for a firm deeply involved in the highly classified ballistic-missile early-warning system. In 1964, he founded Electromagnetic Systems Laboratory (ESL), Incorporated. Located close to Stanford University, the firm grew and prospered in the business of processing digital information from sources such as sensors, radars, and reconnaissance pictures for the U.S. military and National Security Agency.

Perry thus arrived in office with an enduring interest in the ability of technology to cut through the fog of war. "The objective of our precision guided weapon systems is to give us the following capabilities: to be able to see all high value targets on the battlefield at any time; to be able to make a direct hit on any target we can see, and to be able to destroy any target we can hit," he told a senate committee in 1978. Pentagon officials began referring to Assault Breaker as "Bill Perry's wet dream." Comprehensive testing was deferred on the grounds that the system was urgently required in the field. On the few occasions individual components were tested, they tended to fail, and the whole system, with its many steps, was never tested all at once. The General Accounting Office, the watchdog agency that monitors government programs on behalf of Congress, reported in 1981 not only that the system could not tell the difference between armored vehicles and "lower value targets" (trucks or automobiles) but also that these distinctions were "not designed into the advanced development radar and is not part of DARPA's planned testing." In other words, the interests behind the program appeared not to care whether it actually worked.

Assault Breaker was formally canceled in 1984, felled by a combination of ballooning costs, failed tests, and bad publicity. But in its dying days it garnered powerful endorsement from a gilt-edged source. "Precision weapons, smart shells, electronic reconnaissance systems," commented a Soviet military writer in a *Pravda* article about Assault Breaker in February 1984, "could enable NATO to destroy a potential enemy which is still in its rear staging area." The Soviets even coined a helpful catchphrase to describe this claimed ability to see everything, strike anything—the "military technical revolution"—and proclaimed their intention of producing their own versions. In no time, talk of this revolution was gathering momentum in U.S. military commentaries, largely thanks to assiduous promotion by an already legendary Pentagon official, Andrew Marshall. Trained as an economist, Marshall had spent his early career at the Rand Corporation, the famed Santa Monica–based think tank staffed with brilliant minds devising nuclear war strategies for the U.S. Air Force, which financed the undertaking. In retrospect it is clear that Rand's core mission was to devise strategies justifying and whenever possible enhancing the air force budget. When, for example, the navy's development of invulnerable ballistic-missile submarines threatened the air force's strategic nuclear monopoly in the early 1960s, Rand quickly served up a rationale for a "counterforce" strategy. According to this theory, the Soviets could be deterred only by precisely targeted nuclear warheads, which would necessitate a crash air force program for new intercontinental missiles with an accuracy that the navy could not deliver.

In 1973, under the patronage of Defense Secretary James R. Schlesinger (a fellow Rand alumnus), Marshall moved to the Pentagon to head a newly created Office of Net Assessment. He was still there, forty years later, in the second Obama administration. In the intervening period he had evolved into an object of reverence, perhaps because his proposals, despite their iconoclastic flavor, somehow never threatened established interests—and often required lavish additions to their budgets. Marshall's sharp eye for ambitious talent and his skill in the careful deployment of study contracts ensured that, while administrations came and went, generations of mutually supporting graduates of his office were seeded throughout the defense establishment, orbiting between corporations, the bureaucracy, and think tanks.

The eye-catching feature of the revolution in military affairs as popularized by Marshall and others was the emphasis on "precision guidance." This was a long-anticipated development. At the beginning of World War II the air force had claimed that its recently acquired Norden bomb sight, an instrument carried in the plane to enable the accurate launching of bombs, would ensure that 50 percent of its bombs would fall within 75 feet of their target. The boast went unfulfilled. On an infamous raid against the German ball-bearing works at Schweinfurt in October 1943, with the attackers suffering huge losses and little damage to the plants, only one in ten of Norden-aimed bombs fell within 500 feet of the target. (The device was still being used to drop sensors for the electronic barrier in 1967.) While the Norden sight was an attempt to position a bomber in the correct spot to drop a bomb, postwar efforts were concentrated on ways of guiding a bomb after it had left the bomber. In December 1968, John Foster told an interviewer that although bombing Vietnam had produced "meager results . . . we've recently developed a series of weapons that permit us to get incredible accuracies, as compared with normal aircraft delivery systems. Instead of having accuracies of hundreds of feet, we now talk in terms of ten feet."

At the time, this had been another idle boast. Repeated efforts to hit "critical" targets in North Vietnam were still missing by hundreds of yards. One such target was a bridge over a river about one hundred miles south of Hanoi near a town called Thanh Hoa that was supposedly crucial to the enemy supply effort. The air force and navy bombed it obsessively with guided and unguided bombs between 1965 and 1972 to zero effect—apart from the loss of dozens of pilots. Finally, in May 1972, the bridge was cut with two laser-guided bombs. Though hailed as a momentous event then and since, it turned out that the Vietnamese had stopped using the bridge years before, while traffic flowed unmolested across an undetected river ford five miles upstream. Meanwhile the bridge itself was put to use as the center of what Pentagon wags termed "a flourishing anti-aircraft school."

The notion that this triumph of precision might have been irrelevant found little favor where it counted. Under the tutelage of Perry and Defense Secretary Harold Brown (a former nuclear weapons lab director who had also had Perry's job directing defense research and development), billions of dollars poured into variants of precision guidance, some focused on directing the missile via a little TV camera in its nose or by tracking hot shapes with a heat-seeking infrared camera. Others followed the reflection of an infrared laser beam shone at the target by a pilot or a soldier on the ground. Once Ronald Reagan replaced Carter in 1981, defense spending, already inflated, went into a steeper climb, with the costs of all the revolutionary new weapons systems predictably following suit.

Among these were various subsystems of Assault Breaker that took on independent but nonetheless prosperous lives after the program was officially ended. The heart of the original system had been the component that Perry hoped would make it possible to see "all high value targets on the battlefield at any time." This radar was "side looking," meaning that the antenna stretched along the plane's fuselage and thus looked sideways, which, because of its size (bigger is better for radar antennae), promised to deliver sharper images. By filtering the data's echoes to display only objects in motion, the system was billed capable of revealing Soviet tank armies moving up in the rear. Unfortunately, it proved all too efficient at detecting any moving object, not merely tanks, but also automobiles and even trees blowing in the wind. Though the problem proved intractable, the program lived on, to the recurring benefit of the Northrop Corporation, under a variety of code names that ultimately settled on JSTARS for Joint Surveillance Target Attack System.

Soon after his appointment by Carter, Perry began assiduously promoting an even more ambitious concept, pouring huge amounts of money into a technology called radar cross-section reduction. This was first invented by the Germans to make their World War II submarine snorkels harder to detect with special shaping to reflect radar waves away from the sender and special materials to absorb radar. Perry renamed the technology "stealth" and changed the security classification from a low-level "confidential" to the highest levels of "top secret." Intimations that something new and incredibly sensitive was in the works helped to justify the massive funding while simultaneously making test data inaccessible to skeptics. Meanwhile, Perry pursued his grand vision of stealthy cruise missiles and large stealthy aircraft, even stealthy ships. The services were aghast at the impact the inevitably staggering cost would have on more cherished projects, but Perry calmed their fears by promising that the programs would be "technology driven, rather than funding driven," meaning that there would be no limits on spending for any apparently promising advance in technology. Behind the cloak of secrecy the multibillion-dollar B-2 strategic bomber and the smaller F-117 proceeded slowly and expensively toward production, their performance and, more important, their budgets screened from the outside world.

While these technologically ambitious programs were under development, one program founded on radically different principles was quietly entering service. The A-10 Thunderbolt II, to give it its official name, was commissioned to provide "close air support" to troops actually on the battlefield rather than to attack enemy forces far in the rear. Pilots soon renamed it "the Warthog." True to its core belief in waging war entirely independently of the other services, the air force had no interest in such a weapon, but there came a moment in the early 1970s when it seemed possible that the army might capture the close air-support mission for itself with a costly new helicopter, a development that would have deleterious effects on the air force budget. Consequently, the service turned to an analyst then working in the Office of the Secretary of Defense known for his unconventional view on the importance of the close-support mission.

Pierre Sprey, a mathematical prodigy whose parents had escaped to the United States from Nice in 1941, had worked summers at Grumman Aerospace from the age of fourteen, the year he was admitted to Yale. By the time he had left Yale at age eighteen and moved to Cornell for his masters, Grumman was paying him as a statistical consultant on programs that included NASA's Lunar Excursion Vehicle and navy jets. In 1960 he was enlisted to work on an experiment with a direct bearing on "remote sensing" systems of the kind that would one day enable operators looking at a video screen in Nevada to target a truckload of tribesmen on the other side of the world. The experiment was designed to test whether it was worth putting TV cameras in reconnaissance planes to give pilots images better than those they could get with the naked eye.

In a research facility on Long Island a Grumman team crafted a display filled with models of tanks, jeeps, command posts, and other tactical targets, all carefully camouflaged to appear as they would on an actual battlefield. Combat veterans monitored the effort to ensure realism. An observation platform overlooking the display gave observers the same view they would have from an airplane, with a shutter in front of the platform that could be opened to allow only as much time to view the scene, ten or twenty seconds, as a pilot would have as he flew past. In those few seconds the observers were asked to pick out as many targets as they could. Then, for the same amount of time, observers were shown a TV picture using a high-definition camera of a similar display and asked again to look for targets. The results were surprising. Only when the camera had zoomed in enough to show a narrow view, the equivalent of looking down through a soda straw from 15,000 feet up and seeing an area no larger than two tennis courts, were the TV viewers able to find as many targets as those spotted with the naked eye. *But the TV viewers also identified five times as many false targets—tanks and other objects that were not there—as those identified with plain eyesight.* The implications were very clear: electronic imaging does not depict battlefield reality with the same acuity as the human eye, an essential truth long forgotten by the time the U.S. military and CIA began watching the world via drone-fed video imagery, with tragic consequences for many a false target.

Graduating with a masters in operations research and mathematical statistics, Sprey worked full-time at Grumman for two years until, in 1966, he moved on to the Pentagon as a member of the "whiz kids," an iconoclastic team of analysts recruited by Defense Secretary McNamara to bring a fresh look to military thinking. Before long, the young mathematician had earned the wrath of air force generals with a study demonstrating that their plan to fight the Soviets in Europe with long-range bombing was essentially worthless and that the only effective use of airpower was in close support of ground forces on the battlefield. Faced with the political necessity of fending off the army's bid for the close-support mission and the money that went with it, the chief of staff, a devious bureaucratic politician named John McConnell, detailed Sprey, despite the repugnance of his views on air power, to come up with the basic design for a close-support plane that would underbid the army's helicopter candidate.

Endowed with this high-level support, Sprey conceived a design that enabled pilots to operate low and close to the battlefield (thanks to the plane's maneuverability and multiple safety features) and thus be in a position to see *and judge for themselves* what course of action to take. This was a very far cry from the sensor-dependent concepts underpinning the revolution in military affairs, but faced with the threat from the army, the air force went ahead and put the plane into production.

Like all new systems, the A-10, which first flew in 1975, was officially justified by the perennial Soviet threat, which would be confronted in a mighty clash on the plains of Europe sometime in the future. In reality, an actual Soviet invasion of Western Europe seemed highly unlikely (though Andrew Marshall proposed in the 1980s that a weakening USSR might "lash out," thereby generating a billion-dollar nuclear shelter scheme). Then, to everyone's complete surprise, opportunity knocked for a real live demonstration of what the post-Vietnam high-technology military could do, and under near-perfect conditions.

Within a few days of Iraq dictator Saddam Hussein's invasion of Kuwait in August 1990, U.S. Central Command forces had been rushed to Saudi Arabia to prepare the counterattack. Following in their wake came the air force's Deputy Director for Strategy, Doctrine, and War-Fighting, Colonel John Warden, complete with a plan for the air force to win the war on its own. Warden, deeply immersed in the subject of bombing, had long ruminated on the theory that identifying and destroying a limited number of specific "centers of gravity" essential to the functioning of an enemy society would lead inescapably to the enemy's collapse or paralysis.

This was not a new idea; the air force had maintained for years that the destruction of "critical nodes" would ensure such an outcome. The problem had always been how to identify these critical targets, let alone put them out of action. Repeatedly, during bombing campaigns, assaults on supposedly crucial nodes tended to yield minimal effects, so new nodes were designated and targeted. In World War II, for example,

ball-bearing plants were succeeded by rail networks, which were followed by oil refineries. None of them brought about the anticipated
enemy collapse. In addition, a recurring consequence of these campaigns had been an eventual broadening of target categories, so that
in the end, everything got hit. As we shall see, this syndrome applies
even when the targets are individual humans rather than things.

Warden believed that technology had changed the equation. New
methods of intelligence and surveillance, including radars such as
JSTARS, combined with stealth bombers invisible to enemy defenses
and precision-guided bombs and missiles would enable U.S. bombers
to do their job not only rapidly but with a gratifying economy of force:
one plane accomplishing what had required hundreds or thousands
of missions in World War II. As for targets, he had developed what he
called the "five rings" theory, in which the rings denoted targets of progressively greater criticality, with the innermost representing the enemy
leadership. The other rings were "centers of gravity," such as power
plants and communications centers, which, if put out of action, would
lead to enemy paralysis in a neat, surgical, and above all predictable
manner. Resorting to metaphor, Warden compared an enemy system
to the human body, with the brain and nerves representing enemy leadership, bones representing infrastructure, and so on. This sounded like
an "organic" approach to war, except of course the human body cannot replicate or bypass lost parts, whereas enemies like General Nguyen,
defender of the Ho Chi Minh Trail, certainly could.

Untroubled by such quibbles, Warden and a specially assembled
team code-named Checkmate drew up a plan, Instant Thunder, which
he was convinced could defeat Iraq without the army firing a shot. The
targets associated with each ring were duly posted on a board in Checkmate's Pentagon basement office. At the top of the "leadership" list, the
most important target, was a name: Saddam. Critical nodes were no
longer just *things*—bridges, oil tanks, and power plants—now they
could be *people*. Two days later someone remembered that assassination was officially banned as an instrument of U.S. foreign policy.
Saddam's name was erased and the entry changed to "Isolate and
incapacitate Saddam's regime."

Under "Expected results," Warden wrote: "National leadership and command and control destroyed." He estimated it would take six days. After getting an enthusiastic response from the chairman of the Joint Chiefs of Staff, Colin Powell, who exclaimed, "This could win the war!," Warden flew with his team to Saudi Arabia to lay out the plan to General Charles Horner, commander of the coming air war with Iraq.

Horner, a notoriously emotional character, took an instant dislike to the obsessive theorist from Washington and ordered him on the next plane home. However, Warden had brought with him Lieutenant Colonel David Deptula, who had been seconded to the planning team from the office of the secretary of the air force. Deptula, a former fighter pilot like Warden, had developed greater skills as a bureaucratic politician. Earlier in 1990 he had coined the air force's new motto: "Global Reach— Global Power," the title of a manifesto he penned at the secretary's request, touting the air force's unique and enduringly desirable attributes of "speed, range, precision, and lethality" in a changing world when the Soviet threat appeared to be going away. These assets, he noted, offered "decisive capabilities against potentially well-equipped foes at minimum cost in casualties—increasingly important in an era in which we believe the American people will have low tolerance for prolonged combat operations or mounting casualties."

While a despondent Warden flew back to Washington, Deptula had ingratiated himself sufficiently with Horner to stay in Riyadh and was soon ensconced at headquarters as the chief attack planner for the coming war. With Warden's ideas and Horner's backing, he was about to make his reputation.

The air attack on Iraq launched on January 16, 1991, incorporated the basic scheme of Instant Thunder and appeared to be a triumphant success. Lights went out all over the country. Military and other government headquarters were neatly demolished without damage to their neighbors. Within a few days, residential streets in affluent districts of the capital bore the stench of meat that had rotted in freezers left without power. Adding to the triumph were the TV broadcasts of videos beamed from the bombs' cameras as they unerringly zeroed in on their targets. For the first time the public at home could watch and thrill at the air force's "precision and lethality" administered with cool professional efficiency. (The navy, to its chagrin, had not installed the necessary equipment for broadcasting the videos and was thus bested in the public relations war.) Publicity regarding the hitherto highly secret Lockheed F-117 stealth bomber, with its excitingly futuristic design and mystique of invisibility, only added to the allure. As Lockheed publicists reported, on the first night of the war, the plane had "collapsed Saddam Hussein's air defenses and all but eliminated Iraq's ability to wage coordinated war." Not to be outdone, Texas Instruments, makers of the Paveway III laser bomb-guidance system, advertised "one target, one bomb."

Even at the time there were some disquieting indications that not everything was going as predicted. Though the Iraqi air force had been easily neutralized, the Iraqi army remained obdurately in place in Kuwait, clearly still receiving and responding to orders from Baghdad. When Iraqi Scuds fired from mobile launchers started landing on Tel Aviv, intense surveillance efforts using all available technologies failed to find a single launcher. The Iraqi army was driven out of Kuwait only when attacked and outmaneuvered by U.S. and allied ground troops. Saddam, the one-man innermost ring, remained alive and in charge.

Nevertheless, the impression prevailed that the war had been an unalloyed triumph for airborne technology. The promises of Foster, Westmoreland, Perry, and Deptula had been dramatically vindicated, as some of them were happy to point out. Writing soon after the war, Perry celebrated the success of various systems he had fostered and championed, including JSTARS and other surveillance systems—"manned and unmanned"—that had tracked the enemy on a continual basis, not to mention the stealth bombers, 80 percent of whose bombs, he claimed, had destroyed their targets. Andrew Marshall was quick to catch the wave, encouraging a military assistant, Andrew Krepinevich, to pen a pamphlet, "The Military-Technical Revolution: A Preliminary Assessment," that echoed Warden's nostrums about centers of gravity, precision strikes, and other possibilities of the new technology. A year later it was reissued with the catchier title "Revolution in Military Affairs," a phrase that was soon firmly lodged in the defense-intellectual lexicon.

Deptula, who had moved back to the air staff headquarters in Washington, also took to print. The operation he had planned and directed, he began telling the world, had marked a "Change in the Nature of Warfare." The new technologies, especially stealth, had spawned "parallel warfare," whereby it was possible to attack and disable an enemy in one fell swoop, rather than sequentially eliminating air defenses and then other targets, thus foreclosing the enemy's ability to recover.

Over time, Deptula expanded his vision, unveiling the concept of effects-based operations, the notion that precision now made it possible "not just to impede the means of the enemy to conduct war or the will of the people to continue war, but the very ability of the enemy to control its vital functions." In other words, it was now possible so thoroughly to understand the way an enemy system functioned, its "centers of gravity," as he (and Warden) termed it, as to predict precisely the reverberating effects of destroying a particular target. It was a beguiling concept, especially to the air force at a time when the disappearance of the Soviet enemy threatened U.S. military budget cuts.

Unfortunately, the Gulf War as invoked by Deptula, Perry, Marshall, and others was not the war that had been fought. True, most of Iraq's power supply had been knocked out on the first night or shortly afterward, reducing Iraqi civilian society to a preindustrial state in one stroke. All major bridges met the same fate, as did the phone system, TV, and radio. The Iraqi army had certainly been hard hit from the air, though most of the damage was inflicted not by the huge allied fleet of high-speed jets but by a force of 122 A-10s that had been reluctantly dispatched by the air force to the Gulf at the urgent insistence of commander in chief General Norman Schwarzkopf. Thanks to its carefully designed attributes of ruggedness and maneuverability at low altitudes, the plane proved supremely effective at destroying Iraqi armor and other units in the field, so much so that the emotional General Horner was famously moved to signal the Pentagon that "the A-10 saved my ass."

Meanwhile, despite expectations (and media exhortations to "go after" the Iraqi dictator), Saddam Hussein, the "first circle," had been neither hit nor cut off from control of his government. Inevitably, he had reacted and adapted. As former Iraqi military intelligence chief Wafiq al-Sammarai explained to me later, "Saddam would come to my headquarters every day but at random times. He traveled in an ordinary Baghdad taxi, just with a driver. No guards or entourage." Al-Sammarai himself had moved out of his headquarters a day before the war and watched from his new location as the U.S. carefully gutted his empty former office.

Even systems that had demonstrably failed could bask in the warm glow of the technological triumph. Thus JSTARS' side-looking radar, the system originally developed for Assault Breaker to detect Soviet tank columns, could find no sign of the mobile Scud launchers moving stealthily about the deserts of western Iraq, despite their being the highest-priority target of the war. (The two prototypes of this system used in the war zone were inside preowned Boeing 707s. Previously used to ship cattle around the Middle East, they stank of cow manure.)

Needless to say, the various official and semiofficial post mortems did not stress such aspects of the conflict, and so the merits of pinpoint accuracy and invisible planes went unchallenged while the relevant weapons programs, and the corporations that sold them, grew and prospered. Only in 1996, when the General Accounting Office published the results of a diligent three-year investigation, did light dawn on what had actually happened. The F-117 had not flown unescorted and unafraid to its targets. It always needed the company of many escorting planes dedicated to jamming the enemy radars that supposedly could not see the Lockheed plane anyhow. So far from "one target, one bomb," it had taken an average of four of the most accurate laser weapons, and sometimes ten, to destroy a target. Overall, the investigators concluded, "Many of DOD's and manufacturers' postwar claims about weapons system performance . . . were overstated, misleading, inconsistent with the best available data, or unverifiable."

It didn't make any difference. By the time the investigators issued their sobering findings, the revolution in military affairs was carrying all before it. Though defense spending overall sank for a few years—the superpower enemy poised to pour through the Fulda Gap had disappeared, after all—research in and development of all the exciting possibilities foreshadowed in the Desert Storm triumph roared ahead, much of it aimed at the same goals that Igloo White and Task Force Alpha had pursued so many years before.

Catchphrases such as "system of systems" and "net-centric warfare," introduced in the 1990s, were still expressions of the idea that it is feasible to collect, sift, and use information with a minimum of human intervention. "If we are able to view a strategic battlefield and prevent an enemy from doing so, we have dominant battlefield awareness," Admiral William Owens, vice chairman of the Joint Chiefs of Staff, told Congress in 2001, "and we are certain to prevail in a conflict." Owens, an influential figure who talked about RMA (revolution in military affairs) a lot, also coined the acronym ISR for *intelligence, surveillance, and reconnaissance*, a term destined to loom ever larger in intelligence planning and budgets. Other high-ranking officers talked wistfully of how "if we had today's sensors, we would have won in Vietnam."

Another influential admiral, Arthur Cebrowski, is credited with inventing the term *net-centric* to describe the virtues and possibilities of connecting all sources of information—planes, ships, drones, the more the better—to put them in constant communication with a central processor and each other. He drew inspiration from the Wal-Mart chain of superstores, deemed a net-centric organization because every time a cash register rang up a light-bulb sale, a central computer automatically ordered a new bulb from the supplier.

Much of the excitement had been generated by the rapidly increasing power of computers. The Pentium III microprocessor introduced in 1998, for example, had a "clock speed" eighty times faster than that of Task Force Alpha's IBM 360/65 and over a hundred thousand times more directly accessible memory. But while computers had become more powerful, the sensors providing the information, such as infrared and TV cameras, still could not distinguish one hot spot from another or see through smoke or haze. These were facts of life that would not go away.

This inherent problem was apparently lost on Cebrowski, who suggested that if every soldier and warplane was connected up like the Wal-Mart cash registers, an entire force could operate as a coordinated mechanism, identifying and destroying targets with maximum efficiency and discrimination. Jasons pondering how to block the Ho Chi Minh Trail back in the summer of 1966 would have caught on to the idea immediately. Unsurprisingly, the defense intelligentsia was quick to fall into line. Two Rand Corporation researchers, David Ronfeldt and John Arquilla, academic foot soldiers in the revolution in military affairs, popularized the notions of "cyberwar" and "netwar" as well as the catchy slogan "It takes a network to defeat a network."

Meanwhile, politicians were getting in on the act. In 1996 Senators Joseph Lieberman and Dan Coats sponsored a National Defense Panel as a forum to advance "the revolution in military affairs." Andrew Krepinevich, the Marshall aide who had coined the revolutionary slogan, was picked to represent the senate Democrats on the panel. The Republicans selected a burly former naval officer and fellow graduate of the Marshall office, Richard Armitage. Their report, "Transforming Defense: National Security in the 21st Century," was a paean to revolutionary techno-wizardry, thanks to which a transformed military would be able to "project power" around the globe. Prominent in their conception was a huge role for unmanned aircraft—drones—in every aspect of the fight. "Air forces," for example "would place greater emphasis on operating at extended ranges, relying heavily on long-range aircraft and extended-range unmanned systems, employing advanced precision and brilliant munitions. . . . Aircraft, unmanned aerial vehicles, and unmanned combat aerial vehicles operating in theater could stage at peripheral bases outside enemy missile range . . ."

Not everyone bought in. Paul Van Riper, for example, an acerbic and somewhat intimidating three-star marine general, publicly derided the doctrine of "information superiority," as preached by Owens, Cebrowski, and others, which he said consisted of "sweeping assertions and dogmatic platitudes." Nor did Van Riper think much of airpower enthusiasts in general, on occasion delivering a speech entitled "From Douhet to Deptula, a History of Failed Promises" in which he referred scathingly to "those who espouse much of the current nonsense" coming from "organizations within the armed forces that are generally far removed from the confusion and horror of the close-in fighting that occurs in real war. . . . 'Fighting' for them revolves around the movement of icons and tracks on a screen." A Vietnam combat veteran who had made a name for himself as a junior officer for "leading from the front," Van Riper was amazed, as he told me later, "that people who were smart could believe this stuff. The hubris was unbelievable."

Such critiques had little effect, partly because the most influential figure in U.S. defense policy for most of the 1990s was William Perry, who returned to the Pentagon as deputy defense secretary in 1993 and was promoted to secretary the following year. Among his first acts was to direct and subsidize a series of mergers among the major defense contractors on the grounds that the end of the cold war rendered a spending famine inevitable. As it turned out the relatively small decline that did occur lasted only for a brief period in the 1990s, after which spending began once again to edge up and then soar far above even the cold war's bountiful levels. Meanwhile Perry continued to pursue the dream, unrealized in Desert Storm, of seeing "all high value targets on the battlefield at any time."

Perry's undeviating objectives were of course a reaffirmation of those pursued by his predecessor, John Foster, ardent proponent of Task Force Alpha. But Foster, the model-airplane enthusiast, had felt no less strongly about the ultimate weapon that would not only see all those high-value targets but also destroy them. In 1973, in his final session of congressional testimony before a deferential house committee, Foster was asked about his priorities for defense. "To improve surveillance" over land and sea, he answered, and "to get remotely controlled vehicles that can perform that surveillance *and the attack missions.*" The age of drones was not far off.

Foster had hoped that unmanned aircraft might play their part over the Ho Chi Minh Trail, but the effort had proved unsuccessful. Even so, money continued to sluice into drone development for some time after the United States had pulled out of Vietnam, but it was difficult to pretend that drones could defend themselves against Soviet antiaircraft missiles and fighters. For that, a thinking pilot on the scene was obviously necessary. Even so, Boeing and other defense corporations mobilized support in Congress for various drone projects, including Condor, an enormous high-flier proposed by Boeing, with a wingspan wider than that of a 747. None got further than the test stage.

But with the Soviets gone, the U.S. military would now be operating where there was little or no danger from unfriendly fire in the air, a perfect time for drones to flourish. Civil wars in defenseless Somalia, Bosnia, and elsewhere provided a strong rationale for ever more surveillance, for which drones were thought to be ideal.

Perry helped speed the process along by setting up a special office under his direct control called the Defense Airborne Reconnaissance Office to develop and buy a whole new generation of drones. Most of these projects never came into service. One that did was called Predator, the weapon that in the eyes of large parts of the world would one day come to define America.

4

# PREDATOR
# POLITICS

The various drone programs that blossomed during the cold war decades before fading away again in the face of military irrelevance and technical unfeasibility had been supervised by major defense corporations such as Boeing and Northrop, with impressive price tags to match. The machine that captured the twenty-first-century world's imagination, however, originated with an Israeli immigrant with an impressive record of quarreling with employers, and a fringe defense contractor, albeit one with a knack for cultivating useful connections.

The Predator drone was originally designed by Avraham Karem, an Israeli once deemed so irascible by Pentagon overseers they insisted that his daughter be the chief financial officer and spokesperson for his corporation. Born in Iraq in 1937, Karem had grown up with a fascination for model planes, which took him to the Israeli air force and eventually to the design shop of the state-owned Israeli Aircraft Industries. After falling out with his employer thanks, he says, to his single-minded fascination with drones, Karem moved to California in 1977 and continued designing pilotless planes. One potential customer was the U.S. Navy, which was in the process of acquiring large numbers of cruise missiles, one of the projects fostered so assiduously by William Perry. The missiles, themselves essentially self-guiding drones, bore claims of impressive accuracy and gratifyingly extensive range capable of reaching far-off Soviet fleets should the opportunity for a future replay of the Battle of Midway present itself. But the navy had no way of finding the enemy's precise location in real time; hence the promise of Karem's drone. Code-named Amber, it was a cigar-shaped vehicle with an odd-shaped inverted-V tail so that the aircraft could be fired out of a torpedo tube. Once aloft, it had the capacity to beam back video images (though not over long distances). But, as in the case of so many earlier drone programs, after the funding of the design and prototype, official interest flickered and died. However, just as Karem's company, Leading Systems, spiraled into bankruptcy in 1990, a rescuer appeared.

The General Atomics Corporation had begun life in 1955 as an off-shoot of the General Dynamics Corporation whose aim was that of breaking into the nuclear-reactor market. Coincidentally, its initial project, the Triga research reactor, was conceived by a group of nuclear-weapons designers who were active members of the Jasons recruited to the company's San Diego headquarters by fellow Manhattan Project alumnus Freddy de Hoffman. The company also sponsored the same group in Project Orion, a scheme to propel spaceships by exploding nuclear bombs, which never progressed further than the lively imaginations of the physicists who dreamed it up. After parting company with parent General Dynamics, the company passed through the hands of various oil corporations until it was bought in 1986 for $60 million by the Blue brothers of Denver, Colorado. Neal Blue, thirty-five at the time, assumed the office of chairman, while his thirty-three-year-old sibling, Linden, was installed as deputy chairman.

As they have told their story, these scions of a wealthy family were aviation devotees from an early age. By the time Neal was twenty-one, he and his brother were flying a single-prop plane around Latin America. Among the contacts they made south of the border was the long-standing Nicaraguan dictator Anastasio Samoza, with whom they formed a business partnership that lasted right up until Sandinista revolutionaries ejected the Samoza family in 1979. As Neal later told an interviewer, he and his brother were "enthusiastic supporters" of the Contra rebels who sought, unsuccessfully, to overthrow the Sandinistas in the 1980s.

In 1982 Neal was hired by the major defense contractor Raytheon to run their newly acquired Beech Aircraft subsidiary. In this capacity he battled the machinist unions, which were opposed to his plans to introduce labor-saving composite materials. Simultaneously he embarked on a scheme to turn a pristine Alpine landscape abutting Telluride, Colorado, into a major subdivision, complete with condos, hotels, and golf courses. Furious residents blocked the scheme, ultimately raising $50 million to acquire the land through eminent domain, and although Neal battled for twenty-five years, he never realized his dream of the subdivision.

Though the founders of General Atomics had sought to discover new technologies for nuclear power, the Blues initially opted for a more traditional business model, buying a uranium deposit in northwest New Mexico, the largest in the country. The brothers also bought the decrepit Sequoyah uranium-processing facility in eastern Oklahoma that had had a radioactive leak equivalent in size to Three Mile Island just a few years earlier. A nine-legged frog had been discovered nearby. Undeterred, General Atomics kept operating the leaky facility, cranking out specialized uranium metal used in fuel rods and armor-piercing munitions until 1992, before finally shutting it down after the plant experienced yet another major release of radioactive material. An investigation found that groundwater near the plant was 35,000 times above the legal limit of permitted levels of radioactivity and that the company should have known the plant was leaking radioactive waste but did not stop it.

Profitable though mining toxic materials might be (the Blues had another uranium operation in Australia), the mother lodes of government contracts could be at least as rich. Among the brothers' goals in buying General Atomics was the prospect of lucrative business from the Star Wars missile defense initiative launched by Ronald Reagan three years before. To that end they set up a defense programs group within the company with an advisory board decorated with Washington door openers, including former secretary of state Alexander Haig and former Joint Chiefs chairman John Vessey. In 1987 the Blues turned to a recently retired navy admiral, Thomas Cassidy, to helm a newly created "advanced technology projects division." Cassidy, described by subordinates as "not beloved, but admired," had formerly been in command of the nearby Miramar Naval Air Station but had been relieved of his command following an investigation into irregularities in the purchase of overpriced ashtrays and maintenance tools for the base. He was later reinstated after an appeal.

Installed in the General Atomics "campus" on the outskirts of San Diego, Cassidy and the brothers identified unmanned aircraft— drones—as a niche market in which a comparatively small company like theirs might stand a chance against the "primes" (meaning the major contractors). At the end of 1988 the company demonstrated a 16-foot prototype that Cassidy claimed could deliver "300 pounds of explosives, or a small nuclear warhead, to a target 300 miles away for a cost of $30,000." But the Predator, as the device was called, repeatedly crashed and failed to generate any military interest.

Meanwhile Avraham Karem's company, Leading Systems, had slid into bankruptcy when the navy cancelled its order for his torpedo tube– launched Amber drone. Sensing a quick and cheap road to success, the brothers snapped up the assets of Karem's foundering company as well as his own services. One of the assets the Israeli brought with him was an acquaintanceship with R. James Woolsey, a former secretary of the navy appointed to head the CIA by President Clinton following the 1992 election. Woolsey, a protégé of arch-neoconservative Richard Perle, combined eager enthusiasm for spy-craft gadgetry with a strong affection for all things Israeli. Karem's design suddenly became a CIA program, and a prototype was dispatched to Albania to fly over the battlefields of the burgeoning Balkan civil wars. As it turned out, dreams of a persistent bird's-eye view of the complicated ethnic conflicts on the ground were dashed. Of thirty-two flights planned, only twelve were completed, and those reportedly yielded no useful intelligence of any kind. Loath to waste a good name, the Blues called it Predator, after their earlier failed initiative.

Karem's design had the aerodynamics of a glider, its light weight (thanks to the plastics of which it was made) and long, thin wings allowing it to remain aloft for many hours. On the other hand, those wings also made it extremely vulnerable to wind shifts while taking off and landing (especially because it was piloted by remote control), which led to an extraordinarily high rate of crashes. Almost half the 268 Predators ultimately bought by the U.S. Air Force would be involved in major accidents. They were too delicate to fly in anything but perfectly calm weather. In the interests of making the drone's noisy presence less obvious, the CIA demanded the addition of a muffler to its otherwise famously reliable Rotax piston engine. The consequent chronic overheating led to numerous engine failures and crashes, a problem that continues to this day. ("The problem is that nobody is comfortable with Predator. Nobody," said the pilot of a Predator that crashed at Cannon Air Force Base in New Mexico in 2010, calling the notoriously unreliable drone "the most back-assedward aircraft I have ever flown.")

The Predator that first flew in 1994 (Karem had parted company with General Atomics a month before) might have lingered as a historical footnote, like many abortive drone programs before it, had it not been for unrelated advances in technology that opened up new possibilities for drones just as the Predator was ready for market.

Up until this point, all drone projects had faced two major problems. First of all, once the aircraft was out of sight beyond the horizon, it was exceedingly difficult to know exactly where it was and thus navigate it to follow the desired flight path. Second, communicating with the drone beyond the horizon, either to send commands or receive whatever information it might be picking up, was impossible, given that the required high-frequency radio signals would not follow the curve of the earth.

As it happened, the U.S. Navy also had been wrestling with a precision-navigation difficulty. For decades after they were introduced, submarine-launched ballistic nuclear missiles were acknowledged to be less accurate than their rival land-based ICBMs because the launching submarine could not know precisely where it was when firing the missile. The navy's missiles were therefore limited to large targets, such as cities, rather than more precise objectives such as the Kremlin, or Soviet command posts, so the search for a solution was the navy's highest priority. The answer that eventually emerged enabled the navy to claim accuracy on par with that of the air force. Along the way, it changed the way our society functions.

Familiar to anyone with a smartphone, the Global Positioning System (GPS), designed primarily by inventor Roger L. Easton, consists of 31 satellites, each passing overhead at an altitude of 12,600 miles twice a day. Their orbits ensure that, at any one time, at least 4 satellites are in line of sight from any point on the planet. Each satellite continually broadcasts its position as well as the time it is making the broadcast. A receiver on the ground, such as an automobile's GPS or a smartphone, calculates how long it has taken each signal to travel from space, thereby establishing its own position relative to the satellites.

After a period of tests, the air force began launching these satellites in 1989, and by the following year U.S. troops in Saudi Arabia preparing for war with Iraq were using the system to find their way around the desert, though not always with success. By 1993 there were twenty-four satellites aloft. (The thirty-one now in orbit include spares.) Over the following twenty years, GPS would find applications far removed from submarine-launched missiles or even vehicle (car, boat, or plane) navigation. These include bank ATMs, cell-phone networks, stock trading, and the electric power grid, all of which depend on the precise time signals provided by the system for their all-important security encryption.

More or less simultaneous with the GPS-derived revolution in navigation came a revolution in communications technology that was no less vital in promoting the rise of drones. Thanks mainly to exponential increases in the amount of data that could be transmitted via satellite, available bandwidth soared during the 1990s and beyond. Thus the amount of information, quantified in "bits," transmitted by satellite and fiber-optic cable increased forty times just between 1999 and 2002. This was just as well for the U.S. military. "Net-centricity," after all, required vast communication capacity. Thus the comparatively minuscule American force involved in the 1999 Kosovo war—entirely fought from the air—used two and a half times the bandwidth consumed by the force that had fought Iraq in 1991—over half a million men. Thanks to the revolution in communications technology, such extravagance was possible.

Two years after the twenty-fourth GPS satellite soared into orbit in 1993, a small fleet of prototype Predators controlled from a U.S. Army base in Albania was in the air over the Balkans, surveying the ongoing civil war in Bosnia. (The craft now had a distinctive bulge at the front housing a satellite antenna.) Two of these prototypes disappeared during the 1995 missions, either crashed or shot down.

Prone to breakdown and requiring perfect weather, the curiously shaped little airplane might yet have joined the many similarly esoteric prototypes thronging the nation's military aviation museums had it not suddenly been picked up and borne aloft by the underlying currents that propel U.S. weapons development: money and politics. It was an area in which General Atomics was well equipped to compete.

Any veteran of the U.S. defense establishment knows that the fiercest battles and deepest enmities are reserved not for the official enemy but for service rivals in the ceaseless struggle for budget share. Budgets, it should be remembered, are always the source and symbol of power in Washington. For the military services, budget share is largely determined by "roles and missions," control of which in turn determines the strategies that protect service budgets. For example, back in the cold war, the air force initially held the strategic nuclear role and mission, meaning it had a monopoly on funding for delivering nuclear weapons on Russian targets. Then the navy developed submarine-launched missiles, invulnerable to an enemy surprise attack. The air force, its role and therefore a large slice of its budget threatened, quickly devised and promoted a strategy that required precision intercontinental missile strikes, which the navy's less accurate missiles could not

deliver. Thanks to the new strategy, the air force strategic-missile budget was saved. Former air force chief of staff Curtis LeMay expressed
the spirit of interservice camaraderie when he remarked of a forthcoming Army-Navy football game, "I hope they both lose."

In October 1994, when General Ronald Fogleman, a former fighter
pilot and veteran of Vietnam (he had narrowly escaped capture after
being shot down in his F-100 fighter) took over as chief of staff of the
U.S. Air Force, he was shocked upon learning that Predator was under
the purview of the U.S. Army. Ever since the air force had gained independence in 1947, it had jealously guarded its exclusive right to operate all fixed-wing aircraft, including reconnaissance. A lightweight,
unmanned craft that flew at 80 mph would be a very thin end of the
wedge, but the army was claiming a "major breakthrough in UAV
[Unmanned Aerial Vehicle] technology," while publicity over Predator's involvement in actual combat operations was generating attention in Congress.

Fogleman moved swiftly to seize the initiative. Millions of taxpayer
dollars had already been poured into a brand-new training site for
drones at Fort Huachuca, in Arizona, but even though Predators had
not yet been assigned to the air force, Fogelman, acting unilaterally,
set up a special squadron dedicated to drone operations at Indian
Springs, a base outside Las Vegas. The U.S. Army has a long tradition
of bureaucratic defeat that goes all the way back to its loss of what had
been the Army–Air Force following World War II, and Fogleman's
determined onslaught yielded the traditional result. By the end of 1995
the army had caved, ceding control of Predator operations in return
for a vague promise that the air force would respond to its "battlefield
reconnaissance needs."

Victory was not yet total, however. In April 1996, William Perry,
by now defense secretary, signed an order that confirmed the air force
as "the lead service for operating and maintaining the Predator UAV"
but left "responsibility for system development and procurement" with
the navy. This was no good at all, the navy being a much more formidable opponent on the budgetary battlegrounds than the army. Both
Fogleman and General Atomics had need of a higher power, which duly

arrived in the form of Representative Charles Jeremy "Jerry" Lewis, Republican member of Congress for California's Forty-first District and a staunch ally of both General Atomics and the Predator. As Neal Blue, who contributed $100,000 to Republican campaigns in 1988 alone, observed in a rare interview for *Defense News*, "For our size, we possess more significant political capital than you might think."

As originally written, President Dwight Eisenhower's epochal 1961 farewell address had warned of the "military-industrial-congressional-complex" and its "economic, political, even spiritual" influence at every level of government. On delivery, the reference to Congress had disappeared. "It was more than enough to take on the military and private industry. I couldn't take on the congress as well," the president explained afterward. In his years of power, Jerry Lewis amply demonstrated that Ike had been right the first time. First elected to Congress in 1978, Lewis rose steadily through the Republican ranks, securing potent slots in the hierarchy on the appropriations, armed services, and intelligence committees, to the great benefit of his constituents and campaign contributors, who reciprocated his generosity with votes and checks. In 1999 he secured the chairmanship of the House Defense Appropriations Subcommittee, a post that gave him suzerainty over the entire Pentagon budget, then running at $289 billion. "We must provide the resources our men and women in uniform need," he announced to the full House Appropriations Committee the following year, "to maintain America's role as the world's last superpower." In 2005 Lewis took command of the full appropriations committee and in 2006 was nominated, for the first but not the last time, by the Center for Responsibility and Ethics in Washington as one of the twenty most corrupt members of Congress. The honor was bestowed principally in recognition of his tangled relationship with the lobbying firm of Copeland Lowery Jacquez Denton & White, on behalf of which hundreds of millions of dollars in federal contracts were disgorged by Lewis' appropriations committee to the firm's clients while Mr. Lowery, his partners, and their spouses contributed $480,000 to Congressman Lewis' campaign committee and other related funds between 2000 and 2005.

Lewis was a good friend to General Atomics and the Predator. As a colleague no less practiced in the lubrication of defense contracts, the late Jack Murtha (D-Pa), remarked in a 2003 hearing, "The chairman [Lewis] is too modest when he talks about the Predator. If it hadn't been for him there wouldn't be no Predator. He was the guy that pushed it. He was the guy that got criticized and he was the guy that they tried to stop from putting it out in the field. And he persisted and that Predator is one of the most important systems that we have."

Thus it was that Lewis, in his capacity as vice chairman of the House Intelligence Committee, inserted a provision in the 1998 intelligence authorization bill mandating that all authority over the Predator and all its funding be transferred to the air force. Simultaneously, Michael Meermans, an influential intelligence committee staffer, made sure that Big Safari, a semi-secret air force development office empowered to cut corners on development funding (and, coincidentally, Meermans' previous employer), be assigned to oversee Predator development. A Big Safari team accordingly moved into the General Atomics plant in an effort to make the machine perform some useful function, which, as we shall see, was not entirely successful. Meanwhile, General John Jumper, the head of Air Force Combat Command, deputed staffers to begin drawing up official requirements for what the Predator was actually expected to do. Jumper, who would succeed Fogleman as chief of staff, firmly believed that drones were the wave of the future as far as the air force was concerned and was ordering his priorities accordingly.

By 1999, when the Clinton administration led NATO into an air campaign against Serbia, the Predators were ready to play a part.

The three-month war on behalf of the insurgency in Kosovo, an ethnically distinct province of Serbia, put the revolution in military affairs on full display. NATO Supreme Commander General Wesley K. Clark was confident enough at the beginning to predict victory in three days. As in the 1991 Gulf War, "critical nodes"—bridges, TV stations, power plants—were targeted along with Serb army units. Also hit were businesses belonging to President Milošević's friends; strategists assumed that "crony targeting" would generate enough pressure on the Serbian leader to cave. As Deptula, by now a brigadier general, later remarked, particular targets had been attacked "to achieve a specific effect within the parent system." Deptula himself was away in Turkey commanding the no-fly zone over northern Iraq, but as an admiring biographer stresses, "Deptula's ideas guided planning and execution, though he was not present in the command structure." Stealth bombers were once again given a leading role although one was shot down and another badly damaged (Serb radar could track it after all), along with every available tool of ISR, which now included a growing fleet of Predator drones.

Despite Clark's confident prediction of imminent victory at the outset of the Kosovo operation, days turned into weeks as bombs rained down on a steadily expanding list of targets. Eventually, after eleven weeks and one day, President Milošević agreed to evacuate Kosovo. That made it easy for airpower partisans to claim victory, especially as not a single airman had been lost to enemy fire. In fact, Milošević caved only when his indispensable ally, Russian President Boris Yeltsin, withdrew his support following high-level U.S.–Russian negotiations in Moscow. As General Michael Jackson, commander of the British contingent, said afterward, Yeltsin's desertion "had the greatest significance in ending the war" because Milošević had banked everything on keeping Moscow's support.

Nevertheless General Henry Shelton, chairman of the Joint Chiefs of Staff, quickly announced that the happy result was due to NATO bombs and missiles, which, according to Clark, had destroyed "around 120 tanks . . . about 220 armored personnel carriers," and "up to 450 artillery and mortar pieces." Subsequent investigation on the ground by a specialized bomb-damage assessment team concluded that the Serbs had lost no more than 12 or 13 tanks and equally few of the other vehicles and weapons. Clark was outraged and sent the team back to Kosovo for further research. Once again, the team found no evidence that the air strikes had in any way discommoded the Serb military occupation. Ultimately, a U.S. Air Force general, without conducting further research in the field, produced a report with numbers that were close enough to the initial claims to be acceptable and were so recorded as the final, official tally.

NATO staff members were in no doubt as to what had happened. As U.S. Army Colonel Douglas MacGregor, who was director of joint operations at NATO military headquarters throughout the war, later told me, "Pressure to fabricate came from the top . . . the [Air Force] senior leadership was determined that whatever the truth, the campaign had to confirm the efficacy of airpower and its dominance."

Treating the enemy as an inanimate object, something that could be addressed by destroying a set number of targets, had failed once again. The Serb military, it turned out, had followed in the footsteps of General Nguyen in Vietnam. They had put dummy tanks on display, laid out sheets of black plastic to simulate roads, and deployed microwave ovens that emitted decoy signals on the same wavelength as the air force's anti-SAM, radar-homing missiles. None of this was apparent to General Clark as he peered eagerly into his drone video monitor, or to the serried ranks of allied intelligence officers masterminding the "critical node" targeting and bombing.

Unlike the conflicts to come, the Kosovo war caused no bitter debates and left no searing memories. Yet the political effects of the instantly falsified history had far-reaching consequences. The war had been popular with liberals, both the Clinton administration and center-left governments in Europe. The campaign's apparent confirmation that precisely targeted bombs and missiles could achieve victory at no cost in friendly casualties, and in a good cause, too, prepared the political landscape for the wars of the next century.

More hawkish factions were naturally gratified by the vindication of their strategic projections in combat. In September 1999, George W. Bush, then a presidential candidate, introduced his defense program at the Citadel military school in Charleston, South Carolina. Richard Armitage, the former Andrew Marshall subordinate who had cowritten the report on transforming national defense, wrote the speech. "Our forces in the next century must be agile, lethal, readily deployable," said the future president, pledging to "begin creating the military of the next century. . . . Our military must be able to identify targets by a variety of means, then be able to destroy those targets almost instantly.

We must be able to strike from across the world with pinpoint accuracy . . . with unmanned systems." The opportunity to do this, he stressed, had been created by "a revolution in the technology of war. Power is increasingly defined, not by mass or size, but by mobility and swiftness. Influence is measured in information, safety is gained in stealth, and force is projected on the long arc of precision-guided weapons." The lucrative technology dreams of William Westmoreland, John Foster, William Perry, and those they spoke for had now been endorsed at the highest level.

One underpublicized feature of the Kosovo war had especially ominous portents for the future. There had been less of the public bloodlust to "go after" the enemy leader than there had been during the Iraq War. Officially, the highest-priority targets were the enemy's "command-and-control" facilities. But, as one former targeteer remarked to me, "that could mean any place with a phone." So Slobodan Milošević's personal residence was duly destroyed. "We would have been happy to get him," I was told by one former intelligence analyst who had been assigned to a "high-value target cell," a new phenomenon in U.S. intelligence agencies dedicated to tracking the location of high-ranking human targets on an hour-by-hour basis. Assassination, officially forbidden and always denied, was still in the shadows but edging ever closer toward public respectability.

Sharing in the glory of Operation Allied Force was the Predator, which Pentagon briefers extolled as a "CNN in the sky" that "enables us to see things in the battle space in a more human way . . . to use the unmanned vehicle for forward air control, much more efficiently and at much lower risk" than would be the case with manned aircraft. Just as carefully selected video clips transmitted from optically guided bombs and missiles had thrilled audiences during the 1991 Gulf War, snippets of Predator video footage "looking like it was shot from the roof of a fifteen-story building" now performed the same function. As one officer told a reporter, "Kosovo showed that UAVs are perhaps even more useful and can have more missions and roles than we may have thought." Jumper himself excitedly reported to Congress how "toward the end of the war, we equipped the Predator with a laser so that it could place a beam on a target—this identified it so a loitering strike aircraft could destroy it . . . we developed a capability with great potential for rapid targeting."

Such enthusiastic hype, earnestly expressed, is traditional in high-technology defense programs, as demonstrated by the triumphant PR successes of the stealth aircraft and guided-missile systems assiduously promoted to the public during and after the 1991 Gulf War. As we have seen, the actual performance of these technologies was not quite as advertised: stealth planes were not invisible to radar, and precision missiles did not unerringly destroy their targets. It should therefore come as little surprise that the true story of Predator performance in the Kosovo War followed the same path.

Apart from that one incident hailed by Jumper in which an experimental drone laser had assisted in the destruction of a target—an empty barn—the Predators in Kosovo were concerned purely with reconnaissance. As yet unarmed, they beamed streaming video to the JSTARS radar planes, designated to sift information from their own radar scans, from intercepted communications, and from other intelligence sources, and then disseminate the results across the NATO command. In a significant step along the road to remotely controlling the battle via headquarters on three continents, much of this intelligence was transmitted in real time to U.S.-based staffs for analysis and then relayed back to Europe.

Meanwhile, thanks to the same expansion in communications bandwidth that made drones themselves feasible, the generals and admirals running the war were spending much of their days conferring with each other and Washington via video link. When not talking to each other they could watch the drone videos as they were being streamed directly into their offices, inevitably encouraging them in the belief that they had a close-up understanding of the ongoing war. General Clark himself, according to officers on his staff, was fascinated with drone TV and amid his busy days spent many hours glued to the monitor in his office. The general and his micromanaging habits were not universally popular with his brother officers, who were happy to circulate the story of how, one day, he called General Michael Short, the

U.S. three-star commanding the allied air fleets. "Hey, Mike," said the supreme commander, "I'm sitting here at my desk watching the UAV feed on the monitor. When are you going to do something about those two Serb tanks sitting at the end of that bridge?"

In fact, Clark may not even have been seeing any tanks at all. Despite all the high-level enthusiasm and the release of carefully chosen videos, the all-seeing eye in the sky didn't really work very well. We know this because, while Washington was still echoing with those rapturous reports, an organization immune to technohype was taking a cold, hard look at Predator. They were not impressed by what they found.

In the right hands, the director of the Office of Operational Test and Evaluation is the most unpopular person in the Pentagon bureaucracy. Traditionally, the services have cast a benign eye on the actual performance of weapons programs they have fostered and do not welcome independent assessments of whether or not they actually work. That the office exists at all owes a lot in inspiration to John Boyd, the air force colonel who had arrived at Task Force Alpha in the waning days of the Vietnam War, shot the wild dogs, and closed down the essentially futile multibillion-dollar operation. Returning from Southeast Asia, Boyd had begun extrapolating the lessons he had deduced from earlier experiences as a supremely successful fighter pilot into a general theory of conflict that would ultimately earn him the title of the American Sun Tzu, after the legendary Chinese strategist. At the core of his conclusions was the concept of the OODA (the acronym for observation, orientation, decision, and action) Loop, the repeating cycle through which each side in a conflict passes. In air combat, for example, pilots see an enemy, orient themselves (meaning they subconsciously process their observation based on prior combat experience, intelligence, training, etc.), decide what to do, act on that decision, observe the results of that action, and continue retracing the loop. History shows that those who could adapt to changing circumstances— the antagonists' own maneuvers and countermaneuvers—by continually moving through this cycle faster than their adversaries would prevail. Thus Boyd discerned that the F-86 fighter he flew in the Korean War outfought Soviet MiGs because its bubble canopy allowed the pilot a more complete view, while the plane could also transition from one maneuver to another faster than a MiG (partly because its power-assisted controls were easier to shift quickly than the muscle-powered controls on the MiG).

In applying his ideas to organizations, as opposed to one-man machines, Boyd found that the same principles applied and that the overarching need for rapid adaptability to changing circumstances had to be based on a system of command and control that was as simple and harmonious as possible. It was extremely dangerous for the higher commander to try to get involved in the rapid pace and details of the firefight and thereby lose his focus on and grasp of the overall battle. Above all, Boyd stressed the importance of the human, as opposed to the technological, factor in warfare. One of his favorite quotations was Napoleon's: "In war, the moral is to the material as three is to one."

As we have seen in the examples of Task Force Alpha, the Gulf War, and Kosovo, the U.S. military believes very strongly indeed in material, the more complex and technically ambitious the better. Thus Boyd's ideas as well as his emphasis on personal integrity were most certainly not in harmony with the prevailing ideology. Nevertheless, since he applied those ideas with great skill, not to say rigor (once causing a general literally to faint with rage in the course of a telephone discussion), in bureaucratic combat inside the Pentagon, he achieved considerable success in chosen objectives.

Though highly unpopular in the commanding heights of the defense establishment, Boyd's ideas had attracted a growing following in the military, especially among junior officers, as well as in the press and in Congress, giving rise in the late 1970s to what became known as the "military reform movement." This alliance mounted serial campaigns against costly weapons programs of dubious utility, and the customs and practices of the weapons-buying culture that produced and nurtured them, exposing which involved revelations from whistle-blowers prepared, in many cases, to risk or sacrifice their careers for the greater good. For the most part these efforts were eventually defeated by entrenched interests in the military-industrial complex, but the movement, which for a time enjoyed potent support in Congress, did succeed in creating the post of Director, Office of Operational Test and Evaluation, mandated by law to test new weapons systems as a corrective to the services' sorry record of buying systems that worked badly or not at all when deployed. As noted, the office was not popular with the military or with defense contractors, mainly because it regularly disproved claims by contractors and their service sponsors regarding the efficacy of lavishly funded systems.

Even as the smoke of the Balkan battlefields cleared and the Pentagon echoed with claims regarding the success of Predator, a gravel-voiced Floridian mathematician named Tom Christie was taking over as director of the testing office. Christie was a friend and longtime associate of Boyd's, having worked closely with him in the 1960s formulating a theory of air-combat tactics that many years later became official air force doctrine. Analyzing weapons effects at the Air Force Armaments Center at Eglin Air Force Base in Florida, Christie had a front row seat as colleagues worked to implement the high command's obsessive determination to destroy the Thanh Hoa Bridge in North Vietnam. "They even wanted to turn a B-47 (a strategic nuclear bomber) into a drone," he told me. "They'd load it up with high explosives and fly it into the bridge. That never got anywhere, just like all the other crazy schemes they had."

Technically able and skilled in bureaucratic maneuver, Christie managed to advance through the ranks of air force and defense department officialdom. By 1995 he had become director of the Operational Evaluation Division at the Institute for Defense Analyses, the Pentagon's semi-independent think tank. In this capacity he reviewed an air force report on the sterling qualities of the performance of the JSTARS surveillance plane in the Balkans. As an example, the report cited an operation in which the system had detected the movement of a Serb armored unit while it attempted to hide in a cemetery. "We had built this beautiful topographical map of that whole area," Christie told me, "and we knew exactly where the JSTARS had been at any particular time. So we were able to show that at the time they said they had spotted the Serbs in the cemetery, they were on the other side of a fairly substantial mountain. Even the air force couldn't claim the thing could see through a mountain."

When Christie took over the testing office, the very first system that came up for review was the Predator. So, in the mountains and desert that make up the vast Nellis Air Force Base complex in Nevada, Christie's team put the machine through its paces.

The tests, carried out over nine days, mostly in a corner of the Indian Springs drone airfield, which had been activated five years earlier to preempt the army, did not go well. In fact, they were a disaster. One of the weaknesses revealed by earlier tryouts in the Balkans had been the aircraft's vulnerability to ice on its wings, a fatal condition. In response, the technicians at Big Safari had developed a "wet wing" that could theoretically de-ice the wings in flight, and two of the four machines consigned to the tests were so equipped. But they didn't work, a failure, as the testers later reported, that prevented "transition through clouds." In fact the plane could not land or take off in any kind of bad weather, "including any visible moisture such as rain, snow, ice, frost, or fog."

Assuming it did manage to take off and reach enemy territory, the plane had a variety of cameras for viewing the ground and detecting targets. One of these, a "day TV continuous zoom," looked at a 300-yard-wide area of territory in daylight from 15,000 feet. A second, the "day TV spotter," could see in greater detail, but only over a narrower area of 50 yards. An infrared (IR) camera enabled night vision, while a synthetic aperture radar made it possible to see through clouds. To grade the cameras, the testing team relied on the National Imagery Interpretation Rating Scale, which runs from 1, the ability to pick out a large aircraft, such as a Boeing 737, to 9, the ability to recognize a human face. Though the Predator cameras were supposed to score 6, "recognize supply dumps, identify vehicles" at a range of 6 miles, the day TV scored no better than 2.7.

Overall, Predator could find less than a third of its targets. As the testers put it, "[W]hen all targets are considered, only 29 percent of the targets tasked for the 7 days [of testing] were imaged." The "day TV" camera that scanned the landscape could never deliver a picture sharp enough to enable a viewer to tell the difference between a tank and a truck. The infrared camera could manage that feat a fifth of the time. The close-up day TV spotter could tell the difference between a friendly and enemy tank just over two-thirds of the time, but since it captured only a small patch of territory—again, like looking through a soda straw—it was impossible to tell where the tanks were. The infrared camera could detect, as the testers reported, "something versus nothing," but could discern what that "something" was, if a tank or a truck, only 21 percent of the time. Much of the time the aircraft failed to reach the target area, because of bad weather, engine problems (exactly half of the test flights flown under combat conditions never completed the mission), or some other breakdown. One or another component vital to continuing the missions failed on average every 19.5 hours, while some other major system failed every 3 hours.

It made no difference. The drone could relay pictures, in color, of the enemy landscape. In Vietnam, troops fighting on the ground had been supervised by ascending tiers of senior officers hovering high above the battlefield in their personal helicopters, trying to "fight vicariously through that frightened twenty-five-year-old down there beneath the tree canopy," as one veteran later wrote. There were even stories of entire units hiding from micromanaging heli-borne commanders in the sky above. But now, when the weather was fine, four-star generals could take the role of junior squad leaders without having to leave the office and even help destroy targets themselves.

"The air force had had this idea that the [Predator] could be used for detecting patterns on the battlefield," an air force officer intimately involved with the program told me later. "It would send back the FMV [full motion video] from a wide area, and that would be compared with previous video so they could find changes—new units moving in or whatever. But the quality of the video was lousy, as those tests out at Nellis showed."

The testing team had been kept in ignorance of one aspect of the Predator program that was to prove all-important. While they monitored its progress, or lack of it, in the bleak Nevada fall weather, another team had been secretly working to "weaponize" the machine: to arm it with a missile so that it could kill people. The scheme, initially ordered by Jumper in June, had gained urgency following a series of Predator flights flown from a base in Uzbekistan on behalf of the CIA over eastern and southern Afghanistan in September and early October 2000. They had one objective: to find Osama bin Laden, who was a high-value target. An address receiving special scrutiny was a cluster of compounds east of Kandahar known as Tarnak Farms, thought to be frequented by the infamous terrorist leader. Sure enough, on one particular day a Predator beamed back tantalizing images of a figure in white, surrounded by others in dark clothes, moving down a street in the compound.

Those few seconds of footage had momentous consequences. Back at CIA headquarters in Langley, Virginia, officials eagerly interpreted the pictures as showing the six-foot-five-inch Bin Laden himself— the white-clad figure seemed taller than the others—walking to the mosque, surrounded by deferential bodyguards. Just as the muddy pictures from Kosovo had kept General Clark glued to his monitor, so the Tarnak video had a potent effect across Washington. CIA Director George Tenet, who had shown little interest in the drone program heretofore, was suddenly a convert, screening the video for President Clinton and his National Security Adviser Sandy Berger at the White House, declaiming enthusiastically about the drone's capabilities to the intelligence committees on Capitol Hill.

Yet, the closer one looks at those pictures, the less they reveal. The "tall man in white" is actually just a moving white dot surrounded by black dots. It takes imagination to read the black dots as "deferential" toward the white dot and more imagination to define them as bodyguards, since no weapons are visible. Blown up, the images do not reveal more information, but less. The white dot does not turn into a tall man with a beard but merely a fuzzy blur that becomes more indistinct the more it is magnified. Just as the Predator crew in the first chapter of this book interpreted a carload of praying Afghans as Taliban preparing an attack, so eager Washington policy makers saw what they wanted to see and proceeded accordingly. Had the drone only carried a missile, they surmised, the mastermind of the lethal attacks on the U.S.

embassies in Africa and the USS *Cole* off the coast of Yemen could have been eliminated in a single stroke. The pressure to arm the Predator was overwhelming.

Ultimately it turned out to be surprisingly easy, the weapon of choice being a Hellfire missile originally developed by the army for use against tanks. The work went quickly: the first successful test firing of a Predator-launched Hellfire took place the following January. A few months later the air force had also devised the satellite-plus-fiber-optic cable system that transmitted the video feed, allowing a pilot sitting in Nevada to fly and shoot from a Predator thousands of miles away.

"They did it fast," the air force officer closely involved with the program told me, "and that was a pity. It meant that no one stepped back and thought about what it meant to be able to kill someone from thousands of miles away." Such pertinent reflections were not widespread in the air force, not to mention the government at large. As George Tenet later told the 9/11 Commission, "The leadership of CIA reasoned that if we could develop the capability to reliably hit a target with a Hellfire missile and could develop the enabling policy and legal framework, we would have a capability to accurately and promptly respond to future sightings of high value targets."

It is not surprising, therefore, that when Tom Christie presented his team's final report on the Predator tests, Report on the Predator Medium Altitude Endurance Unmanned Aerial Vehicle (UAV), on October 3, 2001, it did not go down very well. It was only three weeks since the 9/11 attacks. With the airwaves full of bloodthirsty threats and promises of revenge, demand for a weapon that promised to deliver what Tenet wanted was unstoppable.

The cover letter of Christie's report, sent to the secretary of defense and the heads of all relevant congressional committees, including Jerry Lewis', stated straightforwardly that "the Predator UAV is not operationally effective. This conclusion is based on poor performance in target location accuracy, ineffective communications, and limits imposed by relatively benign weather." The following sixty-four pages spelled out just how and why the machine was so deficient.

The reaction did not appear until the following morning, but when it did, it arrived with force in the form of Darleen Druyun, the principal deputy undersecretary of the air force, known around the Pentagon as "the dragon lady." Three years later she would be sentenced to a nine-month prison term for corrupt dealings with the Boeing Corporation, but on that October morning she was still immensely powerful and much feared for her commanding role in negotiating prices in multibillion-dollar contracts. The Pentagon building was still smoking from the devastating impact of American Airlines Flight 77 on 9/11 when Druyun marched into Christie's third-floor office with, as Christie later related to me, "four or five sycophant generals trailing behind her." Not known for diplomacy, she came straight to the point. "What the fuck is this?" she shouted at the testing office director. "What do you mean sending out this fucking report saying the Predator doesn't work? Who is the fucking asshole that wrote this report? I'm going to ream him a new fucking asshole."

"Hold on," retorted Christie, unfazed by her foul language. "Have you found anything in this report that's wrong?"

"Er, no," admitted the official. "But couldn't you at least take the bit about 'not operationally suitable' out of the cover letter? (All present were well aware that this was as far as most officials would ever read.) Christie gave no ground; the letter and report stood. But it didn't matter; Washington was already entranced by the notion of killing people at a distance.

In December 2001, President Bush returned to the Citadel, where he had outlined his military program and the virtues of drones two years before. In his speech on this visit he hailed the new weapon and his own prescience: "Before the war, the Predator had skeptics, because it did not fit the old ways. Now it is clear the military does not have enough unmanned vehicles."

An old idea had found its time.

# 5

# IT'S NOT ASSASSINATION IF WE DO IT

He was the ultimate high-value target, the man who by virtue of his personal magnetism and force of will had brought about the most destructive war in history. Even when defeat appeared certain, his absolute control of the nation he ruled meant the fighting dragged on, with millions more dying. "As long as Hitler continues to live among them," wrote Air Vice-Marshal Alan Ritchie of the Royal Air Force in 1944, "the people will have faith and, having faith, they will remain impervious to logical argument or demonstrated fact. . . . Remove Hitler and there is nothing left." Ritchie, a former bomber commander, was a senior official in Special Operations Executive (SOE), the clandestine British warfare agency set up by Winston Churchill in 1940 with a mandate to "set all Europe ablaze." Not only did he believe that the assassination of Hitler would collapse the enemy war machine, but he also became deeply involved in an operation to carry it out.

Along with sabotage, subversion, aid to resistance movements, and other harassing operations against the Germans, SOE was always in search of ways to eliminate leading members of the Nazi hierarchy. By 1944 the agency's most notable success in this regard had been the elimination of SS General Reinhard Heydrich, the ruler of occupied Czechoslovakia, in 1942. Although Heydrich, one of the cruelest of the Nazi bosses, did die from wounds following an attack by Czech partisans dispatched by SOE, the resulting German reprisals were savage in the extreme. Thousands of Czechs, including the entire male population of the village of Lidice, as well as the last surviving Jews of Berlin, were immediately murdered in revenge. The overall ongoing holocaust accelerated.

Nevertheless, the leadership of SOE remained eager to find a way to kill Hitler himself, exploring various possibilities, such as blowing up his train or introducing poison into his tea. By June 1944 serious consideration was being given to Operation Foxley, in which a sniper would infiltrate Hitler's mountain retreat of Berchtesgaden in the Bavarian Alps and shoot him as he took his daily walk, unguarded, to a teahouse a few hundred yards from the main building.

In view of Hitler's status in the pantheon of evil, his elimination would seem to be an obvious and unquestioned priority for the Allies, just as killing Osama bin Laden would be, decades later, for Barack Obama. Such was not the case. Even in the midst of total war against a remorseless and vicious enemy, not everyone agreed that Hitler himself should be on any kind of target list. Major-General Gerald Templer, who, as commander of SOE's German Directorate, would be in immediate charge of the operation, wrote in November 1944 that there was "still a grave divergence of views" on the "desirability and feasibility" of the assassination scheme. The arguments on either side resonate strongly in an age when such targeting has become a fundamental component of U.S. strategy.

"All experts on Germany," noted Templer, agreed that Foxley was "unsound and would not be in the interests of the allied cause." Nevertheless, "among certain members of the SOE Council" and "among the highest in the land in England" were "strong advocates of the operation." The "highest in the land" had to be a discreet reference to Winston Churchill, himself, who not only had already endorsed the notion of assassinating Hitler but also was enamored of schemes for daring and unorthodox military adventures. The SOE council members referred to by Templer included Ritchie, a former bomber commander with a conviction common to his profession that there was a targeting solution to any challenge. Just as his successors fighting the Vietnam War believed that the destruction of the Thanh Hoa Bridge would solve their problems, and their successors pursuing the war on terror single-mindedly hunted the leadership of al-Qaeda, Ritchie took it as a given that Hitler's "mystical hold" was all that was keeping his country together. Given Hitler's absolute domination of Germany and its war machine, who could doubt that getting rid of him would be an unqualified benefit?

However, there were plenty of people with doubts, and they were in a position to express them. Lieutenant Colonel Ronald Thornley, Templer's deputy, was a genuine expert on Germany, since he had traveled there extensively in peacetime as a businessman and spoke the language fluently. Joining the army at the beginning of the war, he had risen rapidly through the ranks of SOE, supervising subversion and sabotage inside Germany itself. In clear, simple prose, he laid out his reasons for why killing Hitler would be entirely counterproductive. Merely disposing of the Nazi leader, he wrote, "would almost certainly canonize him and give birth to the myth that Germany would have been saved if he had lived." Since the overall war aim was to defeat and extinguish Nazism, this would have been a most undesirable development. Furthermore, rather than standing in the way of an Allied victory, Thornley pointed out, the Führer was being extremely helpful. "As a strategist, Hitler has been of the greatest possible assistance to the British war effort. . . . He is still in a position to override completely the soundest of military appreciation and thereby help the Allied Cause enormously." Furthermore, he argued, such an act would cause lasting damage to those who carried it out: "It would be disastrous if the world came to think that the Allies had to resort to these low methods as they were otherwise unable to defeat the German military machine. From every point of view, the ideal end to Hitler would be one of steadily declining power and increasing ridicule." In an age where high-value targeting lies at the core of U.S. strategy against its enemies, Thornley's reasoned assessment still stands as a model of rational rebuttal against the idea.

As it happened, nothing ever came of Foxley, as Hitler stopped visiting Berchtesgaden after July 1944. In any event, SOE was in reality a surprisingly ineffective operation overall, sometimes shockingly so. From 1941 on, its operations in aid of the French resistance had been largely penetrated by German counterintelligence. Agents parachuting into France were met all too often by an enemy reception committee. Shockingly, even when captured agents managed to use prearranged codes to warn they were in enemy hands, headquarters paid no attention and continued to dispatch brave men and women to inevitable torture and death. Dissolved after the war (though not before a mysterious fire had destroyed much of its financial records), SOE left an enduring legacy not only in espionage fiction but also in the culture of another wartime creation: the Office of Strategic Services, precursor of the CIA. The biographer of OSS Director William Donovan summarized the relationship between the two organizations this way: "Each had much to offer the other—the British experience, training, contacts and special equipment; the Americans, manpower, gold and political reputation."

The OSS itself attained legendary status, central to the creation myth of the CIA, although in fact it contributed little in the way of intelligence. For example, though its chief agent in Switzerland, future CIA director Allen Dulles, subsequently made much of his success in inducing the surrender of German forces in northern Italy following months of secret negotiations, this coup preceded the total German unconditional surrender by a mere eight days. The OSS Rome station chief James Jesus Angleton had meanwhile won accolades for recruiting an agent who could supply copies of the Vatican's secret diplomatic correspondence, including reports from the Papal Nuncio in Japan. These were deemed so valuable and urgent that they were rushed straight to the Oval Office. Sadly, the intelligence turned out to be entirely bogus, concocted by the "agent," a forger and pornographer, author of such works as the best-selling *Amazons of the Bidet*.

The great triumph of Allied intelligence of World War II was the comprehensive cracking of German and Japanese codes (not to mention those of most neutral nations as well). This gave U.S. and British leaders an unambiguous insight into enemy plans and dispositions. But the OSS had no access to this vital tool, having been excluded since inception by the military services that had broken the codes in the first place. Indeed, the prevailing attitude of military intelligence toward OSS was contempt. As General Carter Clarke, who headed the vital military intelligence department known as Special Branch, later scornfully informed me, "The OSS did superb work rescuing downed pilots and other unfortunates in Burma, but if they ever produced any intelligence worthy of the name, I was not aware of it." Clarke, a salty-tongued Kentucky native who had risen through the ranks of the prewar army, made no secret of his opinion of William Donovan, the flamboyant lawyer who founded and led the OSS through the war. Clarke's colorful style and views are apparent in his account of an incident when "there were three guys in Dakar that needed to be knocked off, and old Donovan—who was about as useful as a row of tits on a nun—he said, well, the OSS'll do it. So he went over there and they killed three guys all right, but they were the wrong three. Well Roosevelt damn near had a stroke over that."

Special Branch was itself the brainchild of a Wall Street lawyer, Alfred McCormack, a partner in the powerful firm of Cravath, Swaine & Moore, and John J. McCloy, the quintessential insider who became assistant secretary of war in 1940. Following the disaster of Pearl Harbor, intelligence agencies, including OSS, proliferated like weeds in Washington: no less than forty appeared over the following twelve months. Few people even inside the government knew that the Japanese diplomatic code had been broken by a secret army unit and that all Japan's diplomatic traffic had been read for months before the Pearl Harbor attack, priceless intelligence that had been almost entirely wasted. However, McCloy, together with his immediate superior and fellow Wall Street lawyer Henry Stimson, felt that the best way to analyze discreetly what had gone wrong with prewar intelligence and how to proceed in the future was to consult a fellow

Wall Street lawyer. So McCormack was asked to come down from New York and take a look.

Given immediate access to the so-called magic intercepts—there was no nonsense about waiting for security clearance in those days, at least not for a Cravath partner—McCormack soon reported back. Uncowed by his high-level audience, he began by noting that the intercepted material had made it perfectly clear that the Japanese were likely to attack Pearl Harbor, and therefore he asked, "Why were the principal units of our Navy herded together in a harbor from which they could not escape?" The mistakes, he stated baldly, had not been made by the local commanders (who were already being scapegoated for the disaster) but in Washington. Despite this frankness (unthinkable in today's intelligence bureaucracy), McCormack's suggestion that a special and very carefully selected unit be set up to handle the priceless intelligence was heeded. "To do the work well," he wrote afterward, "a man must have not only a broad education and background of information but must have more than his fair share of astuteness, skepticism and desire to solve puzzling problems; and he must have a capacity for laborious detail work that very few people have." The people he had in mind were smart lawyers like himself, many of whom were from the same Cravath firm and almost all of whom were graduates of Yale and Harvard law schools.

The new unit, Special Branch, was soon up and running, commanded by the above-mentioned Carter Clarke, with McCormack as his deputy. As Clarke put it to me many years later, "He furnished the brains, and I did the hatchet work." Hatchet work apparently included not only fighting necessary bureaucratic battles but also executing sensitive missions for Army Chief of Staff General George Marshall, especially when they concerned threats to the great secret of the broken enemy codes. Thus in 1944 Clarke was dispatched by Marshall to dissuade presidential candidate Thomas Dewey from revealing that the United States had been reading Japanese messages before Pearl Harbor. Dewey had learned of this, Clarke explained to me, from General Hugh Drumm, a disappointed candidate for Marshall's post as army chief of staff.

Despite the vital necessity of preserving the supreme secret of the broken codes, it gave way to an overwhelming desire to kill a particular enemy leader. Admiral Isoruku Yamamoto had devised and commanded the surprise Japanese attack on Pearl Harbor, America's greatest-ever naval defeat, thereby earning demonization in domestic U.S. propaganda as "our chief individual enemy, next to Adolf Hitler, leather faced, bullet headed, bitter-hearted Isoroku Yamamoto." By the spring of 1943, however, the Japanese advance had been stemmed. Yamamoto had been decisively beaten in the Midway battle, and more recently at Guadalcanal. Early that April, U.S. naval cryptographers in Hawaii (one of whom was the future Supreme Court justice John Paul Stevens) decrypted a message detailing the Japanese commander's itinerary for a forthcoming inspection tour. American commanders saw an opportunity for revenge. Orders came from on high—by some accounts, from President Roosevelt himself—to "get Yamamoto." His plane was accordingly intercepted and shot down over the Solomon Islands on April 18, 1943, by U.S. long-range P-38 fighters, a feat that rapidly prompted dangerous leaks imperilling the precious secret of the codes.

Yamamoto's death made little or no difference to the course of the war. His successor as commander continued his strategy of piecemeal attacks on the advancing Americans, who as usual in such matters claimed that his death had impacted enemy morale, as always an unverifiable claim. However, the attack would thereafter be cited as a positive example of the merits of high-value targeting.

Overall, the partnership between the ruthless (he thought the commanders at Pearl Harbor should have been executed the morning after the attack) and foul-mouthed Clarke and the white-shoe lawyer McCormack was a great success, in large part because its leaders had direct relationships with the high command, specifically Clarke with General Marshall and McCormack with McCloy. By the end of the war the operation had vastly expanded, covering all theaters in Europe as well as in Asia in profitable partnership with the principal British intelligence service MI6, which itself controlled the legendary code-breaking operation at Bletchley Park. Its Pentagon offices were the most secret and closely guarded in the building, save for perhaps the adjoining suite of offices, the Washington headquarters of the Manhattan Project.

As veterans of Special Branch told me many years later, by the summer of 1945, the team monitoring Japan, which included the eminent scholar and later ambassador Edwin Reischauer, had become convinced that the regime was ready to give up, providing only that the emperor be retained. According to these veterans, this conclusion was relayed to McCloy, who therefore argued at the highest levels that there was no need to drop the atomic bomb. Obviously, his well-informed efforts were of no avail, given that President Truman and his political advisers, as McCloy himself later confirmed to me, were determined to use the new weapon. "I remember when we got the news of Hiroshima," Edward Huddleston, a Special Branch veteran, told me four decades later. "There was incredible shock in the office. People were saying things like 'for god's sake, why?' We all knew perfectly well that the Japanese were only looking for some assurance that we wouldn't hang the emperor, which was what they got in the end anyway."

With the war's end, the Army Security Agency (ASA), the vast organization that intercepted and decoded signals from around the world, remained largely in place. But the men of "broad education" with a "fair share of astuteness, skepticism and desire to solve puzzling problems" who had given the system its brains, largely went back to their law firms and other civilian careers. These included McCormack himself. Following an effort to re-create Special Branch inside the State Department that was crushed by bureaucratic opposition from within the department, he too returned to his practice. Clarke himself was head of the Army Security Agency, and still a powerful figure, but his chief patron, General Marshall, had left the army and could no longer protect him.

Meanwhile, William Donovan, chief of the OSS, had nurtured ambitions to turn his organization into a permanent peacetime civilian intelligence agency and had penned a lengthy detailed memo to President Roosevelt suggesting just that. But the memo was rapidly leaked to Walter Trohan, Washington bureau chief of the right-wing

*Chicago Tribune*, who duly reported that Donovan planned to establish a "gestapo," which would threaten civil liberties. Donovan and others assumed that the leaker was J. Edgar Hoover, protecting the FBI's bureaucratic prerogatives. However, Trohan assured me in 1985 that the source was in fact Steve Early, Roosevelt's press secretary, who handed him the memo with the words "the boss wants this out." The OSS was disbanded shortly afterward. Nevertheless a civilian intelligence agency did eventually emerge, the Central Intelligence Group, which in 1947 became the CIA.

The peacetime agency retained its unequal status vis-à-vis the military. Initially it was manned not only with veterans of the OSS but also with officers detached from military intelligence. As can be the case with any new organization staffed from existing departments, transferees were not necessarily the best or the brightest. As a former military intelligence officer once snidely recalled early CIA staffing to me, "They walked the halls of the Pentagon, calling 'bring out your dead wood!'" Like the OSS, the successor organization lacked any control over communications intelligence and the ever-growing budget that went with it, which remained in the firm grasp of the military, reorganized into the National Security Agency (NSA) in 1952. Only gradually and grudgingly was the CIA permitted access to the actual intercepts.

With the expanding role of ever more costly technical intelligence systems such as surveillance satellites, the CIA's share of the overall cold war intelligence budget, though vast in itself, was a small portion of the amount allotted to the Pentagon. Even when the agency did take a successful technical intelligence initiative with the brilliantly conceived U-2 reconnaissance plane, developed for a total cost of $19 million, it fell under the effective control of the Pentagon, which assigned the targets—bomber bases, missile silos, etc.—useful for military estimates but not for the CIA's allotted task of assessing Soviet intentions. Even more secretly, and dangerously, the commander of the Strategic Air Command, General Curtis LeMay, had his own fleet of reconnaissance planes scanning Russia in the 1950s. Should he conclude that the Soviets were planning an attack, he blithely informed a shocked

White House emissary in 1958, he would immediately launch a pre-emptive nuclear strike without reference to higher authority.

So, while a perennial junior partner in the overall U.S. intelligence apparatus, the agency found function and purpose in the field of under-cover clandestine operations—espionage, subversion, dirty tricks, and manipulation, among others—justified as necessary to maintain America's political and economic influence in the non-Communist world. The Communist world was another matter. Despite constant effort, until late in the cold war the agency had little success in pene-trating the iron curtain. Repeating the precedent of Britain's wartime SOE, the agency recruited hundreds of unfortunate Koreans and Chi-nese as agents and dropped them into North Korea and China during the Korean War, never to be heard of again. "We were following in the footsteps of the OSS," Don Gregg, a young CIA officer engaged in the exercise, later bitterly recalled. "We didn't know what we were doing. I asked our superiors what the mission was and they wouldn't tell us. They didn't know what the mission was. It was swashbuckling of the worst kind."

In parts of the world not under the iron control of the Commu-nists, the agency found a role as the undercover instrument of U.S. control, mainly thanks to its access to ready cash and its willingness to dispense it in large quantities. Thus the CIA's first significant success was to inject money (siphoned off from the vaunted Marshall Plan) into the Italian elections of 1948 in sufficient amounts to defeat the very popular Communist Party. Cash was similarly the crucial factor in the 1953 coup that overthrew Mohamed Mossadeq, the democratically elected prime minister of Iran. CIA officer Kermit Roosevelt financed a network originally assembled by British intelligence that in turn recruited mobs and army units that forced Mossadeq to resign, and ushered in a quarter century of U.S.-supported rule by the shah.

Iran fostered the CIA's legend among Washington's power elite as a silver bullet for fighting the underground cold war. The coup in Gua-temala in 1954 solidified it. Yet in both cases, as one historian of the agency summarized, it was "bribery, coercion, brute force, not secrecy, stealth, and cunning" that won the day. The Guatemalan operation, in particular, was marked by bumbling and misadventure, beginning when plans for the coup mislaid by a CIA agent in a Guatemala City hotel room were splashed across every newspaper in the Western world. Not included among those documents, however, were CIA plans for "low methods" in Guatemala.

Starting in 1952, according to internal agency documents, senior officials in the euphemistically named Directorate of Plans were compiling lists of "top flight communists whom the new government would desire to eliminate in event of successful anti-communist coup." In a later initiative, headquarters ordered the coup-plotters to train two "assassination specialists," a move encouraged by the State Department, while also demanding that a "list of names be compiled for study by staff officers to determine if they meet the latest criteria for inclusion on the Junta's disposal list . . . it is requested that a final list of disposees be approved promptly to permit planning to proceed on schedule."

To aid in training the specialists, someone at headquarters helpfully came up with "a study of assassination" complete with scholarly references to the derivation of the operative word: "thought to be derived from 'hashish,' a drug similar to marijuana." The guide provided useful justifications for the deed: "Killing a political leader whose burgeoning career is a clear and present danger to the cause of freedom may be held necessary." With regard to practical techniques, the guide advised against a manual approach—"it is possible to kill a man with the bare hands, but very few are skillful enough to do it well"—while recommending the "contrived accident . . . a fall of 75 feet or more onto a hard surface" as the most effective technique. Other methods discussed in detail included drugs, "edge" [sharp] weapons, blunt weapons, though these "require[d] some anatomical knowledge for effective use," and firearms of various types.

In the event, according at least to the agency's own review of the episode, none of the listed "disposees" actually were eliminated. On the other hand, human rights groups estimate that the military regimes ushered in by the 1954 coup killed at least one hundred thousand civilians over the next thirty-five years. As the unknown author of the little manual observed: "Assassination can seldom be employed with a clear conscience. Persons who are morally squeamish should not attempt it."

Whereas the quest for victims in Guatemala had been merely a matter of prudent housekeeping, the obsessive targeting of Fidel Castro, leader of the Cuban revolutionaries who overthrew a U.S.-allied dictator in 1959, was something entirely different. The eagerness with which the Kennedy brothers urged the CIA to find a way to kill the Cuban leader, who had turned to the Soviet Union for aid and protection, would not be matched until the hunt for Osama bin Laden a generation later. According to Castro's longtime bodyguard, Fabien Escalante, there were no less than 638 separate plots on the Cuban leader's life, most of them ultimately directed from the CIA. They ranged from the juvenile, an exploding cigar, to the criminal, as in the infamous liaison with mafia hoodlums such as "Handsome Johnny" Roselli and Santo Trafficante, supposedly eager and ready to organize the "hit." There can be little doubt as to the direct personal involvement of the president of the United States. As Richard Bissell, the CIA's deputy director for plans later testified, the orders to set up an assassination squad, known as the Special Group (Augmented), came directly from National Security Adviser McGeorge Bundy and his deputy, Walt Rostow, and "the President's men would not have given such encouragement unless they were confident it would meet with the President's approval."

The Cuban and Guatemalan initiatives were by no means the only assassination plots concocted in the early cold war years. A partial list includes Indonesian President Sukarno, Kim Il-Sung of North Korea, Iranian Prime Minister Mohammed Mossadeq, Philippines opposition leader Claro Recto, Indian Prime Minister Jawaharlal Nehru, General Rafael Trujillo of the Dominican Republic, Francois "Papa Doc" Duvalier of Haiti, and Egyptian leader Gamal Abdel Nasser. Such plans were usually obscured with euphemisms such as "executive action," an evasion disdained by British Prime Minister Anthony Eden in commissioning his own plot against Nasser during the 1956 Anglo-Egyptian Suez crisis. "I want him destroyed, don't you understand?"

Eden bellowed down the phone to his intelligence chief. "I want him murdered."

Until the 1960s, the agency's lethal and paramilitary activities had been largely restricted to variations of the hit-and-run attacks outlined above. (An attempt at something more ambitious, sponsoring the ill-conceived 1961 invasion of Cuba with a force of anti-Castro exiles— the Bay of Pigs—had ended in disaster.) However, expanding wars in Southeast Asia offered fresh scope for such missions. In Laos, for example, a supposedly neutral country where the United States was officially not involved, the CIA ran a full-scale "secret war" using foot soldiers drafted from the Hmong and other indigenous tribes, including many children, some as young as eight years old. This was certainly not a war for the morally squeamish. Anthony Posephny, more commonly known as "Tony Po," who commanded the Hmong effort, once cheerily reminisced to me about the time the U.S. embassy in Vientiane, the Laotian capital, had queried his "body count" of eliminated enemies. "So I sent them a head-count," he chortled, "heads in a bag. But the bag arrived on a Friday and sat in an un-air-conditioned office all weekend until a secretary opened it up on Monday morning. I got into trouble over that!"

The CIA's secret war in Laos was certainly a big operation, costing possibly as much as $100 million a year in 1969 dollars. (At its hub was a base, Long Tien, that grew to a city with a population of 40,000 before an enterprising reporter, T. D. Allman, revealed its existence.) Even so it paled in scope when compared to the U.S. Air Force's campaign in another part of Laos, the automated battlefield of Igloo White and Task Force Alpha, which had cost $2 billion simply to set in motion. However, the CIA was by no means excluded from the trend toward automated warfare, complete with powerful computers. Beginning in January 1967, U.S. officials in Saigon began feeding a list of 3,000 suspected VCI (Viet Cong Infrastructure), into an IBM-1401 computer installed in the "political order of battle" section of the Combined Intelligence Center in Saigon. Officially called the Viet Cong Infrastructure Information System, it has been referred to as the first computerized blacklist. By no coincidence, the initiative came to life at the same time as Task Force Alpha was throwing its invisible net over the Ho Chi Minh Trail.

The ill-fated electronic fence had been born out of Secretary McNamara's frustration at the failure to win the war by bombing the "critical node" of North Vietnamese oil tanks early in 1966. At that same time, the technocratic defense secretary had commissioned a study of means to systematize the counter-guerrilla effort in South Vietnam, eventually spawning the Intelligence Coordination and Exploitation for Attack Against the Infrastructure Program (ICEX).

Just as sensors dropped into the jungle canopy over the Ho Chi Minh Trail would relay signals to the omnivorous IBM-360 machine in Thailand, teams of American and Vietnamese intelligence officials fed dossiers into the IBM-1401 computer in the vast, air-conditioned Saigon intelligence center. Before long the list had grown to 6,000, expanding at a rate of 1,000 a month. In August of the following year, Robert "Blowtorch" Komer, the White House official who had been promoted to supervise the overall pacification effort, mandated a quota of eighteen hundred VCI "neutralizations" per month as a "management tool." So while Igloo White measured success by the number of Vietnamese supply trucks destroyed, the sister program inside South Vietnam counted bodies.

The CIA's neutralizers were initially known as counterterror teams. Rebranded soon after as the functionally equivalent provincial reconnaissance (PRU), they were made up of native Vietnamese who were overseen by American advisers. "Sure we got involved in assassinations," one CIA official, Charlie Yothers, later told a reporter. "That's what PRU was set up for—assassination. I'm sure the word never appeared in any outlines or policy directives, but what else do you call a targeted kill?" News of the program inevitably was leaked to the press, prompting eventual congressional hearings. Just as inevitable, the revelations triggered a concerted effort to portray Phoenix (only one of the successive names for the program) as something much more benign. Thus in 1969 the *New York Times* described it as an initiative to "sideline" members of the Viet Cong infrastructure.

By 1971 euphemism had been cast aside. That year, after William

Colby, later head of the CIA, confirmed that 20,587 people had already been killed under the auspices of Phoenix, members of Congress were openly deriding it as "a program for the assassination of civilian leaders." Alternatively, the program met with wholehearted approval at the other end of Pennsylvania Avenue, where President Richard Nixon reacted angrily to proposed cuts in the PRU program with the straightforward command, "We've got to have more of this. Assassinations, that's what they, the Vietnamese communists, are doing."

The statistics of eliminated Viet Cong "infrastructure" regurgitated by the computers, summarized in the totals solemnly recounted by Colby and other senior officials, gave the appearance of precision and progress, just as the even more powerful computers of Task Force Alpha revealed equally exact numbers of trucks accounted for on the Ho Chi Minh Trail. As with the truck war, the impression of precision cast by the Phoenix computers was misleading. Though large numbers of people were indeed being killed, they were not necessarily the bona fide Communist officials posthumously listed in the account books. Even the program's own statistics indicate that enemy "civilian leaders" weren't in much danger from Phoenix: officially only 150 "Senior VCI" were "neutralized" in 1969. When Komer asked a friend, Colonel Robert Gard, to be the military deputy to the Phoenix program, Gard flatly refused. As he told author Nick Turse years later, "I didn't know a lot about it, except that it was an assassination program, subject to killing innocents." Unsurprisingly, it was well penetrated by Viet Cong agents who could thereby use it to work through their own blacklists. One CIA officer later recalled that Saigon regime officials and even Americans used the PRU for "shaking down the Vietnamese, arresting them if they didn't pay protection money, even taking bribes to free suspects even if they'd already been arrested."

Vincent Okamoto, later a distinguished Los Angeles Superior Court Judge, who in 1969 was a highly decorated combat veteran assigned to a Special Forces unit, has a pungent reminiscence vividly illustrating the chasm between the computerized high-value targeting concept and the murderously haphazard reality of Phoenix in action. "I had never heard of it until they told me I was part of it. I did it for two months and didn't like it at all . . . the CIA and the boys in Saigon would feed information into computers and would come up with a blacklist of Vietnamese who were aiding the enemy. The problem was, how do you find the people on the blacklist? It's not like you had their address and telephone number. The normal procedure would be to go into a village and just grab someone and say, 'Where's Nguyen so-and-so?' Half the time, the people were so afraid they would say anything. Then a Phoenix team would take the informant, put a sandbag over his head, poke out two holes so he could see, put commo wire around his neck like a long leash, and walk him through the village and say, 'When we go by Nguyen's house, scratch your head.' Then that night Phoenix would come back, knock on the door and say, 'April Fool, mother-fucker.' Whoever answered the door would get wasted."

As America withdrew from Vietnam, the assassination program was widely deemed an embarrassment, if not a war crime, and best forgotten. But as the years passed and moral outrage receded along with guilty consciences, attitudes toward Phoenix gradually became more positive. In 2004, for example, David Kilcullen, a highly lauded and influential theorist of counterinsurgency, called for a "disaggregation strategy" targeting insurgent networks on a global scale "that would resemble the unfairly maligned (but highly effective) Vietnam-era Phoenix program."

While the Phoenix operatives were on their killing spree, the CIA's intelligence component was of course tasked to furnish intelligence on every aspect of the war. Thanks to studious scrutiny of captured enemy documents, Sam Adams, a brilliant and dedicated analyst, concluded in 1967 that official estimates of enemy numbers were off by 50 percent. Colleagues and immediate superiors accepted his analysis, which rebutted official pronouncements of impending victory. The military high command, however, rejected it out of hand, a conclusion that was feebly endorsed by the CIA's own leadership. Confronted directly by an indignant Adams, CIA Director Richard Helms revealed a basic fact of life in Washington that did much to explain why the agency has traditionally devoted the bulk of its energies to activities other than intelligence. "Sam, this may sound strange from where you're sitting," said

Helms. "But the CIA is only one voice among many in Washington. And it's not a very big one, either, particularly compared to the Pentagon's. What would you have me do? Take on the entire military?"

Adams suggested that that would indeed be the honorable thing to do, but Helms thought otherwise, as did prior and subsequent CIA directors. When, in the 1970s, other agency analysts began to question inflated estimates of Soviet military strength, powerful interests in Washington moved swiftly to impose a Team B composed of hawkish ideologues to reinterpret the analysts' findings. Suitably chastened, the CIA did not veer significantly from the defense lobby's self-interested assessment of Soviet strength and aggressive intentions right up until the final collapse of the Communist system.

It is a commonly held view that with the exit of U.S. forces from Vietnam, hard-won expertise in fighting an insurgent enemy was discarded and forgotten as the military turned with relief to the simpler task of confronting the cold war enemy on the plains of Europe. But that is not entirely the case. The automated battlefield conceived and executed by Task Force Alpha sprang back to life within a few scant years of the exit from Vietnam as Assault Breaker, with ongoing conceptual resurrections, such as JSTARS in following years, right down to the drone system in the twenty-first century.

The CIA, meanwhile, found itself under severe attack as unedifying incidents from its history, including assassination plots against high-value targets, such as the late Congolese Prime Minister Patrice Lumumba in 1961, became public thanks to zealous congressional investigators, prompting a public ban on such assassinations. The ban, first pronounced by President Gerald Ford in Executive Order 11905 in 1976 and reaffirmed by Presidents Carter and Reagan, stated straightforwardly that "No employee of the United States government shall engage in, or conspire to engage in, political assassination."

It may have been the case that the CIA and the White House took these words literally for a little while, but within a few short years the ban was being creatively reinterpreted. This was made clear in 1983, when "Psychological Operations in Guerrilla Warfare," a CIA instructional manual distributed to the Nicaraguan Contras, surfaced in the press complete with helpful tips on how officials of the Sandinista regime could be "neutralized." Administration officials later explained to the *Washington Post* some of the ways in which the ban might not really ban assassinations, suggesting ". . . the order could be revoked or simply ignored, arguing that covert action against terrorists could be defined as something other than 'political assassination.'"

A pattern was now set: the United States would feel free to target individuals while insisting that the ban was being scrupulously observed—a contradiction in terms that press and public seemed happy to accept. So, in 1986 President Reagan sent a fleet of F-111 bombers to kill Libyan leader Muammar Qaddafi, along with whichever members of his family happened to be present. Spurred by deep-seated misconceptions and distorted intelligence, senior officials convinced themselves that Qaddafi, in the words of Secretary of State Alexander Haig, was "a cancer to cut out." As would later become routine in the post-9/11 era, a state department lawyer obligingly furnished an opinion that the United States had the legal right to preemptive attacks against terrorists, thus justifying killing Qaddafi. State-sanctioned murder, however, was still a touchy subject at the time, so the small group inside the White House promoting the mission, according to an authoritative account published not long afterward, put fake targets on the official orders while simultaneously drafting other secret orders for the pilots to strike Qaddafi's tent. Senior officials were therefore able to plausibly deny that the raid was in any sense an assassination mission. Qaddafi survived the attack.

So it was that the world at large believed that U.S. government-sponsored assassinations had been unequivocally forbidden by presidential edict. W. Hays Parks, a military lawyer working for the army's judge advocate general, had helpfully devised a legal rationale for ignoring the edict in any foreseeable situation. Parks, a former marine colonel whose views on legal boundaries for the use of force tended to the robust, concluded that the ban was indeed intended to establish "beyond any doubt that the United States does not condone assassination as an instrument of national policy." A public relations exercise, in other words. It did, he conceded, "preclude unilateral actions by individual agents or agencies against selected foreign public officials." However, it all depended on what was meant by the word *assassination*. The ban was definitely not intended, stated Parks in his lengthy analysis, to limit "lawful self-defense options against legitimate threats to the national security of the United States or individual U.S. citizens. . . . [Any] decision by the President to employ clandestine, low visibility or overt military force would not constitute assassination if U.S. military forces were employed against the combatant forces of another nation, a guerrilla force, *or a terrorist or other organization whose actions pose a threat to the security of the United States* [author's emphasis]." As Parks later explained to me, his memo was prompted by the increasing number of occasions in which the United States had confronted ter-- rorists overseas. As a particular example, he cited the case of Fawaz Yunis, a Lebanese Shi'ite militiaman wanted on hijacking charges, who was kidnapped by the FBI after being lured to a boat in international waters off Cyprus.

Since the military lawyer's definition left plenty of wiggle room for any president who wanted to murder someone—"legitimate threat" along with "terrorism" and "other" being left undefined—chief counsels at the White House, the departments of Justice and State, the CIA, and the military services signed their concurrence with Parks' judgment, thereby carving a legal highway straight through to the drone assassination programs of Presidents Bush and Obama.

Targeting "high-value individuals" was not yet part of the official U.S. national security lexicon. As we have seen in the evolution of effects-based operations through the bombing wars of the 1990s in Iraq and Serbia, murder attempts on enemy leaders were gradually acquiring the supporting dignity of theory. Prefiguring a twenty-first century fascination with anthropology, CIA officials did advance a rudimentary rationale for the targeting of the leaders' families. According to an authoritative account of the affair, agency officials theorized that in Bedouin culture, Qaddafi would be diminished as a leader if he could not protect his immediate family. The account indirectly quotes an agency briefing at the White House arguing "if you really get at Qaddafi's house—and by extension, his family—you've destroyed an important connection for the people in terms of loyalty." Some things had evidently not changed much since Air Vice-Marshall Ritchie's ruminations in 1944 on the merits of assassinating Hitler.

It would not be long, however, before the CIA, in partnership with a junior but ambitious agency, would discover a whole new field of individual targeting. For once there would be someone watching to see if it worked.

6

# KINGPINS AND
# MANIACS

T he night that North Vietnamese SAM missiles slammed into the B-52s over Hanoi—something that was not supposed to happen—had permanently cured fighter pilot Rex Rivolo of any faith in official military wisdom and promises. A few months later he climbed out of his F-4 Phantom fighter for the last time. After 531 combat missions he was done with war, or so he thought. Heading back to graduate school, he eventually earned a doctorate in physics. The next few years were the happiest in his life, teaching astrophysics at the University of Pennsylvania while probing the far reaches of the universe as a fellow at NASA's Space Telescope Science Institute. "That was a good time," he reminisced fondly one bright winter morning in 2013 as we sat in his northern Virginia office. "All the beautiful space-telescope pictures, that all came out of the Institute." Earlier, as we talked about his time in combat, he pointed to a framed photograph on the wall of a smiling twenty-two-year-old Rivolo standing on the wing of a Phantom. "Can you imagine giving *that* to *this*?" he laughed, indicating the sleek expensive fighter and to the carefree youth in the picture.

By the late 1980s, Rivolo, always enthusiastic about a new project, had conceived an ambitious plan to create the first detailed map of the entire Milky Way, including the vast molecular clouds, billions of miles long, that form the basic building blocks of star systems. Such a map, he thought, could guide astronauts in future space voyages. "We have no idea what's really out there, we are at a stage akin to where geographers of our planet were in the fifteenth century," he said at the time. Simultaneously, he had been exploring the world of graphic art, building up a collection that would grow to over fifteen thousand pieces, including the six signed Miró prints, along with a Picasso and a Braque, that he proudly showed me on the walls of the passage outside his office. Still in love with flying, he joined the New York Air National Guard and flew air-sea rescue helicopters on weekends—"with fighter jets, you need to practice all the time if you want to stay alive"—once making a forced landing on the lawn of Andy Warhol's Montauk estate and being greeted by the artist himself, "a gracious host."

Rivolo's plan for mapping the galaxy involved no less than 5 million observations collected by radio telescopes around the world that would then be analyzed using specially designed computer programs. As with all Rivolo's projects, his approach mandated a rigorous insistence on *hard data*, without which, he would pungently emphasize in his thick Bronx accent, theories and conclusions are *no fucking use.* To that end, he had acquired an expertise in statistics during his years in academia, along with a strong appreciation of how they could yield deeply buried truths otherwise invisible to the untutored eye. Such accumulation and manipulation of data were at the heart of a system he developed in the late 1980s to detect imminent failures in aircraft engines, which he hoped to turn into a profitable business venture. Leaving the stars behind, he launched a business to market it, "which promptly failed. I'm not a businessman."

So, in 1992, he returned to the world of defense, taking a job as an analyst with the Institute for Defense Analysis, the Pentagon's in-house think tank housed in an aesthetically unprepossessing complex of buildings in Alexandria, Virginia, a few miles south of the Pentagon. Fortunately for Rivolo, he landed in the Operational Evaluation Division directed by Tom Christie, the mathematician encountered in earlier chapters as the collaborator of the visionary tactician John Boyd and later a thorn in the side of the military for his unsparing test reports. Rivolo, as it turned out, would provoke equally choleric reactions, not least in his dogged pursuit of the V-22 Osprey, an aircraft under development by the marines that could tilt its rotors to fly like either a helicopter or a conventional plane. Early on, he concluded that the V-22 was dangerously unstable in certain conditions, telling a marine general to his face that the true measure of its performance would be the number of "dead marines per flight hour." (As of 2014, thirty-six people had died in multiple Osprey crashes.)

Meanwhile, though the cold war had ended, America had embarked on another war, the war on drugs. Initially declared by Richard Nixon in 1971 in recognition of the political advantages of being seen as tough on crime, this war had been re-declared by President George H. W. Bush in 1989. Nixon had invoked the specter of heroin as a crime-fomenting menace to society; Bush fought cocaine for the same reason. Money was duly showered on every relevant department of government, including the Pentagon, where an Office of Drug Control Policy headed by a deputy assistant secretary was created to supervise the military's role in the fight. In 1993 the Clinton administration awarded the post to Brian Sheridan, a tough and capable ex–CIA official. Sheridan, according to those who worked with him, was not impressed with what he found. Although Congress had bestowed a billion dollars a year on his office, no one in the government—not even the Drug Enforcement Agency, which could not tell him how many acres of coca plants it took to produce one kilo of cocaine—appeared to understand much about the actual mechanics of the cocaine trade or how to deal with it. More important, no one in the burgeoning drug enforcement bureaucracies seemed to know what the ultimate goal of all this effort might be and still less how to achieve it. Seeking an objective, intelligent analysis, Sheridan turned to the Institute for Defense Analysis and was duly presented with Rivolo and a more politically attentive former air force colonel named Barry Crane.

This was not the first time that IDA had been called in to survey the drug problem. In 1971, while the Nixon administration was promoting heroin addiction as the major cause of crime in America, a White House official had commissioned the institute to study the issue. Unlike law enforcement departments whose budgets were directly impacted by drug policy, IDA had no bureaucratic stake in the matter. So, taking a cool, objective look at the data, the analysts concluded that there was in fact no evidence whatsoever for the claim, accepted unquestioningly by policy makers for half a century, that addiction was a major cause of crime or that addicts were inexorably enslaved to their habit. Since this contradicted the basic premises of all government drug policies then and since, the analysts' report remained classified.

Undeterred by reality, Nixon and his officials pondered means to strike at the drug traffickers who allegedly posed what today would be called an existential threat to American society. The ultimate solution appeared simple and obvious. Cloaked in euphemism as "clandestine overseas law enforcement" with an annual budget of $100 million was a scheme to eliminate the high-value targets (though that phrase had yet to be conceived) of the heroin business. As drug enforcement officials stated confidently in a 1972 meeting, ". . . with 150 key assassinations, the entire heroin refining operation can be thrown into chaos." E. Howard Hunt, later infamous as a key member of the Watergate "plumber" unit, even traveled to Miami to consult with the Cuban exile leader Manual Artimes about supplying killers for drug enforcement work in Latin America. However, Watergate, Nixon's exit in disgrace, and consequent investigations into the darker activities of U.S. intelligence brought trafficker-targeting fantasies to a halt for the time being. Though the congressional enquiries did not uncover the trafficker-targeting schemes, revelations about other plots generated the presidential edict barring assassinations, a ban that, as we saw in the previous chapter, administrations were soon doing their best to undermine.

In the 1980s, cocaine replaced heroin as the officially prescribed menace, especially when ingested in the form of crack by poor people. Predictably, the furor had a nurturing effect on law enforcement as Congress showered money on existing bureaucracies and even created new ones. Coincidentally or not, this was a time when the growing decrepitude of the Soviet Union indicated that the cold war was drawing to a close and that therefore the national security apparatus, including the military and the CIA, should look for other justifications for their budgets. By December 1989, President George H. W. Bush was able to invade a foreign country, Panama, and seize and imprison its leader on the grounds of an antidrug operation. In such an atmosphere, it was hardly surprising that Nixon-era ideas about assassinating major traffickers swung back into fashion in Washington.

In Colombia, the main source of supply for the American cocaine market, the business had been consolidated during the 1980s into a limited number of "cartels," of which the two richest and most powerful were based in the cities of Cali and Medellín. Among these major traffickers, Pablo Escobar, the dominant figure of the Medellín cartel, was to become an object of obsessive interest to American law enforcement as he successfully evaded U.S.-assisted manhunts before negotiating an agreement with the Colombian government in 1991, under which he took up residence in a "prison" that he had built himself in the hills above his home city. A year later, fearing that the government was going to welsh on the deal and turn him over to the Americans, Escobar walked out of the prison and went into hiding.

The subsequent search for the fugitive drug lord marked a turning point. The cold war was over; Saddam Hussein had been defeated; credible threats were scarce; and the threat of budget cuts was in the air. Now the U.S. military, along with the CIA, deployed the full panoply of the surveillance technology that was developed to confront the Soviet foe against a single human target. The air force sent an assortment of reconnaissance planes, including SR-71s that were capable of flying at three times the speed of sound. The navy sent its own spy planes; the CIA dispatched a helicopter drone. At one point there were seventeen of these surveillance aircraft simultaneously in the air over Medellín, although, as it turned out, none of them were any help in tracking down Escobar. The decisive role in destroying his network of power and support was instead played by his deadly rivals from Cali, who combined well-funded intelligence with bloodthirsty ruthlessness. "We used Cali to get Medellín," a former American ambassador to Colombia confirmed to me years later. His once all-powerful network of intelligence and bodyguards destroyed, Escobar was eventually located by homing in on his radio and gunned down as he fled across a rooftop on December 2, 1993. Though the matter is open to debate, a former senior U.S. drug enforcement official assured me unequivocally that a sniper from the U.S. Army's Special Operations Delta Force had fired the killing shot.

Hunting down the leader of the Medellín cartel, albeit with the aid of his business rivals, had been something of an ad hoc affair, but it was nevertheless a showcase for an ambitious bid by the DEA to raise its status in the Washington police and intelligence pantheon. Unveiled the year before Escobar's death under the leadership of Robert Bonner, an ambitious prosecutor appointed administrator of the agency by Bush in 1990, the "kingpin strategy" focused on eliminating the leadership of the major cocaine cartels, along with their key henchmen, either by death or capture. For a DEA case to qualify for support from headquarters, a clear connection had to be made to one of the targeted kingpins. For the agency leadership, the scheme had the merit of shifting power from traditionally influential regional field offices to headquarters, which would control the money for all kingpin operations. Furthermore, the new strategy relied heavily on the use of electronic intercepts, expensive to operate and thereby further enhancing the power of headquarters at the expense of the regions.

Implicit in the concept was an assumption that the United States faced a hierarchically structured threat that could be defeated by removing key components, echoing the core airpower doctrine of "critical nodes" discussed in earlier chapters. In a revealing address to a 1992 meeting of DEA veterans held to commemorate the twentieth anniversary of the strategy's inauguration, Bonner spoke of the corporate enemy they had confronted: ". . . major [drug trafficking organizations] by any measure are large organizations. They operate by definition transnationally. They are vertically integrated in terms of production and distribution. They usually have, by the way, fairly smart albeit quite ruthless people at the top and they have a command and control structure. And they also have people with expertise that run certain essential functions of the organization such as logistics, sales and distribution, finances and enforcement." In essence, this was the same worldview propelling Colonel Warden's "five-rings" strategy for attacking Iraq or Air Vice-Marshall Ritchie's belief that Germany could be defeated by removing the Nazi kingpin. It would also, of course, inspire the targeted-killing strategy pursued by the United States against terrorists and insurgents in the drone wars following 9/11.

For the DEA under Bonner, a canny politician, the strategy was a matter of survival in the face of threats from two larger carnivores stalking the Washington bureaucratic jungle. Between 1981 and 1992, as Bonner related to me in the glass aerie of a giant Los Angeles law firm, the young agency had been effectively under the control of the FBI, with its senior officers drawn from the Bureau. No less threateningly, the CIA had been anxious not to lose out on the bounty of the drug war and in 1989 had created its own special unit, the Crime and Narcotics Center, which was soon running its own version of the kingpin strategy, the "linear strategy." Barry Crane, an air force colonel who later worked closely with Rivolo at IDA, recalls attending strategy meetings as the air force representative at CIA headquarters as early as 1989. The new unit pursued identical targets, at least initially, and took equal credit inside the government for successes against the cartels. Many of the officers assigned to the new entity, such as José Rodríguez, subsequently infamous for his role in the CIA torture program, came from the agency's Latin America Division, known for its rough-and-ready ways in the "dirty wars" of the 1980s. "DEA and CIA were butting heads," recalled Bonner when we met. "There was real tension." Bonner negotiated peace with the infinitely more powerful agency, "so now we had a very important ally. CIA could use DEA and vice versa," by which he meant the senior agency could use the DEA's domestic legal powers to good advantage.

As the DEA commemoration celebration indicates, the kingpin strategy was considered a great success, and in bureaucratic terms it certainly was, bringing great benefits for the DEA, which for years had limped along as a junior partner in Washington's police and national security fiefdoms. "It really brought us closer to the CIA and, through them, the NSA," Bonner told me. A new Special Operations Division created under Bonner to work with these senior agencies superintended the assault on the kingpins, relying heavily on electronic intelligence. The agency budget, always the surest token of an institution's standing, soared by 240 percent during the 1990s, from $654 million to over $1.5 billion ten years later.

Nevertheless, Rivolo was not impressed by the caliber of the drug warriors he was encountering in his new assignment. For a start, they were measuring success in the drug war by the amount of cocaine they seized. To him, this made no sense. "More seizures just indicated that there was more cocaine around. I asked them what would happen if there was no cocaine at all moving into the country. No seizures, right? Seizures were indeed an indicator," he guffawed, "but it indicated exactly the opposite of what they thought." Overall, there appeared to be a disconnect between cause and effect. "What are we trying to achieve?" he continually asked the agency's officials in meetings. "Reduce the supply of cocaine coming into this country, right?" What was the measure of success or failure? For Rivolo, it was clearly the availability of cocaine as signified by its price. If there were less cocaine available, the price would go up, and vice versa. The DEA, he discovered, put enormous effort into monitoring the price of cocaine on the street, using undercover agents to make buys—40,000 since 1980—with the amounts paid laboriously compiled and cross-referenced. However, the portions obtained by these surreptitious means were of wildly varying purity, the cocaine itself having been adulterated to a greater or lesser degree with some worthless substitute. That meant that the price of a gram of *pure* cocaine varied enormously, since a few bad deals of very low purity could cause wide swings in the average. (Dealers tended to compensate for higher prices by reducing the purity of their product rather than charging more per gram.) The implications were considerable, since the agency's price charts showed little movement, thus giving no indication of what events affected the price and therefore the supply.

Having tartly informed DEA officials that their statistics were worthless, mere "random noise," Rivolo set to work developing a statistical tool that eliminated the effect of the swings in purity of the samples collected by undercover DEA agents. Once he had succeeded, some interesting conclusions began to emerge. Rendered in graphic form, the DEA figures revealed only long-term price movements. But following his adjustments, the graph could show short-term price changes, which could be correlated with contemporary developments in the drug war. Most significant, it was now clear that the pursuit of the kingpins was most certainly having an effect on prices, and by extension supply, but not in the way advertised by the DEA. Far from impeding the flow of cocaine onto the streets and up the nostrils of America, it was accelerating it. Eliminating kingpins *actually increased supply.*

It was a momentous revelation, entirely counterintuitive to law enforcement cultural attitudes reaching back to the days of Elliott Ness' war against bootleggers and forward to the twenty-first-century counterinsurgency wars. It might have been possible to arrive at such a verdict intuitively, especially when the kingpin strategy in its most lethal form came to be applied to terrorists and insurgents, but this was a rare occasion in which the conclusion was based on hard data, undeniable facts. For example, in the last month of 1993, Pablo Escobar's once massive cocaine smuggling organization was in tatters, and he himself was alone and being hunted through the streets of Medellín. If the premise of the DEA strategy—that the way to cut drug supplies was to eliminate kingpins—had been correct, his situation should have resulted in a disruption of supply. But the opposite occurred: in that period, the U.S. street price was dropping from roughly $80 a gram to $60, and it continued to drop after his death.

With the elimination of Escobar, the DEA turned its attention to the Cali cartel, pursuing it with every resource: "[W]e really developed the use of wiretaps," Bonner told me. In June and July 1995, six of the seven heads of the Cali cartel were arrested, including the two Rodríguez-Orijuela brothers, Gilberto and Miguel, along with the cartel's cofounder, José "Chepe" Santa-Cruz Londono. Cocaine prices, which had been rising sharply earlier in the year for reasons we shall explore, immediately went into a precipitous decline that continued into 1996.

Rivolo, confident that the price drop and the kingpin eliminations were linked, looked for an explanation and found it in an arcane economic theory he called monopolistic competition. "It hadn't been heard of for years. It essentially says if you have two producers of something, there's a certain price. If you double the number of producers, the price gets cut in half, because they share the market," he explained, making the point appear obvious. "So the question was, how many monopolies are there?" he continued. "We had three or four major monopolies, but if you split them into twenty and you believe in this monopolistic competition, you know the price is going to drop. And sure enough through the nineties the price of cocaine was plummeting because competition was coming in and we were driving the competition. The best thing would have been to keep one cartel over which we had some control. If your goal is to lower consumption on the street, then that's the mechanism. But if you're a cop then that's not your goal. So we were constantly fighting the cop mentality in these provincial organizations like DEA."

Deep in the jungles of southern Colombia, coca farmers didn't need obscure economic theories to understand the consequences of the kingpin strategy. When news came through that Gilberto Rodríguez-Orijuela had been arrested, small traders in the remote settlement of Calamar erupted in cheers. "Thank the blessed virgin!" exclaimed one grandmother to a visiting American reporter. "Wait till the United States figures out what it really means," added another local resident. "Hell, maybe they'll approve, since it's really a victory for free enterprise. No more monopoly controlling the market and dictating what growers get paid. It's just like when they shot Pablo Escobar: now money will flow to everybody." This assessment proved entirely correct. As the big cartels disappeared, the business reverted to smaller groups that managed to maintain production and distribution quite satisfactorily, especially as they were closely linked either to the Marxist FARC guerrillas or to the Fascist antiguerrilla paramilitary groups allied with the Colombian government and tacitly supported by the United States.

Meanwhile, since attacking and dismantling major cartels was clearly counterproductive in stemming the flow of drugs, Rivolo pondered means that would have a positive effect. The key, he concluded, lay in the fact that drug use was clearly linked to its price. The more expensive the drug got, the fewer the number of people able or inclined to use it. "So I said, 'there should be only one goal . . . to increase the price, and the only way to increase price is to increase *risk*.'"

Drug traffickers, obviously, operated between the axis of risk and reward. The greater the reward, the more risk they were prepared to accept, and vice versa. If the risk of doing business increased to the point where traffickers were deterred from continuing to do business, then supplies would decline. This was more than just a hunch, but a conclusion supported by empirical data, including interviews with 112 imprisoned drug smugglers in which they had been asked how inclined to smuggle they would have been had they known the probability of being caught. Eighty percent of them had said that they would have left the business had they known that there was a 10 percent chance of going to prison. Using such data, Rivolo was able to calculate the relationship between risk and reward as curves on a graph, showing when reward trumped risk and vice versa. The graphs showed that as the reward increased, so did people's willingness to take risks. More interesting, they showed that at a certain point, a small increase in risk would lead to a big drop in motivation, and that at another point, where the risk was already high, an increase made little difference.

But where does one apply the risk? The choice was not obvious. Could it be at the ultimate end of the business, the consumers? "How do you put risk on a million people," Rivolo continued as we sat in his quiet office. "More police? Yes, you can do that, but it's not going to work. If you go to the other end of the business, there's only two or three people, the cartel leaders. How do you put risk on two or three? You kill them? That's what the DEA says. But if you kill them, the cartels split into two. So that wasn't it. So the question was, where's the weak link?"

Rivolo figured he knew where to look. Up through the mid-1990s, most of the raw product for cocaine, the coca leaves, had been grown by peasants in Peru, processed into cocaine base in labs in that country, and then flown to Colombia on small planes for final processing into cocaine. That air bridge between the two countries, he concluded, was the weak link. The pilots were willing to charge just $5,000 a trip, "which was nothing," Rivolo points out, because there was little or no risk involved. Once there was risk—of being shot down—they would stop flying or at least charge a lot more, which would increase the price of moving the base to Colombia and ultimately the retail price in New York and Los Angeles.

It was not an easy sell. The State Department objected on grounds that shooting down civilian aircraft was against international law. The DEA, still eagerly pursuing the kingpin strategy, was equally wedded to a theory proposed by the Rand Corporation known as the "additive theory" of drug pricing, according to which profits were so huge for the traffickers that they would easily absorb an increase in the price of cocaine base. Rivolo used his statistical skills to argue that this conclusion was incorrect and that the way the business was organized meant that the effect of cutting the bridge would ripple down the chain of production and distribution and have a major price impact, certainly doing a lot more good than opening treatment centers (a position that irked the Clinton White House, where treatment was a favored option). "Shoot 'em down," he urged, "they'll stop immediately."

When approval finally came from the Oval Office, the results were dramatic. In March 1995 a Colombian A-37 Air Force jet fighter intercepted a Kingair light plane and ordered it to land. As Rivolo recounts the story, the intercepted pilot gave the fighter the finger, whereupon the fighter backed up and shot his wing off. "We watched (on radar) as the plane spiraled into the ground. The next day the radio went from one communication a day to *thousands*. Everybody knew about it. No one flew the next day, the next day, the next day. For the next *sixty days* no one flew. The price of cocaine in New York and LA *doubled*. OK, how clean a story do you want?"

Inevitably, the business adapted to the loss of the air bridge. While Peruvian coca production closed down, coca plantations expanded in Colombia itself. Rivolo thought that a fungus developed by a University of Montana scientist specifically to attack the local coca plant would do the trick. To his disgust, the proposal was rejected in favor of spraying a powerful weed killer over coca farms. Tiring of the incessant bureaucratic politicking that seemed to pervade the world of narcotics enforcement—General Barry McCaffrey, the "drug czar," literally screamed in rage at one of Rivolo's analyses, throwing the paper slides against the wall—Rivolo announced, "I'm done with this business, I'm going back to airplanes." The equations he had painstakingly developed between risk and reward and the nature of underground organizations such as drug cartels went with him. They would be deployed again in a far bigger and more momentous war.

Meanwhile, still at IDA, Rivolo turned his attention to aircraft, finding fresh opportunities to upset received wisdom and established interests. In 1999, his office was asked to monitor an extensive test of various electronic warfare systems, including countermeasures and decoys, installed in naval fighters. The performance of different systems was carefully tracked and graded. Recalling his disillusioning experience when the sky had rained fire over Hanoi, he suggested a variation. "I said, 'Why don't we add another element. Let's just add a test with *no* countermeasures, just doing what pilots always do, which is to maneuver.' So in this huge test we had system X with jammer Y, system Z with jammer X, and then finally we had no jammers at all, just maneuvering. The probabilities of being hit while simply maneuvering were like one tenth of one percent. All the others were ten percent, twenty percent. They claimed great success for some of their systems because they reduced the chances of being hit by eighty percent, but I showed them that it's a ninety-nine percent reduction if you just maneuver, and it doesn't cost you anything! They didn't like that, because a jamming pod costs $3 million and the whole defense business is predicated on selling."

The drug enforcement business he left behind continued to prosper. The formula for the U.S.-sponsored eradication spray used in Colombia remains a closely guarded secret, although it included Monsanto's weed killer Roundup, but the effects were clear enough: destroy peasants' food crops while leaving the resilient coca plant relatively unscathed. The land was thereby cleared of potential support for FARC, the Marxist peasant guerrilla army that had been fighting the Colombian state since the 1960s. However, it was still available for cocaine production, much to the profit of the paramilitary death squads originally founded, ironically enough, in a joint antiguerrilla initiative by the Medellín and Cali cartels. The effect this had on supplies can be gauged very easily by consulting the voluminous and authoritative price charts compiled by the United Nations Office on Drugs and Crime (which had adopted the statistical methodology pioneered by Rivolo). They show that the median price of a gram of cocaine in the United States dropped by 40 percent between 1990, when Escobar and the Rodríguez brothers still controlled their empires, and 2010, when the war against the kingpins had been raging for almost two decades. (Calculated in 2010 dollars, it fell from $278 a gram to $169.)

Even as the Colombian cartels were fading from the scene, their Mexican counterparts, famed for their ferocity, were achieving ever-greater prominence. Urged on by Washington, Felipe Calderón, president of Mexico between 2006 and 2012, had declared war against these new kingpins, a war that to a great extent was guided and serviced by the United States. U.S. spy planes had crisscrossed Mexican skies. Drones operated by U.S. Homeland Security had guided Mexican military and police raids and tracked suspects to establish their "pattern of life." As later reported by the *Washington Post*'s Dana Priest, "The United States had also provided electronic signals technology, ground sensors, voice-recognition gear, cellphone-tracking devices, data analysis tools, computer hacking kits and airborne cameras that could read license plates from miles away."

As his term drew to a close, Calderón broadcast his success in capturing two-thirds of Mexico's most-wanted drug lords without mentioning the key role that the United States had played. However, when Enrique Nieto replaced Calderón as president in December 2012, he immediately announced that he was abandoning the kingpin strategy. Nieto's attorney general, Jesus Murillo Karam, revealed soon after taking office that the kingpin strategy had indeed caused the downfall of a few major cartel leaders. But there were now no fewer than sixty-eighty smaller, but no less violent, criminal drug groups operating in the country. Eliminating kingpins, said Karam, had made matters far worse. "It led to the seconds-in-command—generally the most violent, the most capable of killing—starting to be empowered and generating their own groups, generating another type of crime, spawning kidnapping, extortion and protection rackets."

Such acknowledgments of cause and effect are rare, certainly when the stakes for interested parties are as high and lucrative as they have been in the drug war or would be in the counterterror and counterinsurgency wars to come. As Barry Crane, Rivolo's partner at IDA, a successful habitué of national security culture, emphasized to me, "[H]igh value targeting is required for political sustainability. Promotions are usually in order for those who successfully bring down a significant antagonist."

This point did not escape the DEA's senior partners at the CIA, as they contemplated a mission that would come to dwarf anything the drug warriors had ever contemplated. Yet, as we shall see, the same factors that had undermined the kingpin strategy would apply in the world of counterterrorism, a lesson that was driven home at a very, very high cost in lives.

Counterterrorism at the Central Intelligence Agency had lowly beginnings, born as it was out of William Casey's quest to exercise greater control over the agency he directed. Casey, an ideologically driven lawyer who had managed Ronald Reagan's 1980 presidential campaign, was inclined to weaken the power of established bailiwicks such as the Directorate of Intelligence, which had an irritating habit of (occasionally) serving up politically unpalatable assessments. To run the new Counterterrorism Center he selected one of his favorite operations officers, Duane "Dewey" Clarridge, a flamboyantly irresponsible cold warrior who liked to demonstrate his disdain for authority routinely by showing up for work in a flight suit. Clarridge lived the spirit of the wartime OSS (in which Casey had served) and, among other brain waves, conceived the operation to mine Nicaragua's harbors that earned the United States a condemnation by the World Court in 1986. He was also deeply involved in the illegal Iran-Contra scheme to finance the Nicaraguan Contras through covert arms sales to Iran, which subsequently earned him an indictment on seven counts of perjury (and a pardon from George Bush Sr.). Other senior officials at headquarters approved his appointment, hoping that if Clarridge were confined to the relative obscurity of the new center, he might not cause too much further havoc.

One novel feature of the Counterterrorism Center was that it employed intelligence analysts from the agency's intelligence director-ate as well as operational officers from the Directorate of Operations and reported directly to Casey. This way Casey could more completely control all intelligence on terrorism, molding it as he saw fit. With Clar-ridge, with whom he had formed a close working relationship during the Iran-Contra machinations, helming the new center, he could under-take projects without the bother of interference from agency bureau-crats.

Naturally, this creation did not sit well with established CIA offices, igniting an antipathy that continued after Casey left the scene. Ordered to assign personnel to staff the CTC, they reacted in time-honored fashion by sending over their "deadwood." In addition, as the Soviet empire crumbled and fell, a huge swath of the agency's employees found themselves suddenly without a function. "These were people who had done nothing else but look at Russia and Eastern Europe for forty years," recalled a former senior officer in the agency's clandes-tine service. "They knew nothing about the Middle East or Islam." So it was that, among others, Michael Scheuer, a man who up to that point had enjoyed a relatively placid career as an analyst on the Euro-pean desk, joined the war on terrorism. (Coincidentally or not, a pri-ority cold war mission for the East European Division had been picking out high-value targets to be attacked in the event of World War III.)

Whereas counterterrorism in the 1980s had searched for the con-trolling hand of the Soviet Union, the focus in the early 1990s shifted to Iran, now deemed to be the chief fomenter of terrorist plots. Grad-ually however, the lengthening shadow of Islamic jihadism, marinated in the West's cold war crusade against the Soviets in Afghanistan, fell across Washington, and the Counterterrorism Center found its mis-sion. At the core of the new threat, as perceived in Washington, was the intriguing figure of Osama bin Laden, the charismatic Saudi who had secured the loyalty of the CIA's old Arab Mujaheddin allies from the anti-Soviet Afghan war (a relationship the agency was keen to forget and at pains to obscure) later known as al-Qaeda.

Therefore, encouraged by the White House, the agency set up a special unit in January 1996 solely dedicated to targeting bin Laden and his network. Whether wittingly or not, the kingpin strategy was thus transplanted to the Middle East. Heading the unit, which he codenamed Alec Station after his son, was Michael Scheuer. The new unit, separately housed in a suburban office park a few miles from CIA headquarters and initially employing twelve people, did not impress old hands in the clandestine service. "Scheuer reacted to every threat as if it were existential," one of them told me later. Another station officer, Fred Turco, was nicknamed "Abu Breathless" for his excited and widely broadcast alarms every time he thought he detected signs of al-Qaeda at work. Although Scheuer's unit was supposed to be tracking the terrorist network worldwide, his attention was focused almost exclusively on the individual target of bin Laden himself. "They were really meant to be just analysts, but they got caught up in the idea of being 'operational,' going out in the field and all that stuff, which they really had no idea how to do," recalls one former senior officer.

Scheuer himself paints a different picture, one of an agency and an administration that were halfhearted at best about confronting bin Laden. "When we set up the unit in 1996 we asked the Saudis for some basic material on bin Laden, like his birth certificate, his financial records—obvious stuff," Scheuer told me. "We got nothing. So the next year we asked again, still nothing, and the year after. Finally in 1999, we get a message from the station chief in Riyadh, a Mr. John Brennan. He said we should stop sending these requests, as it was 'upsetting the Saudis.' We had ten opportunities to kill or capture bin Laden. Clinton vetoed every one of them." It should come as no surprise that given their lowly status, the counterterrorists did not fare well in the inevitable battles for budget allocations, and in fact the bin Laden unit's operations were funded not out of the agency's baseline budget but out of a separate supplemental allocation solicited from Congress.

Coincidentally the CIA already had on the payroll a team of Afghan mercenaries originally recruited, funded, and equipped to hunt for Mir Aimal Kasi, a Pakistani who had gunned down a number of CIA employees on their way into work at Langley back in 1993 before he escaped to the Afghan/Pakistani borderlands. Following Kasi's capture (with no help from the Afghans) in 1997, the team, code-named FD/Trodpint, was now available to pursue bin Laden. On two occasions they reported that they had in fact located the elusive Saudi, once at the Tarnak Farms compound, an estate outside Kandahar he often visited, and once in January 1999 in western Afghanistan accompanying a falcon-hunting party of wealthy princes from the United Arab Emirates. Despite Scheuer's heated demands that the United States take the opportunity to strike bin Laden, the White House demurred. Even if the mercenaries' information had proved correct, a missile attack would have inevitably killed a lot of other people as well. Such concerns loomed larger in those days than they would in decades to come, especially when the collateral damage could have included, as with the hunting party, numerous wealthy members of a ruling Arabian Gulf family allied with the United States and well connected in Washington. Even when the White House did authorize a cruise missile strike against a bin Laden camp in Khost in eastern Afghanistan in retaliation for the bloody attacks on U.S. embassies in Kenya and Tanzania in August 1998, bin Laden himself was absent, having decided to visit Kandahar instead of Khost that day. In retrospect, of course, this sporadic and ill-planned pursuit of bin Laden could be made to look good, so in 2006, when "kill" had become a customary boast in presidential vocabulary, former president Clinton told Fox News, "I worked hard to try to kill him. I authorized a finding for the CIA to kill him. I got close to killing him."

Despite Clinton's bravado, there was apparently a legal difficulty. Some CIA officials were leery of pursuing bin Laden to the death on the grounds that this might be illegal. According to one former CIA official, "The directive from the Clinton White House was fuzzy, in part due to the strong reservations of [Attorney General] Janet Reno. The agency understood that it had authorization to capture [bin Laden], but that the references regarding the assassination of OBL were not clear." This official, echoing a common theme, also declared that Scheuer was "typically way off base in alleging that there were good clandestine sources on the actual whereabouts of OBL."

His requests denied, Scheuer rendered himself even more unpopular at Langley by broadcasting angry complaints around Washington, complete with specific criticisms of individual officials. Unsurprisingly, he was soon dismissed from the command of Alec and sent off to a more obscure post. Retiring in 2004 and trading on his counterterrorism credentials to establish himself as an expert commentator, Scheuer grew a long beard and took to respectfully citing bin Laden as enjoying worldwide support from the Muslim community. He even earned a word of commendation from the man himself, who declared in a September 2007 video, "If you want to understand what's going on and if you would like to get to know some of the reasons for your losing the war against us, then read the book of Michael Scheuer."

Just as Scheuer exited the bin Laden unit, a new chief was installed as head of the Counterterrorism Center, Cofer Black. Black had spent much of his career in the agency's Africa Division, engaged in various half-forgotten but often vicious cold war operations, such as the murderous Angolan Civil War, in which the CIA was massively engaged in aiding Jonas Savimbi, an insurgent leader with a taste for burning his enemies alive as witches. Recalled affectionately by a former colleague for his taste for "childish pranks" against the KGB and other opponents, Black was very much in the flamboyant tradition of Dewey Clarridge and other custodians of the old OSS spirit, "an actor," as another former colleague describes him.

The hunt had not yet yielded any significant intelligence on the al-Qaeda leader's plans for future operations. Nor had there been even the slightest success in planting agents inside his network, despite the fact that foreign jihadis, such as the American youth John Walker Lindh, had apparently little trouble in gaining access to extremist camps in Afghanistan. Instead, attention and money were devoted to the Afghan bounty hunters and later an Uzbek group, furnished by their country's dictator, for zero return. The bloody attacks on the U.S.

embassies in Kenya and Tanzania on August 7, 1998, which killed 224 people, had therefore come as a complete surprise. The record did not improve following Scheuer's departure. Though there were fewer histrionics, there was little increase in useful intelligence about al-Qaeda operations, though this was not for want of opportunity.

In December 1999, the National Security Agency intercepted a phone call to a known al-Qaeda safe house in Yemen mentioning that two members were headed to a meeting in Kuala Lumpur, Malaysia. En route, the passport of one, Khalid al-Midhar, who would later help fly American Airlines Flight 77 into the south face of the Pentagon, was copied by Dubai airport security and passed to Alec Station in Washington. Although it bore a multiple-entry visa for the United States that had been issued in Saudi Arabia, the CIA office did not inform the FBI that someone connected to al-Qaeda intended to travel to the United States.

Amazingly, a pair of FBI agents assigned as liaisons to the bin Laden unit knew that two known terrorists were headed to the U.S. but were forbidden to relay this vital intelligence to their home agency, which was responsible for domestic terrorist threats. As Agent Mark Rossini later related, he told a CIA official, "What's going on? You know, we've got to tell the Bureau about this. These guys clearly are bad. One of them, at least, has a multiple-entry visa to the U.S. We've got to tell the FBI," only to be told by the CIA officer: "No, it's not the FBI's case, not the FBI's jurisdiction." Regrettably, Rossini did not dare violate the order. As he later excused himself, "If we had picked up the phone and called the Bureau, I would have been violating the law. I would have broken the law. I would have been removed from the building that day. I would have had my clearances suspended, and I would be gone."

The CIA's determination to keep information about al-Midhar and al-Hazmi (the other al-Qaeda member headed to the United States) away from its domestic intelligence colleagues has given rise to a justifiable suspicion, shared by Richard Clarke, who was at the time the senior counterterrorism official at the White House, that the agency was nurturing plans to recruit the pair as agents, something it had signally failed to do at any time before 9/11. The accusation drew a heated denial from CIA Director Tenet, Cofer Black, and Richard Blee, who at the time of 9/11 had been a lower-ranking official in the Counterterrorism Center. In their statement rebutting Clarke, Tenet & Co. blandly conceded that "In early 2000, a number of more junior personnel [including FBI agents on detail to CIA] did see travel information on individuals who later became hijackers but the significance of the data was not adequately recognized at the time."

The Kuala Lumpur meeting of assorted al-Qaeda operatives was monitored at CIA request by Malaysian security, though without yielding any actual information as to what was discussed, and the resultant reports were eagerly scrutinized in Washington. But when al-Midhar and al-Hazmi left for Bangkok, the CIA lost track of them. Meanwhile, the two proto-hijackers had flown to Los Angeles and then settled in San Diego, where they opened bank accounts and obtained drivers' licenses—even a local phone book listing—all in one or both of their real names. They evidently felt no risk as they waited to gain their reward in heaven.

Two months after the two terrorists had flown out of Bangkok, the CIA bin Laden unit got around to asking Thai security for information on their whereabouts and received word that they had long since departed for Los Angeles and were presumably somewhere in the United States. Though such news would certainly have been of interest to the FBI, it was not passed along, perhaps for unforgivably petty reasons: the CTC had conceived an intense bureaucratic rivalry with and dislike of the chief of the FBI National Security Division in New York, John O'Neill, and therefore felt justified in withholding what was clearly vital information. Had the bureau been aware of their presence, they might have made inquiries of a regular informant in San Diego, Abdusattar Shaikh, from whom, as it happened, al-Midhar and al-Hazmi had rented a room. Shaikh, who later recalled the pair as being "nice, but not what you call extroverted people," apparently forgot to tell his FBI handler his tenants' last names or the fact that they were taking flying lessons.

Settling into their new home, the terrorists stayed in regular contact with the organization by phoning al-Midhar's father-in-law's house in Yemen, which served as an al-Qaeda message center. These conversations were duly swept up by the NSA's omnivorous global eavesdropping system, but the intelligence went no further. Many years later, the electronic intelligence agency, under fire thanks to whistle-blower Edward Snowden's revelations of its mass surveillance programs, would claim that had such programs been in place before 9/11, they would have nipped the attacks in the bud. President Obama himself, in defending the massive domestic "metadata" phone records program, repeated this canard. But, as a number of former senior NSA officials swiftly pointed out, the NSA not only had been intercepting calls to and from the Yemeni house since 1996 but also could very easily have traced them back to San Diego. As it was, the pair was left unmolested, with al-Midhar even taking time to return to Yemen and spend time with his family before moving to temporary lodgings—a motel in Laurel, Maryland, within sight of NSA headquarters—in preparation for that last fatal flight.

Late in the evening of 9/11, the man who succeeded Scheuer as head of the bin Laden unit stopped by the office of an old colleague, a senior agency official not involved in the counterterrorist mission. "We're fucked," he said simply, explaining that intelligence about al-Midhar and al-Hazmi living in San Diego and calling al-Qaeda in Yemen had been ignored.

With scenes of the collapsing trade towers and the burning Pentagon endlessly replaying on the TV screens to a traumatized public, the official was entirely justified in assuming that he and his colleagues who had missed all the warnings would suffer severe consequences. But he was entirely wrong. Far from ignominy and sanctions, the CIA's counterterrorists had a glorious future ahead of them. As a former senior CIA official who watched the process with cynical detachment later described it to me: "On the morning of September 11, 2001, the Counterterrorism Center was a collection of rejects and cast-offs. On the morning of September 12, it was the most powerful organization in the country. Before, they had had to scramble for pennies; now they could ask for billions of dollars and get it. They were briefing the president of the United States." The briefings struck just the right note with the president, who loved hearing Cofer Black's macho posturing about "when we're through with them they will have flies crawling across their eyeballs" and "bringing bin Laden's head back in a box." Speaking with regretful affection of the CTC leadership, the former official remarked, "They were my friends. I had worked with many of them. After 9/11 they turned into," he paused, seeking the right word, "maniacs."

Formalizing the matter, on September 17, 2001, President George W. Bush signed a secret "Memorandum of Notification" giving the CIA carte blanche to hunt down and kill high-value targets in the al-Qaeda leadership. Bush also approved a list of about two dozen people whom the CIA was authorized to kill or capture without further presidential review and allowed the addition of names to that list with no permission necessary. On the day he signed the document, Bush spoke with reporters at the Pentagon, saying "I want justice, and there's an old poster out West, as I recall, saying 'Wanted, Dead or Alive.'" Reporting on the presidential "kill list," the *New York Times* noted: "Despite the authority given to the agency, Mr. Bush has not waived the executive order banning assassinations, officials said. The presidential authority to kill terrorists defines operatives of Al Qaeda as enemy combatants and thus legitimate targets for lethal force." The legal fig leaf outlined by Hays Parks was still respected. To keep track, Bush drew himself a diagram listing potential victims in order of importance, which he kept in a drawer in his office. It was in the shape of a pyramid, with bin Laden's name at the apex.

The counterterrorists had clearly failed miserably in their appointed task. But their mission was now a national goal. Within a few months of 9/11 their numbers had swelled from three hundred to twelve hundred and would soon soar to over three thousand. They had near-limitless resources. They still had little or no intelligence about the enemy, but they did have what seemed to be the perfect weapon, the newly armed Predator, and a license to kill. The list of targets could only grow.

To accommodate the change, *target* as a verb took on a new meaning. Traditionally, *targeting* meant "focusing intelligence resources on some item of interest," such as the Soviet Muslim population or the Italian Communist Party or a likely prospect for recruitment as a spy.

Now the targets were individual humans, and a new profession of "targeters" was born. Their task was to assemble information on a future victim, his movements, associates, and habits, in order to set him up for the kill. Just as the counterterrorists had been called in from the moribund Soviet and Eastern European desks, targeters were recruited from the ranks of "reports officers." This comparatively lowly occupation involves editing and rewriting case officers' reports of intelligence from agents to obscure any clue that might hint at the identity of the source. Now, many of them would be retasked in this new specialty of targeter, which within a few short years would become the fastest career track in the agency, involving fully 20 percent of all CIA analysts. Many targeters spent their entire professional lives doing nothing else, rising steadily through the ranks as they developed greater expertise at hunting people, one by one.

Since many people still thought there was a blanket ban on assassinations, despite Hays Parks' pronouncement, a name change was clearly called for. So the A-word was supplanted by the more palatable "targeted killing," which gradually crept into official and popular lexicons. In this, as in so many other aspects of the strategy, the trail was blazed by Israel, whose founders had been well versed in the practice of assassination, as in the killing of UN mediator Folke Bernadotte in 1948, from the earliest days. In fact, within weeks of Bush unleashing the CIA's counterterrorists, Israel was already moving ahead, at least in the art of euphemism. For many years the preferred Hebrew term for assassination had been *Hisul Memukad*, meaning "targeted extermination." But in November 2011 Attorney General Elyakim Rubinstein decreed that that term "wrongs" Israel and mandated substitution of the phrase *Sikul Memukad,* meaning "targeted prevention," which duly became both the official and popular term.

In 2005, Avi Dicter, the retiring head of Israel's internal security service, Shabak, was asked, "Do you have a problem with a state becoming an executioner?"

"No," he replied. "I'm telling you, foreign delegations come here on a weekly basis to learn from us, not just the Americans. It has become the sexiest trend in counterterrorism. Its effectiveness is amazing . . . the state of Israel has turned targeted preventions into an art form." Dicter's philosophy, as explained by another Israeli intelligence chief, was that "all the time we have to mow the grass—all the time—and the leaders with experience will die and the others will be without experience and finally the 'barrel of terror' [a Dicter analogy] will be drained."

"If you do something for long enough," later observed Colonel (Res.) Daniel Reisner, former head of the IDF's Legal Department, "the world will accept it. The whole of international law is now based on the notion that an act that is forbidden today becomes permissible if executed by enough countries. . . . International law progresses through violations. We invented the targeted assassinations thesis and we had to push it. [Now] it is in the center of the bounds of legality."

Immediately following his retirement, Dicter spent several months as a visiting scholar at the Brookings Institution in Washington, DC, where he coauthored "Israel's Lessons for Fighting Terrorists and Their Implications for the United States." The paper reiterated his "barrel of terror" thesis, stating as a first principle that "the number of effective terrorists is limited," thereby rendering their elimination especially productive.

His argument found fertile ground. Discussing the post-9/11 U.S. assassination timeline, a former senior White House counterterrorism official drew my attention, unprompted, to the influential role played by both the kingpin strategists and the Israelis. "The idea had its origins in the drug war. So that precedent was already in the system as a shaper of our thinking," he explained. "In addition, the success of the Israeli targeted-killing strategy was a major influence on us, particularly in the Agency and in Special Ops. We had a high degree of confidence in the utility of targeted killing. There was a strong sense that this was a tool to be used." Echoing Dicter's notion that the enemy has only a limited number of effective leaders, he noted that by targeting the "seconds in command, you force the organization to put up its third string, and so you get a steady decline in quality."

So, within a few short weeks of 9/11, the newly emboldened assassination machine began to crank into action, firing the first shot in a war that may never end. It missed.

7

# LEGALLY BLIND

O n the night of October 7, 2001, the U.S. military and intelligence high command at the Pentagon, CIA, and various headquarters across the globe were gazing attentively at the video screens that had lately become such a prominent feature of their offices. The recent collapse of the dot-com boom meant that a huge amount of commercial satellite bandwidth capacity had become available for use by the military to transmit all the exciting video streamed by drones to an ever-wider audience. They were watching a grainy infrared video relayed from a Predator drone armed with two Hellfire missiles over the outskirts of Kandahar, in southern Afghanistan. The drone "pilot" was sitting in a trailer in a parking lot at CIA headquarters in Langley, although CIA drones in the war zone were under military control. The silent picture showed three vehicles and a motorcycle leaving a mud-walled compound and heading toward Kandahar.

Among the far-flung spectators was General Tommy Franks, the four-star general commanding the assault on Afghanistan from his wartime headquarters in Tampa, Florida. "I felt a familiar rush of

adrenaline," Franks wrote later, for the spectacle took him back to long-
ago days watching battles from a helicopter in Vietnam. "This target
has all the characteristics of a leadership convoy," reported a CIA counterterrorism officer who was watching from the trailer, a former day-
care center, in the Langley parking lot. "This could be Mullah Omar's
personal vehicle." Mullah Omar was the Taliban leader, a very high-
value target. Here was a chance to eliminate the heart of the enemy
war machine at a blow.

"Valid target," pronounced a military lawyer standing at Franks'
side.

The convoy entered Kandahar and drove through the predawn
streets, then stopped as some of the passengers got out and entered a
building. "Valid target for Hellfire," said the lawyer, but the vehicles
moved on before the drone could fire. When the convoy stopped again,
several passengers entered a mosque, off-limits for a strike without special permission. Meanwhile, David Deptula, mastermind of the 1991
Iraq bombing campaign and theorist of effects-based operations who
was by now a two-star general directing all allied air forces in the
Afghan War, was also glued to the Predator video feed at his headquarters in Qatar. As he told me later with some irritation, he had four planes
over the mosque, waiting for clearance to obliterate the building. "Suddenly a vehicle parked outside the building blows up. I said, 'Who the
hell ordered that?'" It turned out that Franks himself, chafing at the
delay, had ordered the drone operator to fire a Hellfire missile at
the vehicle, a Toyota Corolla. Like many people, Deptula was not
used to the notion that commanding generals were now bypassing
the entire chain of command to blow up cars. Minutes later, the
remainder of the convoy came to a halt and various passengers disappeared inside a large building. Would it be in order to kill everyone
inside, including innocent parties? Franks thought he had better consult Secretary of Defense Rumsfeld.

Rumsfeld announced he was going to refer the matter to the president. Five minutes later he reported back that Bush had agreed the
building could be hit. Then the CIA officer monitoring the video
reported that the building might be a mosque. Franks, as he wrote later,

"swore silently," concluded that it didn't look like a mosque to him, and ordered a waiting Navy F-18 fighter-bomber to bomb the building forthwith. "You're still good," said the lawyer. A few minutes later, Franks received a call from Air Force Chief of Staff General John Jumper, who had been watching the entire episode on the Predator screen in *his* office and who smugly informed him that he thought he had seen the high-value targets escape from the building before the strike. Enraged, Franks demanded that the chairman of the Joint Chiefs of Staff have Jumper's screen removed. In this new kind of war, video conferred power, at least in Washington.

Unbeknownst to the high-ranking audience gazing at their separate screens, Mullah Omar had indeed been in the convoy. Earlier that evening an American missile had plowed into his home compound as he huddled in the basement, sparing him but mortally injuring his ten-year-old son. According to the Mullah's driver, later interviewed by journalist Anand Gopal, the Taliban leader had set off with his family and dying child in the Corolla. But the child could not be saved. When the car exploded from the missile strike while he was inside the building, he and the rest of his family ran off (leaving the remainder of the convoy to proceed on its way), and he has not been seen by any Westerner since that day.

Overall, the initial campaign in Afghanistan was deemed a great success, particularly by Rumsfeld, who relished the notion that it was all thanks to "a combination of the ingenuity of the U.S. Special Forces, the most advanced precision-guided munitions in the U.S. arsenal, delivered by U.S. Navy, Air Force and Marine Corps crews, and the courage of valiant one-legged Afghan fighters on horseback." (Rumsfeld had been taken by reports of one Northern Alliance fighter charging the enemy despite a prosthetic limb.) There was a certain amount of truth in this. Resistance to the U.S.-supported Northern Alliance did collapse when the Taliban lost the northern city of Mazar-e Sharif. But most casualties came after the Taliban surrendered, when many prisoners were crammed into shipping containers and left to suffocate. Had the air strikes really had the devastating effects as claimed in Rumsfeld's history, there would have been a large number of wounded.

Yet in the north, where the bombing had been most intense, there were very few fighters to be found among the casualties at local hospitals, even within days of the fighting. Elsewhere, where U.S. planes caught Taliban formations in the open, such as in front of the town of Tirin Kot in Uruzgan Province, they did inflict heavy casualties, but at Ghazni, which had been heavily bombed thanks to the large number of Taliban tanks based there, the total number of casualties, according to postwar local testimony, was three. More important contributions to the victory were the orders from the Taliban's overseers in Pakistani intelligence to give up the fight and go home as well as the hefty cash payments handed out by the CIA to various Afghan warlords to abandon their Taliban allies.

Meanwhile, the hunt for high-value targets was pursued with unrelenting but somewhat indiscriminate vigor. Bin Laden himself had slipped the net with relative ease. Having evaded efforts to corner him in his Tora Bora mountain redoubt, he took himself off to the mountainous and heavily forested Kunar Province and thence across the border to Pakistan, settling in the pleasant district of Haripur, where he lived in wedded bliss with his youngest wife for two years before moving to a purpose-built compound in equally pleasant Abbottabad. His immediate subordinate, the Egyptian Ayman al-Zawahiri, also escaped. Less fortunate was Mohammed Atef, another Egyptian, who in addition to being generally considered the military commander of al-Qaeda was also a valued mentor to bin Laden. (Atef's daughter married Mohammed bin Laden, Osama's son.) He was killed along with seven associates in a drone-assisted bombing strike during the initial American air assault, but was swiftly replaced as military commander by another Egyptian, former army colonel Saif al-Adel.

The list in Bush's desk had originally contained some two dozen names, but although the president carefully updated the list with excisions whenever news of a fresh kill came in, the number of nominated high-value targets continued to grow. Just as strategic bombing campaigns that commence with a limited number of select targets have traditionally tended to expand, the attack on Afghanistan that began as a hunt for the perpetrators of 9/11 inexorably widened. In part, this was a function of demand, as the number of hunters eager to join in the chase proliferated. In particular, Defense Secretary Donald Rumsfeld, irked by the prominent role played by CIA paramilitary teams in the initial overthrow of the Taliban, was eager to enhance the U.S. military role in covert operations. "Have you killed anyone yet?" he would query General Charles Holland, chief of Special Operations Command, whenever they met. In December 2001, a Joint Special Operations Task Force, code-named Task Force 11 for the occasion, with personnel drawn from elite units of all three services, arrived in Afghanistan with the specific mission of killing or capturing al-Qaeda and Taliban "HVTs" (high-value targets).

Task Force 11 appeared to embody the vision of a twenty-first-century military as described in George W. Bush's September 1999 speech at the Citadel: "agile, lethal . . . able to identify targets by a variety of means, then be able to destroy those targets almost instantly . . . able to strike from across the world with pinpoint accuracy . . . with unmanned systems." Not only did the task force have the services of the CIA's Predators, armed and unarmed, the intensely trained elite troops also carried high-tech radios and satellite phones designed to put them in instant communication with commanders near and far. At their disposal were AC-130 Spectre gunships, which could not only lay down withering fire against enemies on the ground but also provide close-up pictures of any area a unit might be thinking of occupying, thanks to the profusion of TV and infrared cameras on board. The NSA and service communications intelligence assets vacuumed up targets' radio communications and tracked their location. The drones rolling off the General Atomics assembly line gave commanders up to the level of Tommy Franks and beyond a bird's-eye view of unfolding battles.

Despite the profusion of sensors, it was still hard for the task force to find targets, because in the immediate aftermath of the fall of the Taliban regime, there were few to be found. The al-Qaeda leadership had disappeared to Pakistan and elsewhere, as had many of the leaders of the regime. Most of the Taliban had simply retired from politics, at least for the time being, accepting that Afghanistan had entered a new era. Nevertheless, a central war aim of the U.S. military machine had been "to capture or kill as many Al Qaeda as we could," according to General Richard Myers, chairman of the Joint Chiefs of Staff. The targeting apparatus embodied in organizations such as Task Force 11 and the CIA paramilitary squads demanded victims. Therefore, supply met demand. Strongmen and warlords found they could dispose of two birds with one stone by denouncing rivals in local power struggles to the credulous Americans as Taliban or al-Qaeda leaders and thereby ingratiate themselves with the country's new rulers. Even those with ironclad proof that they were not al-Qaeda or Taliban were swept up, including a Syrian named Abdul Rahim al-Janko, who had been arrested by al-Qaeda on suspicion of being a Western spy and tortured into giving a videotaped confession that he had been sent by the CIA and Mossad to kill Osama bin Laden. In a jail in Kandahar when the Taliban regime fell, al-Janko was handed to the Americans, who sent him to Guantánamo. U.S. Attorney General John Ashcroft later played part of the tape of his confession to journalists, claiming it was a would-be suicide attacker's martyrdom video. The audio was muted, on the excuse that it might contain coded messages for other terrorists.

Meanwhile the search teams thirsted for bigger game. "By February 2002," Army Special Operations Colonel Andrew Milani drily noted in a later report, "the Joint Special Operations Task Force (i.e., Task Force 11) had become frustrated by the lack of actionable intelligence for high value targets."

Even genuinely active Taliban leaders were at this point hard to find. One such was Saifur Rahman Mansoor, a youthful son of a famous anti-Soviet fighter who had risen to be a mid-level Taliban commander. Following the fall of the Taliban regime he had retreated with a few hundred followers, including assorted Uzbek and Arab jihadis, to his father's old redoubt during the Russian war, a remote, narrow mountain valley close to the Pakistani border called the Shahikot. Finding his arrival unpopular with local tribes, he opened negotiations with the authorities in Kabul, using tribal elders as intermediaries, offering "to end his armed defiance of the interim government."

Mansoor's surrender offer was quickly brushed aside, for the U.S. military, eager to "flush out" such a conveniently consolidated collection of the enemy, was preparing a major assault. A surge in cell-phone traffic from the area and sightings of a number of SUVs had convinced the CIA and Task Force 11 that one or more of the highest-value targets of all—Osama bin Laden, his second in command Ayman al-Zawahiri, or Mullah Omar (quickly dubbed "the big three")—might be wintering there, protected by a large force of body-guards. According to the plan, conventional U.S. Army troops would drive down the valley from the north in expectation of pushing the enemy, or at least their leaders, into the arms of other units blocking escape routes through the mountain passes leading toward Paki-stan. The special operations units, U.S. Navy Seals and others, would be waiting on observation points, ready to scoop up or kill flee-ing high-value targets. In keeping with the exclusive and obsessive focus on these particular targets, the Task Force 11 teams were under an entirely separate chain of command from the conventional force, free to act as they chose. Code-named Operation Anaconda, it would be the largest U.S. military ground operation since the 1991 Gulf War.

The ensuing battle featured almost all aspects of the remote-control high-technology approach to war, notably the abiding faith in remote sensing as a substitute for the human eye. The results were instructive, if tragic.

Overlooking the southern end of the valley was a 10,000-foot moun-tain, Takur Ghar. Task Force 11 planners thought the summit would be an excellent spot for an observation post. "Unfortunately," as Milani noted in his report, "the enemy thought so too." Just to make sure, the task force dispatched one of their favorite tools, a four-engine AC-130 plane, to make a reconnaissance of the mountaintop and confirm that it was unoccupied. The plane carried a formidable amount of firepower, including heavy machine guns and a cannon. But Special Forces esteemed the aircraft even more for the array of surveillance devices it carried, including electro-optical and infrared cameras as well as radar. Relayed back to task force headquarters, the pictures showed no sign of any human presence, nor did any other intelligence report from the various surveillance aircraft and other systems blanketing the area. But they were wrong. In fact, as the elite Navy Seals were shortly to discover, several dozen of the enemy, highly trained Arab and Uzbek fighters, were well dug in, complete with a heavy machine gun in a fortified bunker, concealing themselves with the low-technology aid of snow, trees, and a tarpaulin.

To the naked eye, on the other hand, the enemy force was by no means invisible. There was snow on the mountain, and trails of footprints showed up clearly, as did goatskins and other detritus left in plain view by untidy jihadis. These were exactly the kind of telltale signs that Marshall Harrison, the forward air controller prowling the skies over South Vietnam in his wide-observation little plane, had been ready and able to pick up: a trail of footprints left in the mud after early-morning rain, extra clothes on a washing line, and other indications visible to a well-trained human observer. Staring at the images from Takur Ghar on their (relatively) high-definition video screens, the task force mission planners saw no such signs. Believing these systems to be infallible, the commander ordered the SEALs to head for the mountaintop.

So it was that on the night of March 2, 2002, a helicopter flew a SEAL team directly to the summit. They noticed the fresh tracks and goatskins the moment they touched down, but a discussion on whether to quit the scene was interrupted when a rocket-propelled grenade hit the helicopter, which was simultaneously ripped with machine-gun bullets. The pilot quickly took off again, flying the badly damaged craft to a landing several miles away on the valley floor. But in the sudden jolt of the takeoff, a SEAL, Petty Officer Neil Roberts, who had been standing on the rear exit ramp, fell off, stranding him alone amid the hornets' nest of aroused jihadis.

Both Roberts and the team leader with the damaged helicopter switched on their high-tech infrared strobe lights, visible to the AC-130 gunship circling overhead. This was a means of revealing location to friendly forces and was much valued by the special operators. It had, however, never been tested in actual combat. Thanks to the images, ascending levels of Special Operations command were aware of these distress signals, but none of them were clear as to whom each light belonged, thus generating a spiral of confusion.

Down in the valley, the officer in immediate command of the unit that had tried to land on Takur Ghar quickly devised a plan to deal with the emergency. He did not have any sophisticated surveillance equipment, merely a radio and a satellite phone to talk to higher headquarters, but he had been in the area for some days and had a clear grasp of the local geography, what had happened, and what could and should be done. None of that mattered, however, because buzzing in the freezing darkness two thousand feet above the mountain summit was a Predator drone, its infrared camera streaming video up to a satellite high above and then across mountains, deserts, and oceans to Task Force 11 headquarters on Masirah, a desert island off the coast of Oman in the Arabian Gulf, a thousand miles from the battle on Takur Ghar. The hypnotic allure of close-up video gave commanders the illusion, not for the last time, that they were in close touch with the battlefield and had a better understanding of events than anyone actually on the scene. They felt they had "total situational awareness," wrote one historian of the battle later, "making them like gods, omniscient and all-seeing," and consequently better equipped to manage a complicated and fast-moving series of events far away. "We don't need you getting all worked up on the radio," the officer on the scene was curtly informed. "Get off the Net, we've got it."

The chair-bound staff on Masirah, not to mention the technicians and officers at assorted other headquarters in Bagram, Florida, and the Pentagon who were also watching the pictures (Special Operations Command was by now spending $1 million a day renting satellite bandwidth), were in fact glued to a strange depiction of reality. Dawn was hours away, and the silent stream of images generated by warm bodies against a cold background that was filtered through security encryption and satellite relays before ultimate translation into viewable pictures was indistinct at best. Just as Tom Christie's testers had honestly reported two years earlier (to air force fury), the images gave only a "soda-straw" view of events, with a visual acuity of 20/200. As it so happens, this is the legal definition of blindness for drivers in the United States.

To make matters worse, the people operating this drone were CIA employees sitting in the trailer park at CIA headquarters who felt free to shift the direction in which the drone camera was pointing without reference to the staff trying to coordinate troops and helicopters on and around the mountain. So each time this happened, the headquarters staff on the island off Oman had to contact the CIA trailer park and request a change of camera direction, a process that sometimes took twenty minutes.

Apart from the quality of the pictures, the command post on Masirah should in theory have been able to communicate easily with troops on the scene thanks to the wonders of the radio communications net, which was designed to bypass mountains and other obstacles by relaying signals via satellites. But this system was notoriously unreliable, and true to its reputation, conversations were repeatedly interrupted or broken off completely, causing endless repetition and confusion during the operation. Nevertheless, so determined were the members of the task force battle staff to supervise the battle through the Predator drone, they settled for the deficient satellite radio with its unfulfilled promise of direct and instantaneous communications over long distances. The officer on the scene who had been rudely displaced from command did have direct and instant communication where it mattered, inside the valley and surrounding mountains, because his radios were comparatively simple and could easily reach anyone who was in line of sight, but this advantage was considered secondary to the omniscience conferred by the Predator.

The helicopter carrying the first SEAL team had flown off the mountaintop when attacked and crash-landed in the valley, leaving Roberts behind. A second helicopter, having picked up the survivors from the first, landed on the same spot in hopes of rescuing Roberts. Under heavy fire and taking casualties, including Technical Sergeant John Chapman, an air force combat controller responsible for coordinating air support who was left for dead, the team retreated down the mountain and called for reinforcements, which were dispatched after some delay. But thanks to the confused communications among all concerned, the incoming rescue force of U.S. Army Rangers did not understand that the team had left the mountaintop. They therefore landed on the very same spot where the first two groups had already been attacked. Sure enough, they were met with a blizzard of rocket-propelled grenades and machine-gun bullets. Within a few minutes several men were dead and the survivors pinned down. Poor communications made it difficult for them to call in air support until late in the day.

Elsewhere in the Shahikot valley, the U.S. offensive was not going any better. By the afternoon of the second day of the operation, senior officers were seriously discussing a complete retreat from the valley to regroup. The best intelligence that satellites, reconnaissance planes, signals intercepts, and CIA agents could supply had reported that there were some 250 enemy fighters overall in the valley. In fact there may have been as many as 1,000. It had also been reported that there were about 800 civilians living in villages on the valley floor, but there were none. It was believed that the enemy would also be sheltering on the valley floor, but they were dug in on the high ground and far better armed than predicted. The army commander had been confident that the operation would be over quickly because the enemy would cut and run. But the foreign fighters had determinedly stood and fought, despite a rain of bombs from dozens of planes crowding the air over the valley, including B-52 bombers cruising 7 miles above the fray.

Anaconda's overall commander, Major General H. L. "Buster" Hagenback, was not helping this disordered state of affairs by devoting a lot of attention to the individual manhunt. A vivid dispatch by an embedded reporter at his headquarters described the pursuit, via Predator drone feed, of a "late-model SUV" as it drove toward Pakistan. Among those inside was a man wearing a white robe and turban, a sure sign, according to the senior intelligence officer at headquarters, of a "liaison" between al-Qaeda forces in the field and the terrorist organization's senior leadership. As described in the dispatch, the entire staff at headquarters was engrossed in the video of the car as they all waited impatiently for strike aircraft to appear on scene. "Go get 'em," yelled Hagenback. Eventually, a B-1 bomber unleashed 16 tons of bombs, obliterating the car and surrounding landscape. As the smoke cleared, the deputy commander addressed the headquarters staff: "If you haven't done it recently, reach around and pat yourselves on the back. This is hard stuff. Hell, I've been trying to shoot a truck on that damned road for two days!" he said to appreciative chuckles.

In theory, the relentless air attacks were being coordinated by two huge aircraft designed specifically for "battle management" and orbiting ceaselessly above the battlefield. One was a $244 million JSTARS (Joint Surveillance Target Attack Radar System). Readers may recall that this system was originally developed to track Soviet armored divisions racing across the plains of northern Europe by collecting radar images of moving objects and processing them with on-board computers in order to target the advancing formations. Conceptually descended from Task Force Alpha and the electronic fence of Vietnam days, it had never worked properly (being unable, for example, to distinguish a moving tank from a tree waving in the wind). Tom Christie had caught the air force pretending that it could see through mountains in the Balkans in 1995. But as always, the dream that sensors could make centralized battle management possible had never been allowed to die, so now JSTARS was supposed to be tracking sandal-clad guerrillas hiding behind rocks. Joining it in orbit over the battlefield was a $270 million AWACS (Airborne Warning and Control System), an airborne air traffic control system designed to manage aerial battles.

Despite this costly deployment of advanced technology, when Scott "Soup" Campbell arrived on the scene, he found chaos. An air force captain, Campbell flew an A-10 "Warthog," which could maneuver at low level with relative impunity, allowing the pilot to survey the ground with the naked eye, unlike the sensor-rich AC-130 that led the SEALS to disaster on Takur Ghar.

Campbell and his wingman had been dispatched to Afghanistan on a few hours' notice late in the morning of the third day of Operation Anaconda. The long journey down the Gulf, necessarily skirting Iran, and across the Arabian Sea and then Pakistan, took 5 hours, with repeated hookups to an accompanying tanker aircraft. As ordered, he flew straight to the battle without landing. At the time he arrived, the sun was sinking behind the mountains, so the valley below, as he told me later, was in deep shadow, and everything was in a state of utter confusion. On the ground, 39 separate Joint Terminal Attack Controllers (whose job is to call for air support) in the 5-by-9-kilometer "killbox" were radioing urgently for air support: "we're getting mortared, Dshk [machine-gun] fire . . . we're getting hammered." In the gathering darkness, fighters, gunships, and helicopters thronged the airspace, moving at hundreds of miles an hour, all ignorant of each other's position and missing each other often by mere yards. A navy fighter shot between Campbell and his wingman: a Predator "practically bounced off my canopy." In his vivid recollection, "weapons coming off the jet(s) fall through that sky. . . . All of a sudden a 2,000-pounder blows up just as I'm sitting there looking down at the ground. That means it probably just dropped right through my formation off a bomber at 39,000 feet. So it quickly dawned on us that this is a mess and the threat is not from the ground really, from guys shooting at us, it's from each other."

In theory, everybody would have been coordinated by an Air Support Operations Center relaying requests from the ground in an orderly fashion. But the colonel in charge of the air operation had elected to direct matters from many miles and several high mountains away at Bagram, the main American base in Afghanistan. This system depended on line-of-sight radios so, thanks to those mountains, it was effectively out of action, and without it, the beleaguered soldiers on the ground had no way of communicating directly with the planes overhead . . . until Campbell showed up. His A-10 had radios that could talk to both ground units and other aircraft. So he and his wingman became a two-man air traffic control center, relaying the frantic calls for help from the ground to the circling planes while warning bombers off strikes that might hit friendly positions. He could achieve this because his plane was designed, and he was trained, to enable a "fingertip feel" of the immediate surroundings.

Campbell was able to form a three-dimensional mental picture of who was where in and above the valley, coordinating and directing air strikes accordingly, an impressive feat considering that when he finally landed at a base in Pakistan he had been in the air for a total of twelve hours. Over the next few days he returned to the valley, where conditions were slowly stabilizing, until he was urgently dispatched, along with a multitude of other fighters, gunships, and SEAL teams, to pursue a white van on an Afghan back road rumored to contain Osama bin Laden himself, which of course it did not.

Operation Anaconda, which officially ended on March 18, was declared an unqualified success, with over seven hundred enemy casualties in exchange for eight U.S. dead (seven on Takur Ghar) and seventy-two wounded. Others, including friendly Afghan commanders, reported that the number of enemy casualties had been far, far lower. It turned out that none of the "big three" had been anywhere near the battle. For some time it was claimed that Saifur Rahman Mansour, whose foiled attempts to surrender had preceded the operation, had indeed been killed. But he lived to fight on many more days, his reputation reportedly bolstered to hero status by his stand against the Americans in the Shahikot. He finally died in a battle with the Pakistani military in South Waziristan in 2008.

Even as silence descended over the valley, the hunt for targets went on. Joining the effort in June was a new force grandly titled Combined Joint Task Force 180 whose mission was "to conduct operations to destroy remaining Al Qaeda/hostile Taliban command control and other hostile anti-Islamic Transitional Government of Afghanistan elements." It was also tasked to help establish a "stable and secure Afghanistan able to deter/defeat the re-emergence of terrorism." But it was the "kinetic" part of the mission that occupied the energies of the force, especially its chief of staff, a tough, aggressive two-star general named Stanley McChrystal. "I always thought Stan was responsible for the Afghan war we ended up with," a former army general who served in Afghanistan at that time told me. "All we had to do was leave the Afghans alone; they weren't any threat to us. But Stan insisted on doing all these raids, busting into villages, arresting people, killing people. Pretty soon they were all riled up at us and the whole thing went south from there on in."

In the weeks following Anaconda, Special Operations Command undertook an intense postmortem into the debacle on the mountain, paying particular attention to the ultimate fate of Neil Roberts, the

SEAL who fell from the first helicopter. Fortunately, or so it seemed, the Predator video was available as a firsthand record of what had actually happened. Careful scrutiny of the footage satisfied commanders that he had died a noble death, taking the fight to the enemy despite several bullet wounds and even storming a machine-gun nest. At his crowded memorial service his deputy commanding officer spoke movingly of how the video "shows the mortal wound and Neil falls to the ground . . . he had expended all of his ammo, both primary and secondary, as well as all his grenades."

But this was an illusion. As Colonel Milani, the Special Forces officer tasked with assessing the events on Takur Ghar reported (much to the irritation of the SEALs), nothing of the kind had happened. Roberts' body was discovered very close to where he had landed in his fall. Postmortem examination of his wounds indicated he had been shot almost immediately. On the other hand, the body of Sergeant Chapman, who had been left for dead in the hurried flight following the second landing on the mountain, was discovered in a bunker several yards from where he had been seen to fall and from where he may have been firing on the enemy. The wounds that actually killed him apparently came from the U.S. bombs that destroyed the bunker. Given that Chapman, wounded in the initial attack, had been abandoned on the battlefield, this was not an appealing conclusion. As Milani ultimately concluded in his unsparing after-action report, "Roberts' colleagues desperately wanted to see him alive and taking it to the enemy. They not only saw what they wanted to see, they saw what they needed to see." They were, he wrote, "necessarily enmeshed in a network of preconceptions."

Those officers saw what they needed to see even though they had the leisure of several weeks to review the video in minute detail. But more and more, drone pictures were guiding life-and-death decisions made in a matter of hours or minutes, with consequences that would endure for years.

8

# KILL THEM!
# PREVAIL!

George W. Bush had arrived at the White House with a pledge, as outlined in his 1999 speech at the Citadel, to "begin creating the military of the next century" as well as to boost overall defense spending. The Afghan operation had put precision-guided bombing on display, but the revolution in military affairs held the promise of further wonders. "Millennium Challenge 2002," the largest and most elaborate war game ever held, was accordingly designed to put the revolutionary "military of the next century" on full display. Three years in the planning, budgeted at $250 million, involving 13,500 participants waging mock war in 9 training sites across the United States as well as 17 "virtual" locations in the powerful computers of the Joint Forces Command, the exercise, to be held in the summer of 2002, enjoyed the personal attention of Defense Secretary Rumsfeld himself. As Rumsfeld declared during a visit to Joint Forces Command headquarters in Norfolk, Virginia, where the major players in the game would be based, the game would show "the progress that we have made this far in transforming to produce the combat capability necessary to meet deep threats and the challenges of the 21st Century."

Escorting Rumsfeld round the premises, the commanding general, William Kernan, took care to keep his distinguished guest away from a tall, bald-headed man with a military bearing but clad in civilian clothes; he was the enemy. Paul Van Riper, the three-star marine general, now retired, who had poured such scorn on David Deptula's theories in the years following Desert Storm, had been called back to command the red team in the Millennium war game. In such exercises, the enemy is always red; the U.S. side is always blue. But Van Riper was a twofold enemy; not only was he playing the role of an opponent, he also was making no secret of his contempt for the concepts underpinning the blue team's plan for the game.

"None of it was scientifically supportable," he told me later, after delivering a droll recitation of the full range of acronyms pumped out by the command. "They claimed to be able to understand the relationship between all nodes or links, so for example if something happened to an enemy's economy, they could precisely calculate the effect on his military performance. They talked about crony targeting [the destruction of the property of Slobodan Milošević's friends' property during the Kosovo conflict in hopes of affecting his behavior] a lot." In short, the blue plan encapsulated the core belief system of U.S. military doctrine. High-value targeting, as Van Riper was well aware, was inherent in the official doctrine's assertions of the capabilities of effects-based operations. But given his low regard for the entire concept of "total situational awareness," he was not unduly worried.

In the scenario designed by the exercise planners, Van Riper was playing the role of a rogue military commander somewhere in the Persian Gulf who was willfully confronting the United States. Though there were thousands of troops as well as planes and ships taking part in the game across the country, much of the action would be "virtual," occurring in computers and displayed on monitors. It was to be the ultimate video game. Needless to say, each of the services foresaw a useful role for their expanding fleets of drones as well as for other novel systems.

Among the digital tools available to the blue team was an enormous database labeled Operational Net Assessment (ONA), which they believed contained everything they needed to know about their opponent and how he would behave. But they did not even know what he looked like. The blue commander, a three-star army general, worked in full uniform, surrounded by his extensive staff. As the game was getting under way, Van Riper, dressed in casual civilian clothes, took a stroll, unrecognized, through the blue team headquarters area to take the measure of his opponent. With his own staff, he was informal, though he forbade the use of acronyms. "We'll all speak English here," he told them.

In the first hours of the war, the blue team knocked out Van Riper's fiber-optic communications, confidently expecting that he would now be forced to use radio links, which could be easily intercepted. He refused to cooperate, however, turning instead to motorcycle couriers and coded messages in the calls to prayer from the mosques in preparing his own attack. He was no longer performing an assigned part in a scripted play. Van Riper had become a real, bloody-minded, Middle Eastern enemy who had no intention of playing by the rules and was determined to win.

Just a month earlier, the Bush administration had unveiled a new national security policy of preemptive attacks, justified as "our inherent right of self-defense." So, when a blue team carrier task force loaded with troops steamed into the Gulf (at least in the computer simulation) and took up station off the coast of his territory, Van Riper assumed that they were going to follow the new policy and attack him without warning. "I decided to preempt the preempter," he told me. Oddly enough, the blue general sensed this, saying: "I have a feeling that Red is going to strike," but his staff was quick to assure him that their ONA made it clear that this could not happen.

Van Riper was well aware of the U.S. Navy's Aegis antimissile capabilities and of how many missiles it would take to overwhelm them. "Usually Red hoards its missiles, letting them out in dribs and drabs," he told me in retracing the battle. "That's foolish, I did a salvo launch, used up pretty much all my inventory at once." The defenses were overwhelmed. Sixteen virtual American ships sank to the bottom of the Gulf, along with twenty thousand virtual servicemen. Only a few days in, the war was over, and the twenty-first-century U.S. military had been beaten hands down. Van Riper, who had been an attentive student of the theories of John Boyd, the fighter pilot and theoretician of conflict, won by adapting quickly and imaginatively to changing circumstances (such as his use of motorcycle messengers and calls from the minarets of mosques when his phone links were destroyed). In contrast, his opponent's rigid "effects-based" approach had locked him into a preset vision of how the battle would play out.

For General Kernan, the Joint Forces commander, there could be only one solution to this crisis. Van Riper was informed that the sunken ships had magically refloated themselves, the dead had come back to life, and the war was on again. But this time there would be no surprises. He was not allowed to shoot down vulnerable blue team V-22 troop transports. The red team was ordered to switch on their radars so that they could be more easily detected and destroyed. The umpires announced that all of the red team's missile strikes had been intercepted. The game was now unashamedly rigged to ensure a U.S. victory as well as validation of the new theories. Van Riper resigned in disgust as red leader but stayed on to monitor the predictable rout of his forces under these new conditions. Afterward he wrote a scathing report, documenting how the exercise had been rigged and by whom, but no outsider could read it because it was promptly classified.

Undaunted, in the very next real war, the March 2003 invasion of Iraq, the U.S. military deployed many of the same concepts recently deployed in the Millennium Challenge. Initially, things appeared to go well. The invasion was planned strictly in accordance with the concept of rapid dominance, defined as "near total or absolute knowledge and understanding of self, adversary, and environment; rapidity and timeliness in application; operational brilliance in execution; and [near] total control and signature management of the entire operational environment." This happy state being achieved, the enemy must inevitably be reduced to a state of "shock and awe."

Decapitation fit neatly into this approach, indicating that the planners misunderstood how useful it would be to keep Saddam alive and in command of enemy forces. According to a postwar Pentagon assessment, "The largest contributing factor to the complete defeat of Iraq's military forces was the continued interference by Saddam (Hussein)," posthumously affirming the argument advanced by British intelligence officer Lieutenant Colonel Thornley against killing Hitler in 1944 on the grounds that the Nazi leader's blunders were of inestimable help to the Allied cause. Nonetheless, despite Saddam's previous demonstrations of military incompetence during the 1991 war and before, the U.S. pursued a decapitation strategy to an almost obsessive degree. Attempts to kill the Iraqi leader in 1991 had been lightly cloaked in euphemism, but this time there was little such pretense.

In the first minutes of the war a fusillade of bombs and no less than forty cruise missiles rained down on a collection of farm buildings on the outskirts of Baghdad, prompted by a CIA report that Saddam and his sons were lurking there in an underground bunker. Early reports were optimistic. "We were sure we'd got him," one of the targeting team told me. "Cheney came out and said he was dead. It took us three days before we were sure he had survived." In fact, neither Saddam nor either of his sons had been at the farm. Nor did it have a bunker.

The effort was coordinated by a High-Value Target Cell in the Pentagon, an elaboration of the system that had tracked Milošević in 1999. The office coordinated other such cells at CIA, NSA, and Centcom, the military command overseeing the Iraq and Afghan wars. "Between 1999 and 2002 it was growing into a new science," a Pentagon analyst formerly assigned to the operation told me. "If you're doing HVT, on Saddam Hussein, for example, you have to know where he is at all times, who are his security retinue, where they are. You look for patterns, but our predictive ability was low. We got very, very good on where he had been; sometimes we knew where he was. But predicting where he would be, that was hard, and we needed that because at that time the kill chain, the time between getting the intelligence and the bomb or missile impacting, was too long, a minimum of forty minutes, and often more. The shortest kill chain we managed in the 2003 war was forty-five minutes," the analyst recalled. "That was the strike on the al-Saath restaurant in Baghdad. We thought that Saddam was there. He wasn't, but we did kill a bunch of civilians."

"I did not know who was there. I really didn't care," Colonel Fred Swan, weapons officer on the B-1 bomber that hit the restaurant, later told reporters. "We've got to get the bombs on target. We've got to make a lot of things happen to make that happen. So you just fall totally into execute mode and kill the target."

Drones, with their ability to wait and watch for a target to appear and then launch a missile can, at least in theory, shrink the kill chain almost to zero. "But that means you're taking the decision on the fly, with no time to really assess potential collateral damage, like who else is in the house or whatever," the former inmate of the High-Value Target Cell pointed out to me.

The former specialist raised another occupational hazard of this particular strategy: the difficulty of assessing success. "After that first strike, it took three days before we knew for certain he wasn't dead. Even when he appeared on TV, sitting at a desk, reading a speech, with glasses on, a lot of people in the office were saying 'It's not him, it's a double,' or even suggesting it was prerecorded earlier in case he got hit. We even had analysts going over the video to see if the angle of light in the window was right for that time of year."

Precision strikes were targeted over the ensuing weeks of the invasion on the purported lairs of various Iraqi commanders, though without success. According to the former Defense Intelligence Agency analyst Marc Garlasco, the United States selected fifty specific "high-value individuals" to be targeted and killed during the invasion. All survived. Not so lucky were the "couple of hundred civilians, at least," according to Garlasco, who were killed in the strikes. Many of them may have died thanks to what appeared to be an ingenious innovation in targeting technology. The war coincided with the introduction in the Middle East of a new model of satellite phone for civilians, the Thuraya. Unlike its unwieldy predecessors, this device, about the size of an old-fashioned telephone handset, could be easily carried and used, and it was believed that many of the fugitive Iraqi leadership carried them. Like all such devices, the Thuraya inevitably transmitted information regarding its location, thus providing a convenient mark for GPS-guided bombs. In effect, the target would be guiding the bomb that killed him. But there was a flaw: the Thuraya's GPS system was not so precise in fixing its position and was accurate only within a 100-meter (109-yard) distance, which meant that the bomb could land anywhere within an area of 37,500 square yards. This was lucky for the target but not so lucky for innocent passersby who happened to be in that area. In other words, as a Human Rights Watch report subsequently observed, innovative technology had turned "a precision weapon into a potentially indiscriminate weapon."

The United States was not unmindful of collateral damage, going to some lengths to preserve a degree of proportion. Regulations stipulated that civilians could be killed but not too many, at least not without clearance from higher authority. "Our number was thirty," explained Garlasco. "So, for example, Saddam Hussein. If you're gonna kill up to twenty-nine people in a strike against Saddam Hussein, that's not a problem. But once you hit that number thirty, we actually had to go to either President Bush, or Secretary of Defense Rumsfeld." As it happened, approval from higher authority was pretty much pro forma; following the invasion, General Michael Moseley, then vice chief of staff of the U.S. Air Force, reported that the necessary clearance to risk thirty or more civilian lives in this manner had been requested at least fifty times. In no case had it been refused.

Following the defeat of the Iraqi military and the installation of the occupation regime in Baghdad, the manhunt for Saddam continued. Spurring such efforts was the widespread belief that the source of the escalating insurgency was the deposed leader and his diehard followers. So when he was finally run to ground on December 13, 2003, his capture inevitably monitored in real time via Predator by generals at their U.S. headquarters, hope blossomed that resistance might now begin to taper off. As Colonel Jim Hickey, the Chicago-born leader of the unit that unearthed Saddam, remarked the day after his capture, "From a military point of view, if you lop the head off a snake, the snake's not going to be so viable after that."

But that turned out not to be the case.

At the end of March 2004, four employees of the Blackwater military contractor corporation were ambushed and killed in the town of Fallujah, their incinerated bodies strung up for all to see. Meanwhile the popular Shi'ite cleric Muqtada al-Sadr threatened to ignite an uprising among the previously quiescent Shia population. All the while, the number of lethal attacks with homemade bombs against American soldiers had been ticking remorselessly upward. The mounting chaos sparked a heated reaction in Washington, where the administration had hitherto believed that the insurgency was largely the last gasp of Saddam's defeated regime. On April 7, a week after the Fallujah ambush, Bush, Rumsfeld, and Secretary of State Colin Powell held a videoconference with General Ricardo Sanchez, the overall commander in Iraq. As later related by Sanchez himself, Powell (often cited as the cerebral moderate in that administration) set an emotional tone, declaring: "We've got to smash somebody's ass quickly. There has to be a total victory somewhere. We must have a brute demonstration of power." As Sanchez recalled, the meeting became even more bellicose. "Kick ass!" exclaimed the president. "If somebody tries to stop the march to democracy, we will seek them out and kill them! We must be tougher than hell! . . . There is a series of moments, and this is one of them. Our will is being tested, but we are resolute. Stay strong! Stay the course! Kill them! Prevail! We are going to wipe them out! We are not blinking!"

That same month the commander of the Joint Special Operations Command, General Stanley McChrystal, moved his headquarters to Iraq. As in the unhappy saga of Task Force 11 at Takur Ghar, the elite JSOC had been active in Afghanistan. McChrystal himself, though not directly engaged in Special Operations there, had been the aggressive chief of staff of Combined Joint Task Force 180, which according to a later report by officers who served in it, had conducted its affairs according to the principles of effects-based operations, defined in a military publication as "producing desired futures." The principal effect of these operations was of course to embitter the population. Thanks to a steady surge of ill-judged arrests and incarcerations, the Taliban was reviving.

In Iraq, JSOC components such as the elite Army Delta Force and Navy Seal Team 6 had been initially engaged in rounding up the "deck of cards," the leading officials of Saddam Hussein's defeated regime whose names and faces had been printed up by the Pentagon as playing cards and distributed to soldiers before the invasion. But that was about to change. A new kingpin had appeared on the scene, a suitable candidate to succeed Saddam as the advertised source of all evil in occupied Iraq.

The Jordanian Abu Musab al-Zarqawi (a nom de guerre, his real name being Ahmad Fadeel al-Nazal al-Khalayleh) had been a petty criminal in his native country before moving to Afghanistan, arriving too late to join the anti-Soviet jihad but staying on to train with members of al-Qaeda. In early 2003, he was plucked from obscurity by Secretary Powell, who, in his notorious UN address justifying the upcoming attack on Iraq, singled out Zarqawi as the link (nonexistent in reality) between Saddam and al-Qaeda.

A gifted organizer and propagandist, Zarqawi appreciated that self-promotion, as a ruthless champion of fundamentalism, would attract funds and recruits to his banner. In May 2004, a gruesome video appeared online with the caption "Abu Musab Al Zarqawi slaughters an American," the American in question being Nicholas Berg, an independent civilian contractor kidnapped in Baghdad the month before whose head Zarqawi sawed off with a carving knife for the benefit of the camera. This and other videos had wide distribution and impact thanks to one of the occupation's few success stories, the construction of cell-phone networks in Iraq, none of which had existed in the old regime. Inaugurated in February 2004, the Egyptian-owned Iraqna network, which covered Baghdad and central Iraq, was soon attracting subscribers at the rate of 100,000 a month. Insurgents rapidly adopted it as a tool for detonating bombs, while Zarqawi and others utilized its potential for communication and propaganda. Soon, it would become the most essential tool in the U.S. counterinsurgency arsenal.

Thanks to his carefully crafted public relations campaign, Zarqawi was soon cast in Saddam's old role in U.S. demonology. In many ways he was ideally suited for the part. Along with his evident psychopathic cruelty, his former association with al-Qaeda bolstered the notion that Iraq and 9/11 were somehow linked, while his foreign origins and the foreign volunteers in his group could be taken as demonstrating that the insurgency was the work of international terrorists, not disaffected Iraqis. To guarantee his high-value status as the cause of all ills, beginning in 2004 the U.S. military mounted a propaganda campaign aimed not only at Iraqis but also at Americans: internal military documents cited the "U.S. Home Audience" as one of the targets of the campaign.

Paradoxically, having created a larger-than-life high-value target, the military command themselves came to believe in it. By 2005, according to a British report, Zarqawi was dominating the command's thinking about the war almost to the point of obsession. A participant at the two morning videoconferences held by General George Casey (who replaced Sanchez in June 2004) reported: "[I]t was mentioned every morning [in both venues] in the mistaken belief that if you got him the insurgency would collapse."

Marketed as a master-terrorist, Zarqawi was an ideal target for Joint Special Operations Command and its ambitious commander. Rapidly jettisoning the redundant "deck-of-cards" targets, McChrystal set to work reorganizing his command for a confrontation with the foe. JSOC moved out of its initial Camp Nama headquarters at Baghdad airport, where investigators had discovered prisoners being tortured with electric shocks and held in cells the size of dog kennels, to a new headquarters at Balad, the sprawling air force base forty miles from the capital. Impatient with the cumbersome system by which intelligence collected by the elite Delta Force, SEAL, and Ranger units was shipped off elsewhere for analysis, he promoted a "flattened" system in which intelligence was analyzed on the spot and acted on immediately, producing further intelligence for instant analysis, and so on. Communal spirit among the headquarters staff was enhanced by the new working space, a single large room without partitions, in which everyone could watch the fruits of their efforts on "Kill TV," large plasma screens on the office wall streaming video footage of air strikes and raiding parties in action. It was a very self-contained operational headquarters, with all components of the JSOC machine, including aircraft and helicopters as well as the men of the elite special operations units, together in one facility. Prisoners were also housed there, although for some time British special operations units were forbidden to hand over any prisoners to McChrystal's command on the grounds that prisoners at the new headquarters were again being held in "tiny" dog kennels.

The operation ran twenty-four/seven, three shifts a day. Although he was a two-star general overseeing a far-flung operation, McChrystal immersed himself in the day-to-day battle, working right next to officers, planning and directing the night's raids, and often accompanying them himself. A videoconference, starring the general—one camera was trained on McChrystal throughout—and linking thousands of people across the globe, from intelligence agencies in Washington (timed to suit their convenience) to forward-operating bases in the mountains of Afghanistan, occupied several hours of his day and consumed unimaginable amounts of bandwidth. By 2007, writes McChrystal in his memoir: "[T]he O&I (operations and intelligence) was a worldwide forum of thousands of people associated with our mission."

This was indeed net-centric warfare in action, complete with all the esoteric (and costly) technology associated with the concept. The underlying premises of the revolution in military affairs had been that information is the key to victory and that it is possible to have near-perfect intelligence concerning the enemy, thereby enabling precise military operations, including the targeting of precision weapons with accurately predicted effects. Tellingly, McChrystal, at that time and since, liked to repeat the mantra "it takes a network to defeat a network," referencing the theories propounded by think tankers John Arquilla and David Ronfeldt, academic popularizers of "netwar" and staunch adherents of Andrew Marshall and the revolution.

Successful net warriors of course demand "information dominance" (Arquilla served as a Pentagon adviser in that field during the Kosovo conflict). But despite repeated promises, such high-level target intelligence never quite materialized, as had been apparent in Vietnam, 1991

Iraq, and the Balkans. The arrival of the cell phone in war zones held out the prospect of a giant leap forward, rendering it possible, in theory at least, to map the enemy network, to determine desirable targets, and to target them. In the days of Task Force Alpha, sensors were distributed across the landscape in hopes that they would detect the enemy and signal his whereabouts. Later, as with JSTARS, the sensors became airborne. Now the enemy was obligingly carrying their own sensors—cell phones—with them at all times, not only continually broadcasting their location but also continually updating connections among individuals in the target network: who was calling whom, how often, who got the most calls, and so on.

In the 1990s the leadership of the Drug Enforcement Agency had forged a profitable relationship with the National Security Agency following its adoption of the kingpin strategy. JSOC under McChrystal's command similarly turned to the powerful National Security Agency, exploiting its technological resources and bureaucratic clout. NSA, under the ambitious command of General Keith Alexander, responded readily, instituting a program called Real Time Regional Gateway to collect every Iraqi text message, phone call, and email on the principle that it was better to "collect the whole haystack" rather than look for a single needle.

No less prized than the actual recordings was the "metadata" of all calls made and received. So-called traffic analysis has long been an intelligence tool: the British, for example, used it in World War II to track German submarines via their radio transmissions even when unable to read the actual messages. Now, computer-aided analysis made it possible to display instantly patterns of communication within the relevant population. By looking at these links it supposedly became possible to construct intricate diagrams of the enemy network.

First, however, it was obviously essential to find out people's phone numbers. Zarqawi was unlikely to list his number in the phone book, and neither would anyone else of interest. That was where a classified technology developed by NSA and known by a variety of names, including Triggerfish, Stingray, and IMSI Catcher, was introduced. These devices in essence mimic a cell tower, getting a cell phone or cell phones, even when several kilometers away, to connect and thereby reveal the respective number(s) and location(s). Portable (very little power is needed to override the real tower's signals) and functioning even when the targeted phones are inside buildings, this technology rapidly became central to JSOC's manhunts. "It's simple," a former intelligence operative in Iraq explained. "I've walked past buildings with the device in my backpack and scooped up the numbers of all the people inside. So you have the numbers. Then, later, when we went to get one of those people, the device pings his phone and tells us where he is." The devices, also known generically as "virtual base-tower receivers," could be carried not only by a person or vehicle but also in a pod mounted on a drone.

The implications of these developments in tracking technology were thrilling, at least to the NSA and its partners. An NSA document dated March 3, 2005, and later released by the whistle-blower Edward Snowden asks rhetorically:

> What resembles "LITTLE BOY" [one of the atomic bombs dropped on Japan during World war II] and as LITTLE BOY did, represents the dawn of a new era (at least in SIGINT and precision geolocation)?
>
> If you answered a pod mounted on an Unmanned Aerial Vehicle (UAV) that is currently flying in support of the Global War on Terrorism, you would be correct.

If and when everything worked as planned, the drones would not only help locate targets via their cell phones but also stream video of them and their locations before they finally broadcast dramatic imagery of their destruction for screening to an appreciative audience on Kill TV. But of course things did not always go as planned. Clearly, a lot depended on the phone being correctly associated with the target. But the target might easily have passed his phone on to someone else, or the original link between phone and person could be in error.

Technology, whether in the form of signals intelligence or pictures, was always central to JSOC, whether in Afghanistan or Iraq. Artful jockeying of high-level connections back in Washington ensured McChrystal a disproportionate share of technical resources: at one point the entire non-JSOC U.S. force in Iraq had just one Predator drone for all purposes. The forceful Irishman, Michael Flynn, McChrystal's intelligence chief, elevated this hoarding of resources to a matter of doctrine, claiming that "Intelligence, surveillance, and reconnaissance [predominantly drones] are most effective against low-contrast enemies (i.e. people) when *massed*. . . . It is not enough to have several eyes on a target—several eyes are needed on a target *for a long period.*" By these statements he meant that he needed three Predator drones watching a target 24 hours a day, 7 days a week. Given that 168 support staffers were required to keep one Predator 24-hour Combat Air Patrol in the air, this was clearly an expensive undertaking.

A high-ranking British visitor to JSOC's Balad operation commented that it smacked of "industrial counterterrorism." He did not mean it as a compliment, but many in the system took it as one. Some spoke approvingly of the "machine." McChrystal himself could wax lyrical about his creation. Reminiscing years later about happy days at Balad, he described his impressions thus:

> . . . *as night fell, the operations center hummed with serious, focused activity. Soon, the rumble of helicopters and aircraft, some throaty, some a high whine, bounced across the darkened gravel and off the cement walls and barriers of our compound. The sound grew in layers, building like a chorus singing a round, as one set of rotors, propellers, or jet engines came alive, joined the cacophony, and then departed the airfield. Gradually, the chorus dissipated until silence returned to the darkened base.*

The entire operation was very self-contained and secretive, with little news seeping into the outside world of what was going on apart from discreet references by privileged insiders. Even other components of the occupation regime were largely left in ignorance; McChrystal communicated with the regular forces only at the highest level. A "flimsy" (a printed message on a secure fax) would arrive each morning in the Baghdad military headquarters' SCIF (Secure Compartmented Information Facility), the repository for especially secret material detailing the previous night's JSOC raids. The paper had to be destroyed in the classified shredder by noon at the latest. "It was bad stuff," said one former inmate of the SCIF who made a point of perusing these short-lived documents. "They were really running riot, shooting up rooms-full of people, massacring families, night after night after night."

Such mayhem denoted what McChrystal later described as an artful shift in strategy. Despite the resources directed against him, Zarqawi had survived and expanded his operations, helping to kill hundreds of Shia in suicide bomb attacks and most dramatically blowing up the much-venerated Al-Askar Shi'ite shrine in Samarra in February 2006. The revised JSOC strategy, according to McChrystal, was to "disembowel the organization by targeting its midlevel commanders. They ran AQI day to day and retained the institutional wisdom for operations. By hollowing out its midsection, we believed we could get the organization to collapse on itself."

Such an approach indicated the influence of social network analysis, a fast-growing discipline in the world of counterterrorism in which esoteric algorithms were deployed to probe the structure and dynamics of enemy organizations. A leading pioneer had been the mathematician and social scientist Valdis Krebs, who deployed such analysis on the 9/11 hijackers' relationships with each other to demonstrate, by using elaborate diagrams, that their conspiracy was undetected because they adopted a low profile and kept to themselves. Central to this approach was the focus on what was called relational analysis—the links between different "nodes" rather than "attributes"—meaning who or what these nodes actually were (so heaven help a pizza-delivery store owner getting a lot of calls from a terrorist cell). Thanks to such studies, the business of assassination, or targeted killing, could move beyond a crude fixation with killing enemy leaders to more elaborate scenarios for "shaping" the enemy network by killing carefully selected individuals whose elimination would make the entire structure more fragile and thus easier to disrupt. This theoretical approach was becoming ever more fashionable, spreading into every nook and cranny of the national security apparatus. A classified study commissioned by the Pentagon's Strategic Command in 2008 found that there were no less than "185 separate Attack the Network efforts across the military that are not consolidated, centralized, or coordinated." The study's authors referred to this structure as "ad-hocracy."

Following such an operation, the social network charts, based on the intelligence monitoring of the network's phone links, showed the disappearance of such links, indicating that the network had been disrupted. But the vanished links might have been equally likely indications that survivors had sensibly concluded that they should stay away from the phone and find some other way to get in touch. The network had not fragmented, even though it might have looked as if it had on intelligence diagrams of the network, which of course showed only those links known to intelligence. As Keith Dear, a Royal Air Force intelligence officer formerly serving in Iraq and Afghanistan, has acutely pointed out: "Targeted killing is often justified by the display of a social network chart before and after a targeted killing in order to explain how the group fragmented." But, he explained, the charts ignored the fact that the group was probably using other ways to communicate. "The illusion that they fragment is based on the acceptance of the abstraction [of the chart] as reality."

While the happy operation at Balad was doing its work, another campaign was under way to promote the notion that the United States could turn the tide of the war by adopting COIN, a doctrine of counterinsurgency that emphasized the cultivation of popular support as an essential tool. David Petraeus, the ambitious officer who parlayed COIN as a means to a rapid ascent through the ranks, succeeded in enshrining its precepts into an official U.S. Army Field Manual, FM3-24, published to rapturous public acclaim in December 2006. In the section devoted to "targeting," intelligence analysts are required to identify "targets to isolate from the population, and targets to eliminate . . . the targeting board produces a prioritized list of targets and a recommended course of action appropriate with each."

McChrystal's shift to targeting midlevel commanders would appear to have rested on this sort of carefully considered approach. However, as a former Pentagon analyst with an institutional memory stretching back to the days of the Phoenix program observed to me with some amusement, "You could suggest any set of targets and say their loss would collapse the organization—low level, middle level, top level, it can all be made to seem equally valid. In the end it always comes down to this: the poor sap with the most links gets iced!" Seeking to verify such a cynical conclusion, I asked a JSOC veteran who had worked closely with McChrystal in Iraq if there had indeed been a thought-out plan as to whom to target, with careful consideration of how that would affect the enemy network. "No," he replied after pondering the matter for a few seconds, "it was all kind of ad hoc." Fundamentally, McChrystal's campaign was following the same trajectory of previous "critical node" campaigns stretching back to the strategic bombing of Germany in World War II.

Ultimately, Zarqawi was run to earth and killed, though largely thanks to old-fashioned human intelligence rather than elaborate technology. His isolated safe house, located thanks to a tip-off, was hit with two precision-guided 500-pound bombs, shortly after which he expired. At the subsequent press briefing the military displayed a twice life-size matte photo-portrait of the dead jihadi in a large gilt frame that reminded some who viewed it of a hunting trophy. President Bush, who had promoted McChrystal to three-star rank in February, called with congratulations. The *New York Post* headlined "Gotcha!" and *Newsweek*, in its cover story, speculated that Zarqawi's demise might be a "turning point in the long, frustrating war on terror."

"Things changed when we got Zarqawi," the former Pentagon-based specialist in high-value targeting told me. "Morale was getting a little low, at least in the military, up to that point. There was a kind of fatigue setting in—I remember people were saying 'It's always failing, maybe it's not worth it.' After all, we'd had fifty HVTs on the Iraq blacklist in

2003 and hadn't killed a single one of them. We hadn't gotten Osama bin Laden, or Mullah Omar. So Zarqawi was the first really high-value guy we got, and we had several successes shortly after that. Zarqawi—that was when it changed."

A week after their leader's death, al-Qaeda in Iraq named his successor, an Egyptian with an impressive jihadi record named Abu Ayyub al-Masri.

Zarqawi had been dangerous. Al-Masri was worse.

Whereas Zarqawi, as a former associate told American interrogators, had the prime goal of fighting for the Sunnis in Iraq, al-Masri saw Iraq as only part of a wider war against the West. Al-Masri repaired relations with al-Qaeda's distant senior leadership in Pakistan, boosted his group's revenues from various criminal enterprises, and cracked down on careless cell-phone use. He insisted on truthful reports from subordinates and improved the group's digital operations. Suicide bombers were put to work editing and uploading propaganda videos while they waited to carry out their terminal mission. IED attacks and American casualties went into a steep upward curve.

The U.S. military did not mount a propaganda operation to raise al-Masri's profile.

# 9
# KILLING
# EFFECTS

I n the summer of 2005, a small group of Americans gathered in the
Jordanian desert to test a revolutionary weapon. If it worked, they
expected to change the shape of the ongoing war next door. Among
the testing party was Rex Rivolo, still working as a senior analyst with
the Institute for Defense Analysis.

The weapon was an airplane, a very small, cheap, simple plane
designed to fly low and slow. Built by a Jordanian company, the $200,000
Seeker looked like a helicopter but with high wings and a pusher propeller behind the fuselage so that the view from the cockpit was wide
and unobstructed. It could stay in the air for as long as 7 hours and 15
minutes, land on a narrow road or the open desert, and refuel with
regular 87-octane gas from any gas pump. Its camera could transmit
infrared and daylight color imagery direct to the SUV that served as
its ground station. The pictures could be screened on an ordinary PC.
It carried a pilot and an observer, and required a maintenance crew
of just one. With an enhanced camera and other accoutrements the
entire system still came to no more than $850,000, less than a third of

the price of a Predator (which required a support staff of 168) and a tiny fraction of the bill for an air force jet fighter.

Underlying the simplicity was a subtle concept. As weapons systems became more complex and expensive, they were bought in progressively fewer numbers. Because such systems were costly and scarce, their control tended to be pushed ever higher up the military hierarchy. But of course at that level control is exercised through mechanisms that are themselves complex and expensive. Think General Franks and his link to the trailer in the CIA parking lot, which was in turn linked via satellite to the Predator, which he could fire only after asking his lawyer, the secretary of defense, and the president. Meanwhile, U.S. soldiers, especially road convoys, were being shredded by a proliferation of roadside bombs. Rivolo and his teammates, led by a former navy F-18 pilot named Dan Moore, believed that an aircraft that could be bought in quantity and efficiently watch over a convoy or whatever else required attention would make a profound difference.

Their experiment, in which Jordanian Special Forces "ambushed" road convoys protected by the Seeker, was a great success. Time and again, the attacks were thwarted by warnings easily communicated from the plane to the ground commander. The aircrew, as the test report noted afterward, could scan an entire area with the naked eye (using night-vision goggles when it was dark) and then use the sensor to focus on objects of particular interest. A drone, as the report noted, "would require systematic search of the same wide area through a small aperture (the soda straw), which would make the mission much more difficult or impossible to conduct from a UAV ground station."

The exercise was a triumphant endorsement for putting human eyes and brains close to the battlefield rather than filtering information through layers of imperfect video, fallible communications, and command bureaucracies. Accordingly, the team concluded their report by recommending that the plane be put into service in Iraq and Afghanistan. They printed multiple copies of the report and prepared to distribute them around the Pentagon. The response was swift. Orders came down that all copies were to be collected by a senior official in IDA and destroyed immediately. Higher authority evidently did not want publicity for a successful demonstration of a cheap and effective counterinsurgency weapon.

Meanwhile in Iraq that summer of 2005, bomb attacks edged past forty a day. The country was awash in explosives, largely in the shape of artillery ammunition looted from Saddam's arsenals. Thanks to what had been a very capable education system and a universal military draft, there were large numbers of technically proficient Iraqis with military training ready to resist the occupation with a cheap, easily obtained, and highly effective weapon. *Improvised explosive devices*, a term originally coined by the British when combating the IRA in Northern Ireland, had already plagued U.S. soldiers during the ill-fated Somalia expedition ten years earlier. A strongly worded after-action report on the Somalia mine experience had even described the ubiquitous U.S. Army Humvee as a "death trap" when struck by a mine. A decade later, soldiers and marines were dispatched to patrol Iraqi roads in these same vehicles, with predictably bloody results. Just as the blue force commander had been discommoded by Van Riper's unexpected use of messages via motorcycles and mosque minarets, so too American generals were now nonplussed by guerrillas using doorbell ringers and cordless phones to detonate bombs made from recycled artillery shells. Even more confusingly, the enemy was not a single snake with a head that could be cut off but a plethora of self-contained groups around the country.

In June 2004, General John Abizaid, overall commander in the Middle East, called for a Manhattan Project (the original World War II program to build the atomic bomb that had employed 135,000 people) to find a solution to the threat of the homemade bombs. Naturally, such urgency could prove highly lucrative for some. In November 2003, for example, Lieutenant Colonel Christopher Hughes, an army officer who had recently returned from Iraq, was commanded by his superior in the Pentagon to "stop the bleeding" from bomb attacks. Hughes had experience in the counterterror world and accordingly sought out some old friends, graduates of Special Operations units—"people who know how to shoot people," as he described them to me—who were now working with a small Virginia-based security company, Wexford

Group International. Hughes arranged a $20 million contract for Wexford to deploy teams to Iraq who, when they encountered an IED, were to "track, hunt down, and kill those who emplaced it, built it, financed it, and finally those who were actually responsible for it." Soon, a number of teams, at a cost, according to Hughes, of some $200,000 per man, were in place in Iraq. By 2006 the company's revenue had grown 500 percent to $60 million. The following year, still flush with counter-IED contracts, employee-owned Wexford was bought by CACI, a billion-dollar security contractor notorious for supplying interrogators to Abu Ghraib, for $115 million.

To detonate their bombs by remote control, attackers were using low technology such as garage door openers and radio-controlled toys. The United States responded with high technology, which was good news for many. The well-connected EDO Corporation, for example, which boasted several retired three- and four-star officers on its board and important politicians on its list of PAC recipients, garnered a handsome contract to produce a jammer that would block the detonator's radio signals. Adapting a system originally developed by the army for use against radio-detonated artillery shells, EDO soon began churning out thousands of $100,000 Warlock jammers. By early 2005 they were being mounted on Humvees and other vehicles. When they were switched on and working, bomb-triggering radio signals were indeed masked from the bombs by the jammer. As rush orders for more and higher-powered Warlocks poured in, EDO revenues soared from $356 million in 2003 to $715 million in 2006.

Unfortunately, not only did the jammers mask the bomb-detonator's signals, they also cut off all radio contact between the soldiers they were protecting and the outside world. Brandon Bryant, a "stick monkey" (drone sensor operator), witnessed the lethal consequences one day while watching streaming video of a military convoy in northern Iraq in 2005. The picture on his screen revealed what was almost certainly a mine buried in the road ahead of the vehicles; insurgents had burned a tire to melt the tarmac, leaving a telltale heat signature. From Nevada, Bryant and his fellow crewman tried frantically to alert the soldiers as they rolled inexorably toward the buried bomb. Their efforts were in vain; the convoy was deaf to outside warning thanks to its own technology. As Bryant watched in agonized frustration, the first vehicle rolled over the bomb without mishap. The second exploded in a ball of flame, killing two soldiers and wounding three more.

The men did not have to die; their jammers were already irrelevant. Less than two months after their introduction, the Iraqi insurgents largely stopped using radio signals and switched to other methods. The bomb that Bryant saw explode was almost certainly detonated by a nearby "triggerman" via a buried command wire. Soon, Iraqi highways became so strewn with old detonator wires that bomb makers simply recycled them. Meanwhile, jammer production rolled on. In September 2007 the giant defense contractor ITT announced it was buying EDO for $1.7 billion. By that time practically every Humvee in Iraq was sporting two $100,000 Warlocks.

Thanks to the weight of tradition and its obligations to corporate partners, the U.S. military machine was clearly adapting more slowly than its light-footed opponents, incapable of absorbing unconventional concepts such as the Seeker, which could at a pinch have landed on the highway and warned the doomed vehicle. The Warlocks may have been profitable for EDO, but even bigger money flew overhead in systems such as Compass Call Nova, a $100 million cornucopia of electronic wizardry assembled by the $10 billion contractor L-3 Communications under the aegis of Big Safari, the secretive air force unit that had overseen development of the Predator drone. Originally designed to jam the communications of a Warsaw Pact army rolling across Germany, these aircraft now patrolled the roads and towns of Iraq and Afghanistan at the significant cost of $34,000 per hour, seeking not only to jam the tiny, distant pulse of a garage door opener before it could detonate a $25 bomb but even to "predetonate" buried bombs before they could harm any friendly forces.

Amid the torrent of resources being flung at the bomb problem, Rex Rivolo got an invitation to go to Iraq. It came from Jim Hickey, the colonel who had led the final successful search for Saddam and who thought cutting off the head of a snake made the rest of the snake less viable. Soon after that triumph, Hickey's tour in Iraq had ended, and he was posted back to Washington, temporarily assigned to IDA, the Pentagon think tank where Rivolo worked. As well as being a fighting soldier who relished combat, Hickey was also a military intellectual. Fluent in Russian, German, and French, he liked nothing better than a weighty discussion on operational intelligence and similar topics. By the fall of 2005, however, he was keen to return to the war zone and assess progress. Like Rivolo, he had a habit of delivering home truths regardless of the rank of the listener, a trait that was not necessarily beneficial to his career. Perhaps because he recognized a kindred spirit, he got the former fighter pilot assigned to accompany him on a battle-field investigation of the IED problem.

In mid-October 2005, the pair flew into Baghdad. Skipping the headquarters briefings, they headed out into the field, touring belea-guered army bases across Iraq, a dark and ugly world far removed from Washington, or the requisitioned Baghdad palaces from which the U.S. generals thought they were managing the war.

"It was a terrible trip," recalls Rivolo. "We went from base to base to base, sleeping in sleeping bags in the corner of dirt fields. Stuff that I would have done gladly when I was twenty, not when I was sixty." But he found out a lot, mostly because of whom he was with. Hickey was from the tribe, someone whom the combat soldiers recognized as one of their own. "Hickey knew everybody," explained Rivolo. "Once you showed up with Hickey, they would tell you the truth. If you showed up without Hickey, they wouldn't tell you anything. Normally when you show up and say 'we're a team from the Pentagon and we're here to investigate,' they just blow you off because they don't trust you. But once you show up with one of *them*, you've been anointed."

So officers and men in the forward operating bases talked freely about the realities of the war: the pointless "presence patrols" they were ordered to lead through the hostile streets, enclosed in their steel vehi-cles while waiting for the searing blast of an IED; the futility of pana-ceas such as the million-dollar observation balloon that could spot mine layers but couldn't tell ground troops where they were; the eighteen-year-old female air force reservist left alone for an entire night guarding an incinerated corpse in a bombed-out Humvee while different headquarters bickered over who was responsible for rescuing her.

When the topic of conversation came around to ways of defeating the bombs, everyone was in agreement. "They would have charts up on the wall showing the insurgent cells they were facing, often with the names and pictures of the guys running them," Rivolo remembers. "When we asked about going after the high-value individuals and what effect it was having, they'd say, 'Oh yeah, we killed that guy last month, and we're getting more IEDs than ever.' They all said the same thing, point blank: '[O]nce you knock them off, a day later you have a new guy who's smarter, younger, more aggressive and is out for revenge.'"

For Rivolo, this sounded all too familiar. The U.S. strategy to overcome the Iraqi insurgency looked like a rerun of the DEA's kingpin strategy. In fact, the more he thought about it, the more it seemed that the insurgency had a lot in common with the narcotics business. In each case, the activity was carried out by a number of organizations, each with a similar hierarchy. All of them shared the same objective: for the drug dealers it was selling drugs and making money, whereas for the insurgents it was keeping Iraq in a state of chaos, killing Americans, and hopefully gaining power. They were "self-organizing," meaning that no outside force had set them up, and they were "self-healing," meaning that when they were damaged by the loss of a member, they adjusted by compensating with recruits and promotions. Most fundamentally, both activities induced different trade-offs between risk and reward at different levels. The bosses of the cocaine cartels accepted a lot of risk because the rewards were so huge: billions of dollars. The insurgent leaders directing IED attacks were equally immune to risk because they were driven by ideology and therefore willing to die for the cause.

Lower down, the trade-offs shifted. In the drug business, pilots had been willing to fly cocaine base from Peru to Colombia for little reward because there was minimal risk. Once that risk went up, as it did when they started getting shot down, the reward for the pilots became insufficient, and they refused to fly. In the insurgency it was people who were working for the money, such as the men digging holes to bury the bombs, who were susceptible to increased risk.

Returning to Washington, Rivolo briefed his superiors on his conclusions, bluntly suggesting that the "attack-the-leaders" strategy enjoying the highest priority was "completely unproductive." Far better, he insisted, to concentrate on those lower down. Later, he would calculate the precise degree of risk involved in planting a bomb. When just fewer than 70,000 bombs had been placed in Iraq, four hundred Iraqis had been killed or wounded while planting those bombs. Therefore, the probability of getting killed or wounded while planting a bomb was 1 in 175, or just under 0.6 percent. In addition, many of those killed or wounded had been doing something in addition to planting the bomb, such as engaging in a firefight with U.S. forces. So, he concluded triumphantly, the risk of simply planting a bomb was close to zero! That was why, he noted, people were doing it for as little as $15.

The emplacers, along with the "triggermen," who actually detonated the bomb when a suitable target presented itself, were the frontline troops of the insurgency. Although there were dozens of separate IED networks, they tended to operate in the same way, which was to hand the emplacers a bomb and give them a month to use it, wherever and whenever they chose. In a sense, the insurgents had the same advantages as the system Rivolo and his colleagues had tested in the Jordanian desert, or that Pierre Sprey had in mind for the A-10 close-support plane so many years before. Those were based on the belief that the only way to have what the German army had called "fingertip feel" for the battlefield was to have a thinking human brain right there, with the maximum facility to observe and react. The crews in the planes could pick up footprints in the snow, or notice vehicles driving in a suspicious pattern, or people walking faster past a particular building as if they knew that it contained something dangerous such as a weapons cache or a bomb factory. The bomb planters and triggermen were similarly ideally placed to watch their enemy and react immediately to any change in the situation. Both were "bottom-up" approaches to war, very different from the centralized "top down" system embodied in official doctrinal notions such as Operational Net

Assessment, or for that matter drones controlled from a trailer in Nevada, multiple time zones away.

Since the IED networks were not controlled by some central authority, Rivolo wondered how it was that they all seemed to operate in much the same manner, sharing the same tactics and techniques. When new techniques appeared in one area, they appeared to spread, sometimes overnight, to other regions and even to groups on the other side of the sectarian divide. Eventually, he believed he found the answer in *stigmergy*, a theory originally developed by French biologist Jean Pierre Grasse to explain how it was that insects that were apparently working alone nevertheless worked—Grasse used termite nests as an example—in a manner that appeared to be coordinated.

Stigmergic systems use simple environmental signals to coordinate actions of independent agents (each with their own decision-making process). Termites building a mound, for example, leave a chemical trace on each piece of mud they add to the mound that is attractive to other termites, who add their own attractive piece of mud on top of it. Rivolo thought that independent insurgent groups were somehow communicating in the same way, their efforts appearing coordinated, and therefore inducing the U.S. to believe it was facing some sort of unified operation with a leader who could be targeted.

Perhaps unsurprisingly, this sophisticated theory failed to gain traction when Rivolo proposed it on his return to Washington. His observations on the benefits, or lack thereof, of high-value targeting, did receive a receptive hearing from IDA Director Dennis Blair, a blunt-speaking former four-star admiral. Blair found Rivolo's arguments on this score "completely convincing," and tried to interest others in the military high command but without success. As he afterward opaquely explained to Rivolo, there were "too many layers of command" to effect any change in policy. Rivolo and Hickey did better with a simple suggestion that Iraqi cell-phone companies put a random delay of a few seconds on the time it took a call to go through. This would automatically end the use of phones as detonators, since the triggermen could not time the blast on a moving target. This idea, which was adopted, was a lot cheaper than $100,000 Warlocks, but the counter-IED business was already too valuable for alternative, and simpler, solutions. In January 2006, proclaiming the defeat of the homemade bomb to be a major national priority, Congress approved the creation of a whole new bureaucracy, the Joint IED Defeat Organization (JIEDDO). Adopting a mission statement of "Attack the Network, Defeat the Device, Train the Force," the new bureaucracy rapidly swelled to more than 3,000 people and an annual budget that equally rapidly climbed to over $4 billion.

Rivolo never thought much of JIEDDO, deriding it as a flaccid bureaucracy serving the interests of the contractors who feasted at its brimming trough, but in a roundabout way, it brought him back to Iraq. In December 2006, General Ray Odierno was appointed multinational corps commander–Iraq to command the day-to-day war. As such, he would inherit a large staff, including intelligence. But like many other leaders, military and civilian, he saw the need for a personal intelligence team headed by someone he could trust to be his "eyes and ears" on what was really going on. So he picked Jim Hickey, an old friend who had served under him in other commands. Hickey, in turn, recruited Rivolo as chief analyst.

The essential point of such a team was that it should be outside the formal bureaucracy, operating as much as possible under the radar. Hickey therefore needed a cover, an excuse for his handpicked team of a hundred people to be in Odierno's headquarters. So he approached the JIEDDO director, a grandiloquent retired general named Montgomery Meigs, and proposed that Meigs authorize and pay for an intelligence unit at the Baghdad headquarters that would ostensibly be working for JIEDDO. He stipulated that Meigs could not attempt to exercise any control or interfere with its operations, but could claim credit for any success it might enjoy. Meigs agreed.

Installed at Camp Liberty, the vast U.S. military headquarters on the outskirts of Baghdad, Rivolo had total access to all information, classified or otherwise, in the Iraqi theater of operations, and he settled down to learn all he could about the IED war. There was plenty of information on hand. Every significant incident, bombing, firefight, accident—all inevitably jargonized to SIGACTS (the after-action reports that units were required to file on all incidents)—was assiduously noted and entered into the record. But as had been his reaction when introduced to the DEA, Rivolo was not impressed with the army's staff work, especially when he discovered that their ignorance of basic statistics left them incapable of making the simple calculations necessary to account for "statistical fluctuations" in the reports of bomb attacks. "Odierno would get a chart with bullets that said 'IED activity today is up 37 percent.' Well, shit, that looks pretty bad. The following day they would say 'oh we had a great day, IED activity was down 90 percent.' True, but irrelevant."

Rivolo bluntly informed them that there is a standard statistical formula for eliminating fluctuation to reveal an underlying trend and that the erratic numbers they were solemnly briefing meant nothing. In truth, the underlying trend was bleak. Shorn of scatter, the charts of bomb attacks and the resulting killed and wounded followed an undulating but inexorably upward slope. There had indeed been a decline in casualties in the spring of 2005, the clear result of a belated decision to "up-armor" the Humvees that soldiers had previously tried to protect with scrap metal and sandbags encased in plywood. But the ominous trend soon resumed, ticking up in a saw-toothed pattern, month after month, peaking at Ramadan in the fall, then dropping sharply as the Iraqi weather turned unpleasant before starting another upward climb in the spring.

"Apart from when we first put armor on the vehicles," recalled Rivolo, "nothing else we were doing was making much difference." This was certainly not for want of effort by the burgeoning anti-IED military-industrial complex, now lavishly nurtured by JIEDDO's multibillion-dollar budget, as well as a host of other centers and task forces across the military bureaucracy. Multiple initiatives funded by the organization included the training of bees to detect homemade bombs (soldiers had to watch screens with magnified images to see if the insects stuck their tongues out when close to explosives), sniffer dogs, and "Fido," a $25,000 "molecular sniffer" designed to duplicate canine detection capabilities.

Apart from such eccentricities, more substantial efforts were being introduced in the form of vastly heavier armored vehicles known as MRAPs. In his memoir of his time as secretary of defense, Robert Gates writes movingly of the death and suffering inflicted on troops by inadequate armor, and his pride at having forced a crash MRAP program on a reluctant military. However, according to a former senior staff officer at army headquarters in Baghdad, the initial requirement that MRAPs be built to withstand an explosion of several hundred pounds was progressively and quietly scaled back by developers to a more modest thirty-five pounds. Since many insurgent bombs were far more powerful than that, these massive and costly vehicles in fact made little practical difference to the number of dead and wounded GIs coming home from the wars. An exhaustive analysis of the number of killed and wounded per successful attack on the commonest type of MRAP compared to those suffered by Humvees equipped with additional armor in 2007 revealed that while the Humvee suffered 2.4 killed and wounded, the equivalent number for the MRAP was 2.3. Nevertheless, no less than 27,000 of these massive vehicles would be built and fielded for use in Iraq and Afghanistan. The total cost came to $40 billion.

Meanwhile, jostling for airspace above the bomb-pitted highways of Iraq were growing flocks of ISR, the acronym for "intelligence, surveillance, and reconnaissance" coined in the 1990s by Admiral William Owens, the apostle of net-centricity. Drones, U-2 spy planes (some operated by the air force, others by a specialized army unit), Task Force ODIN ("observe, detect, identify, and neutralize"), an operation dedicated to tracking down the deadly IEDs and the groups behind them—all were thrown into the mission. JIEDDO even embarked on an effort to deploy satellites on the fringes of space, once dedicated to seeking our Soviet ICBMs with thermonuclear warheads, to search for men digging a hole in the road.

Occupying space, the surveillance industry was also moving into time. Adopting an initiative originally conceived to track loose nuclear weapons, the military poured money into "change detection." The concept was simple: if you had constant surveillance of every conceivable location where a bomb might go off, then, following an explosion, you merely had to rewind the tape to see who buried the bomb and follow the tape back in time to retrace the offender's steps to wherever he picked it up. The possibilities were potentially limitless; sufficiently extensive surveillance would reveal the bomb maker's lair, the origins of his materials, the home base of his financiers, and ultimately the location of his leaders. In a story called "On Rigor in Science," the Argentine writer Jorge Luis Borges conceived of an empire "in which the cartographers' guilds struck a map of the empire that was the exact same size of the empire and that coincided point for point with it." In effect, this was the goal that the proponents of change detection, or "ground movement target indicators" as the concept was also known, were seeking to achieve by watching and recording ever-greater areas in hopes of providing the answer to everything. Year after year, new programs to achieve this goal were unveiled, though on close examination they usually turned out to be the same concept but with a different name. The goal may have been impossible, but the attempts were very profitable.

The army's initiative, Constant Hawk, billed $84 million for 2007, while the air force's offering, Angel Fire, garnered $55 million. Meanwhile the air force research laboratory in Dayton, Ohio, was hard at work on developing the Gotcha radar system. Mounted on a drone that resembled a miniature B-2 bomber, this was billed as capable of remaining aloft for 24 hours or more, beaming back a constant stream of radar, video, and infrared images of an area 20 kilometers wide to a specially designed $2.2 million supercomputer, all in hopes of catching the bomb layer at work. "The capability to scan an entire city from the air in any weather and detect any movement of any object as small as a cockroach is a goal of the Gotcha radar program at the Air Force Research Laboratory," ran an air force promotional release.

Further inquiry reveals that Gotcha was in fact a variation on our old friend JSTARS, once conceived to observe and target advancing armored Soviet hordes. The dream of seeing everything, targeting everything, hitting anything had, with "rewinding the tapes," now extended into four dimensions.

There was much in this enormous and expensive effort to impress outsiders. Defense Secretary Gates, for example, was beguiled by Task

Force ODIN's videos. "It was amazing," he recalled in his memoir, "to watch a video in real time of an insurgent planting an IED, or view a video analysis tracing an insurgent pickup truck from the bomb-making site to the site of an attack. It was even more amazing—and gratifying—to watch the IED bomber and the pickup truck be quickly destroyed as a result of this unprecedented integration of sensors and shooters."

Reality was less gratifying. In May 2007, some months after arriving in Baghdad, Hickey enlisted Odierno to sponsor a meeting at which the units that were deploying various technologies could present their results and make their case. When it came to their turn, Task Force ODIN displayed Constant Hawk videos of the type that so impressed Gates. Then Rivolo asked an awkward question: How many bomb planters had they actually tracked back to their point of origin? The task force representative came clean: one. Other vaunted technologies emerged with even less credit. Compass Call Nova, for example, a major air force contribution to the anti-IED effort, was cruising the skies at $34,000 per hour, year in and year out. Rivolo had made careful study of its performance by correlating specific missions flown with what happened on the ground below. The results were painfully clear: in the period he examined, between October 2006 and May 2007, hundreds of bombs had gone off or remained quiescent completely regardless of the $100 million planes overhead pulsing out their electronic commands. As he tersely informed Odierno, Compass Call Nova had "no detectable effect." However, when queried at the meeting as to why they continued to fly these pointless and expensive ($100 million per year) missions, the air force representative replied, "[T]he field commanders want it." (Rivolo later discovered that an inquisitive researcher at the Center for Naval Analysis had done a similar study a year before and had come to the same conclusions, which were duly ignored by high authority.)

There was, however, no mistaking who controlled the principal strategy for defeating the IED. It was evident even in the furniture. Most of the equipment around the base was "pretty beat up," according to one of the tens of thousands of Americans who passed through its heav-

ily guarded gates during the years of the occupation. The office equipment, furniture, and electronics were worn, much of it old, having been
hurriedly shipped in from other bases around the world as the occupation army settled in for the long haul. One single-story building close
by Odierno's office was different, though. "You walked in there, and
everything was brand new," remembers a visitor. "They had the most
up-to-date computers, big servers, nice big plasma screens in full working order on the walls. You could tell it had priority."

This was the home of the High-Value Targeting Cell, a counterpart
to the cell in the Pentagon that had tracked Saddam and, before him,
Milošević. Here, analysts tracked individuals on NSA "manhunt" lists
while others combed through reports from units around Iraq for sightings of the wanted men or others to be added to the Joint Priorities
Effects List, the JPEL, a constantly refreshed master list of targets slated
for elimination. All around Iraq and Afghanistan, every unit maintained its own list of high-value targets, also known as high-value individuals, each death or capture dutifully recorded in the SIGACTS. For
example, a May 5, 2006, report on the shooting of Allah Harboni, spotted from a U.S. army observation post and shot as he tried to escape
by car, was summarized as: "AT 0810C, A 3-187 OP ENGAGED AND
KILLED ONE OF THEIR BN [Battalion] HVI'S IN THE SALAH AD
DIN PROVINCE IN SAMARRA VIC 38SLC9652784715."

Meanwhile, on the expansive grounds of Camp Slayer, yet another
of the sprawling bases in Baghdad housing the military occupation
regime, stood an ornate, domed building known as the Perfume Palace. Originally constructed for the pleasure of the notorious Uday, elder
son of Saddam, it had escaped the "shock and awe" bombing and was
now occupied by U.S. military intelligence. Jerry-built, with questionable drains, it was not a popular place to work: the chief of military
intelligence in Iraq at one point decreed a weekly Be Happy Day as an
initiative to raise morale. Although many of the inmates were servicemen and women, civilian contract employees occupied several
floors. They were there thanks to JIEDDO, which was sluicing money
into Attack the Network along with the rest of its mission statement.
Most of them were retired U.S. policemen, retained by defense

contractor SAIC to analyze intelligence dossiers in search of high-value targets. All commanded high salaries, as much as $300,000 a year, though their employers charged JIEDDO far more. Target hunting had become a profitable business. (Asked if their nominees ever found their way onto an actual target list, a JSOC officer bluntly answered, "No.")

For the HVT industry, the benefits of hunting down leaders of the "IED networks" appeared self-evident, as had assassinating Hitler, Patrice Lumumba, or Pablo Escobar in years gone by. Since the elimination of formerly critical nodes such as Saddam and Zarqawi had paid little dividend, the target list was expanding, as such lists always do. Toward the end of 2007, Rivolo, already dubious about the presumptions behind the strategy, began to look for data that could reveal whether or not the strategy worked. He found it in the SIGACTS.

With full access to the SIGACT database, Rivolo extracted the records of 200 cases in which high-value targets had been killed or captured between June and October 2007. Then he went through the records again to see what happened in the neighborhood where each leader had operated. This was the crucial question. Had his elimination made a difference in the fight against the insurgents? Rivolo counted the number of IED attacks against Americans in the 30 days following each high-value target death or arrest within a given distance from the event and compared it to the number in the 30 days before the death or arrest as a percentage of change. Repeating this procedure for different distances, Rivolo plotted the results on one axis of a graph and the distance on the other. When complete, the graph delivered a simple, unequivocal message: the strategy was indeed making a difference but not the one intended. Hitting HVIs did not reduce attacks and save American lives. It *increased* them. Each killing had quickly prompted mayhem. Within 3 kilometers of the target's base of operation, attacks over the following 30 days shot up by 40 percent. Within a radius of 5 kilometers, a typical area of operations for an insurgent cell, they were still up 20 percent. Summarizing his findings for Odierno, Rivolo added an emphatic punch line: "Conclusion: HVI Strategy, our principal strategy in Iraq, is counter-productive and needs to be re-evaluated."

How could the removal from the scene of ringleaders of attacks on Americans generate such a counterintuitive result? Just as the field officers had told Hickey and Rivolo during their 2005 trip, dead leaders were invariably replaced quickly, "usually in twenty-four hours, always in forty-eight," recalls Rivolo. For a variety of reasons, new commanders were almost always eager to press the fight harder. Often, they would be relatives of the dead man and hot for revenge. In addition, having just succeeded to the command, they would feel the need to prove themselves, especially if the late leader's martial energies had been faltering due to battle fatigue or other interests, highlighting the need for a new broom. Always, they were more deadly.

A week or so after submitting his findings, Rivolo asked Odierno if he had read the study. "Yeah," replied the powerful commander shortly, "there's a limit to what I can do." Bureaucratic politics, it seemed, superseded empirical truth. Odierno's reliance on Hickey's operation to tell him what was going on rather than the elaborately staffed formal apparatus was ruffling feathers. "Hickey was going directly to Odierno every day and Odierno was just ignoring the other people and they knew that and they weren't happy about that." Returning to Washington in February 2008, Rivolo presented his conclusions on the strategy to his superiors at IDA. Unfortunately, IDA Director Dennis Blair was gone, having been replaced by former air force chief of staff Larry Welch, who appeared disinclined to challenge established doctrine; there were by now too many vested interests involved in targeted killing. Some thought it didn't matter anyway. "When you mow the grass," the senior counterterrorism official who had drawn my attention to Israeli influence on the strategy remarked offhandedly to me, "you don't expect the grass not to grow again."

As the American war in Iraq wound down—Rivolo's scrutiny of IED statistical trends gave early warning that the majority of Sunni insurgents were changing sides—the targeting machinery redeployed with renewed vigor to Afghanistan, its masters convinced that they had found the key to victory.

# 10

# A PIECE
# OF JUNK

Despite accounting for almost half the world's arms spending, in much of the country the U.S. military establishment is largely invisible. There are exceptions where landscape and politics have resulted in an evident military presence. One of these is Virginia's Southern Neck, the long peninsula jutting out into the Chesapeake Bay. An archipelago of bases and forts, as well as the CIA's Camp Peary, it stands as a testament to the enduring power of the state's congressional delegation. Whole communities were swept away in the headlong militarization of the area during the hot and cold wars of the twentieth century, periodic outbreaks of peace occasioning only minor shrinkage before a fresh cascade of appropriated dollars rained down to irrigate the area's economy.

In July 1921, General Billy Mitchell of the Army Air Corps took off from the corps' Langley Field at the tip of the peninsula to prove his theories regarding the omnipotence of airpower by bombing and sinking a number of surrendered German warships anchored in the bay. Mitchell is one of the patron saints of the U.S. Air Force, as it was founded on the presumption that airpower can win wars unaided by interventions from armies and navies. Down through the years, this conviction has underpinned the doctrines and budgets of the service. For true believers, presumptions about technology embodied in the revolution in military affairs and David Deptula's theory of effects-based operations, and further expressed in the drone-assisted manhunts of the twenty-first-century wars, merely reaffirmed Mitchell's contentions. "Find, fix, finish," Deptula remarked to me one day over lunch. "We spent a hundred years working on finish. We can now hit any target anywhere in the world, any time, any weather, day or night."

So it was fitting that when I visited Langley Air Force Base it was on an introduction from Deptula himself, who had retired in 2010 and was appointed dean of the Air Force Association's Mitchell School of Airpower Studies two years later. I came to the base to view the Langley "node" of the Distributed Common Ground System, the "system of systems" that General Deptula had been promoting since 2003. In essence, the DCGS is the repository of the oceans of data flowing from "platforms," drones, spy planes, and satellites in an endless stream of video as well as electronic signals and conversations.

Earlier, we saw analysts at the DCGS node at Florida's Hurlburt Air Force Base in Florida monitor video from a Predator drone as it stalked a little convoy of Afghan civilian vehicles in the mountains of Uruzgan. But DCGS (pronounced *D-sigs*) does more than that, collating imagery from different platforms in order to identify targets or just watching a house, a vehicle, or a person to monitor "pattern of life" or logging archived material for later reference. There are five principal and forty subsidiary sites within the network. Each of the principal system "nodes" is co-located with a specific air force unit, thus the site at Hurlburt Air Force Base pairs with the air force special operations headquarters in support of Special Forces missions. Even so, this is a network in which all the parts are interchangeable, all having equal access to the same material, all enabled to coordinate lethal strikes. The air force calls this a "weapons system," with a unit cost of $750 million for each of the principal sites. At $4.2 billion for the air force— and $10.2 billion across all services—when completed, it will represent a far more substantial financial prize for major corporations than drone programs. The contractors who shared in programming and building those "weapons"—Raytheon, Lockheed, L-3 Communications, Northrop, Hughes—are among the titans of the defense complex. Further monies are being garnered (at least $63.5 million in 2013) to support the enterprise. Recipients are many of the above as well as General Dynamics, SAIC, CACI, and Booz Allen along with smaller fry. "It's the key to the whole system," Deptula told me, "drones are just fiberglass in the sky."

Prior to his retirement, Deptula had risen high in the air force, gaining his third star by 2005. Along the way, he had continued to spread his gospel, encouraging Wesley Clark in the air strategy of the Kosovo conflict and for two months directing the air operations staff doing the targeting for the 2001 air campaign against Afghanistan. An admiring air force biographer summarized that war as one in which "small teams of special forces on the ground had supported airpower as it dispersed Taliban forces. . . ." Ground forces *supporting* airpower rather than the other way around was the fulfillment of a dream going back to Mitchell himself. Subsequent developments appeared no less gratifying. Deptula's friend General Michael Moseley, supervising the air component of the 2003 Iraq invasion, had, according to that same biography, very properly "employed stealth with precision weapons" in the initial attempts to kill Saddam. Thereafter, as implemented by Moseley, Deptula's "vision of parallel warfare and effects-based operations resulted in devastating the Iraqi ability to defend itself."

With the ensuing insurgency having dashed American hopes for a trouble-free occupation, Deptula was nevertheless confident that he had the answer to this very different kind of war. "Like a liquid that gravitates toward our weakest points, they aim to defy our grasp," he wrote in 2007. "Because they infest urban areas and hide among the civilian populations, finding the enemy has become a great challenge. In this sense knowledge is assuming precedence over kinetics as the prerequisite 'weapon' of war . . . victory will go to those who create and exploit knowledge faster than their opponents." If knowledge were more important than "kinetics," meaning physical force, then whoever collected, analyzed, and distributed the knowledge would be in a very powerful position and worthy of a commensurately sized budget. "When we took out Abu Musab al-Zarqawi," Deptula liked to tell audiences, "that operation consisted of over 600 hours of Predator time, followed by about ten minutes of F-16 time." Traditionally, the collection of intelligence, especially about underground insurgents, had been in the hands of signals and human intelligence collectors, that is, NSA, CIA, and DIA. The advent of drones with their enticing streams of video, not to mention their ability to collect signals intelligence and track people through Stingray technology, meant that the air force was expanding its role and therefore entitled to a bigger share of the pot.

Offered the powerful position of deputy chief of staff for intelligence in 2006, a position traditionally occupied by a mere two-star general, three-starred Deptula had successfully negotiated an expansion of the title to deputy chief of staff for intelligence, surveillance, and reconnaissance. This was more than just an exercise in title inflation. In air force terminology, *reconnaissance* has heavy implications of space and satellites, usually the purview of other agencies, including the young and expanding National Geospatial Agency, which supposedly had responsibility for analyzing and distributing satellite pictures. *Surveillance* also had interesting implications, since it was traditionally associated with monitoring the borders by land and sea. Indeed, at this time Deptula was also leading a push for the air force to be nominated as the "executive agent" for all medium- and high-altitude drones, meaning that it would hold the purse strings on other services' drone programs. This was not, obviously, an initiative welcomed by the other services, which lobbied furiously and effectively to kill the proposal.

Central to the argument that these activities and responsibilities be combined was the notion of *jointness*, a term that might suggest a spirit of benign interservice cooperation. Deptula invoked it to mean, among other things, "an arrangement where one service oversees the acquisition and standardization of theater-capable UAVs." Simply put, this meant that the air force should own all the important drones. As a serving air force officer familiar with this approach remarked to me,

"Deptula was one of the generals in the air force that were at war, first and foremost, with the other services. More than Russians or Chinese or Al Qaeda or anybody else, Deptula's main enemy was the United States Army, and after that the Marine Corps, and after that the Navy."

Deptula's attitude toward the marines may have been colored by rhetorical salvos regularly loosed off in his direction by his old nemesis, retired marine general Paul Van Riper. In a 2005 email exchange between the generals, Van Riper once again derided the airman's claims to have changed the nature of war with choice observations such as "let me say that your description of an approach based on 'control of the enemy' demonstrates, at least to me, your lack of understanding of non-linear or structurally complex systems." Van Riper's friend and fellow marine General James Mattis, who had been appointed to lead the Joint Forces Command formerly humiliated by Van Riper in the Millennium Challenge war game, gave what he thought was a death blow to Deptula's *effects-based operations* doctrine by issuing an order banning the use of the term in his command. Among other pungent critiques of the concept ("Assumes a level of unachievable predictability") Mattis pointed out that its wholehearted embrace by the vaunted Israeli Defense Forces prior to the 2006 Lebanon War had proved disastrous. "Although there are several reasons why the IDF performed poorly during the war," noted the general, "various postconflict assessments have concluded that overreliance on EBO concepts was one of the primary contributing factors for their defeat."

The Distributed Common Ground System headquarters at Langley is not an institution comfortable with outside scrutiny. Throughout my visit, I was an alien presence. Touring the facility with a squad of escorts, my little phalanx was preceded at all times by a serviceman holding high a red torch to signify that an interloper from outside the classified universe was in their midst and therefore that nothing secret should be shown or uttered. The huge rooms, lined with workspaces crammed with multiple screens, resembled nothing so much as a Wall Street trading room, except that here the screens display images of Afghan hillsides collected by a Reaper drone or a patch of the Pacific ocean sent by a Global Hawk drone at 60,000 feet or the horn of Africa from an orbiting satellite or the coast of Iran from a U-2 spy plane, any and all of which, in theory at least, could be called up by the young men and women consigned to gaze at the screens day after day. They may be coordinating a strike, archiving video so that it can be called up later, or simply gazing at a targeted house, car, or person far away. Larger screens high on the walls displayed the location of "platforms," the drones and planes and satellites gathering the knowledge being piped into the system in a ceaseless torrent, the equivalent, so the air force informed me, of 700 copies of the *Encyclopedia Britannica* per day.

It is a system of extraordinary complexity and expense. Simply to ensure that all the different nodes and sites remain interconnected at all times involves a massive investment in bandwidth and fiberoptic communications. Even rendering the incoming imagery viewable requires a considerable engineering effort to "clean up" what may arrive as unintelligible images.

Thus, ever since William Perry championed the privatization of defense operations and support functions in the 1990s, outsourcing key missions to civilian contractors has taken up an ever-increasing share of military operations and budgets. This makes it legally difficult, given the sanctity of contracts and corporate litigiousness, to cut spending in this area. The esoteric world of "D-Sigs" is no exception. Just as private contractors handle drone takeoffs and landings before handing them over to the military crews to conduct actual strikes, so corporations not only built this complex electronic nervous system but also to a considerable extent operate and maintain it.

A simple check on Internet job postings from corporations on contract to service the system helps to convey the scale of the business. Openings at just the Langley node, for example, were appearing daily, with no sign of a slowdown even as Washington rang with talk of austerity and "a hollowed out military." A typical day's sample in early March 2014 advertised openings for, variously, a "systems administrator" (the position that Edward Snowden put to good use) required by CACI International, a "subject matter expert" sought by Sehike Consulting, an "intelligence capabilities analyst" required by Digital

Management, while General Dynamics was looking for a network engineer. All positions required at least a Top Secret Clearance, and most mandated SCI (special compartmented information), which usually meant signals intelligence. Salaries ranged between $120,000 and $170,000 annually, though of course the contractors would be adding a hefty overhead when submitting bills to the taxpayer.

The Langley unit has a resident chaplain and a psychologist who patrol the area between the computer banks ready to offer counseling to anyone unduly distressed by scenes of remote death and destruction in which they may have participated via video. But though much has been made of the combat stress suffered by servicemen and women in such conditions, Colonel Hernando Ortega, surgeon for the Air Force Intelligence Surveillance and Reconnaissance Agency, has expressed a different view of the stresses of what he calls "tele-warfare." Addressing a Washington think-tank seminar in 2013, he divulged the fact that "our guys are below the general civilian population as far as risk for PTSD." To murmurs of disbelief from his audience of defense intellectuals he insisted that "we haven't had any pilots with PTSD. . . . We had, I think, one sensor operator, maybe."

One side of the huge room at Langley was reserved for the signals intelligence workstations where NSA assignees monitored the cellphone locations of targets, eavesdropped on their conversations, or checked links based on calling patterns, all crucial elements in Deptula's drive to fulfill his thirst for "knowledge." They enabled the marriage of visual and signals intelligence, so that a specific SUV in a wedding-party convoy can be pinpointed thanks to signals from the high-value target's cell phone and then incinerated with a Hellfire missile. This does indeed constitute an impressive feat of technological intelligence, assuming, of course, that they have the correct phone number.

"I overhauled the system," Deptula told me, "made it global, so that any station could be involved in any operation with a phone call." The scale was impressive—the whole world enclosed in one thinking spiderweb—even if the end result was a tsunami, a thousand hours *per day* of full-motion video (defined as 24 frames per second) plus further streams of intercepted calls and associated signals intelligence that the current 5,000-strong complement of air force Distributed Common Ground System analysts will never have time to review.

Lamenting the quantity of information collected, whether images or signals, is a traditional meme of intelligence officials. Deptula, for example, liked to warn that "we will soon be swimming in sensors and drowning in data." However, neither he nor any of his fellow generals has ever suggested that the answer might be to collect less. As General James R. Clapper, future director of national intelligence, once said, "I cannot see a situation where someone is going to say, 'Hey, I can do with less of that.'" This statement suggests that perhaps the object of the exercise, wittingly or otherwise, is not the production of useful information but simply the building of a bigger bureaucratic empire with a bigger budget. Clearly, however, no one could admit to this. Therefore the orthodox response to the "drowning-in-data" lament has been to invoke the urgent need and imminent prospect of turning the business of analysis over to machines. As Deptula himself has declared, "making this automatic is an absolute must."

This is the Holy Grail, pursued ever since the distant days of Task Force Alpha, with ever-more participants joining the chase. Exponential expansion in processing power and software improvements has certainly made it easier to extract relevant items from a mass of data and "connect the dots," as the hackneyed phrase has it. Yet this program embodies a mechanistic approach to warfare, as in the 1941 air-war plan that projected the defeat of Germany with the destruction of a set number of targets, or Warden's "five rings" concept for defeating Iraq in 1991. Lack of information leading to misidentification of truly critical nodes has been routinely blamed for the long string of post-1941 failures of this target-list approach to war.

This mind-set has been extremely beneficial for the various interested parties, including most recently the contractors who are building and servicing the air force DCGS (Distributed Common Ground Systems) as well as those (largely the same cast) who are creating its army and navy counterparts, DCGS-A and DCGS-N. While the air force version primarily serves to assist in the execution of airstrikes, the $2.3 billion army system is supposed to help soldiers on the ground assess present and future threats, such as the names, faces, relationships of known enemies, favored sites for planting IEDs, and so on. DCGS-A attracts a great deal of well-merited abuse from a host of critics, in and out of uniform, who attest to the difficulty of using it and its frequent breakdowns.

Many of these critics, including soldiers in the field, swear with equal vehemence to the merits of the data-analysis system offered by Palantir, a Silicon Valley corporation with origins in the PayPal fraud-detection division. Much of its appeal derives from its ease of use: "It's a database with an Apple-ish interface," one contractor in the automated intelligence business told me, "and they're really good at selling themselves." Palantir, like DCGS, is an intelligence fusion system but one that has applications across a wide range of fields, from Wall Street to disaster relief. "Palantir works because it's a commercial system, constantly refined," one longtime Pentagon consultant explained to me. "The army system is produced by a bureaucracy that works in partnership with the usual suspects, Northrop, Raytheon, General Dynamics, Lockheed, and they put together something horribly complicated, unwieldy, and expensive."

In its early years Palantir worked exclusively for the CIA, which had initially funded it through its In-Q-Tel start-up arm. Basically, the system categorizes information in an easily readable form, making use of whatever disparate databases the user can access and wants to use. So, for example, it could display a list of cities in Libya ranked according to the number of suicide bombers they have produced or in graphic form to show maps of where the most productive cities are. An army officer in Afghanistan sent me a Palantir-generated color-coded display, showing which senior officers in the Afghan unit he was advising had good relations with senior officials in the Kabul government and which did not. Bolstered by intelligence agency accolades for its undisclosed feats in tracking al-Qaeda terrorists, Palantir has expanded its market to Special Forces, law enforcement, and JP Morgan, where it detects mortgage fraud (by outsiders). I queried a marine friend serving in an isolated Afghan outpost about its alleged ability, as one enthusiastic congressman put it, to "detect IEDs." He responded that it is indeed a "great system . . . since the enemy in this part of the world is habitual, you can 'predict' where possible and likely IEDs will be, based on historical trends."

This is clearly an eminently useful function, as long as enemy habits don't suddenly change and as long as the hard data, in this case records of previous IED attacks, have been correctly entered. There is no reason to suppose this would not be the case; bombs, especially when they kill and maim, are easy to define and record. But even at the simplest level, the automation optimistically foreseen by Deptula and others represents a more ambitious goal: a system that will "extract insight from information" (as the Palantir website neatly defines *analysis*) from sensors in real time, painlessly delivering prepackaged analyses to "customers" for further action as desired.

Ruminations on the problems of managing enormous quantities of surveillance data and the exciting possibilities for analyzing it automatically are a frequent topic on those occasions when inmates of the military-intelligence-industrial complex meet and confer, such as at the annual GeoInt convention in Florida (dubbed by insiders "the intelligence community's spring break"). Less attention is paid to more mundane matters, such as the shortcomings of existing systems for reasons of technical unfeasibility, incompetence, or greed. The MQ9 Reaper drone, for example, General Atomics' successor to the Predator, was introduced into service in 2005 and is now the backbone of the drone fleet. "They developed and fielded it in a hurry," an official in the Office of the Secretary of Defense explained to me. "Jumper [the air force chief of staff who promoted Predator] was retiring. He was an enthusiast for UAVs, but they knew Moseley, the incoming chief, was not so keen, so they pushed it on Jumper's watch." Larger and heavier than the Predator and capable of carrying more weapons (including 500-pound bombs), Reaper is extremely expensive to buy (more than $30 million a copy) and maintain ($5 million per year), much greater than older manned combat planes such as the F-16 and A-10. Though advertised as capable of patrolling for up to 30 hours, it manages less than half that when carrying its limited load of armaments, and it crashes at least twice as often as F-15 and F-16 manned fighters.

Nor should it be assumed that the Reaper is better equipped than Predator to survey the ground beneath and thus avoid confusing women and children with "military-aged males," a problem known in the video-surveillance world as "slants." In fact, it carries essentially the same sensors as the Predator that killed a marine, staff sergeant Jeremy Smith, and a navy corpsman, [medic] Benjamin Rast, in Upper Sangin, Helmand Province, Afghanistan, on April 6, 2011, because it could not distinguish their distinctive helmeted and armored profiles from turbaned Taliban. The engagement was monitored by a DCGS substation in Terre Haute, Indiana, manned by the Indiana Air National Guard, where an "imagery supervisor" concluded that the two men in the process of being targeted by the Predator appeared to be shooting *away* from fellow marines, indicating they were friendlies. He communicated this to the "tactical communicator," who passed the information on to the Predator base in Nevada, but the message was received by two mission intelligence coordinators who somehow failed to communicate this important news to the Predator pilot and sensor operator sitting a few feet away. They were looking at exactly the same video but were convinced that the muzzle flashes indicated the men were shooting *toward* the marines, hardly a testament to the much-touted resolution of drone videos. Furthermore, as the pilot subsequently told investigators, he thought the targeted men were enemy partly because, on infrared, their images tended to be "much hotter than friendly forces." The subsequent investigation concluded that no one was to blame. Nor did anyone seriously question the baroque complexity of these arrangements, with "imagery supervisors" trying (via a "tactical communicator") to get a vital message to "mission intelligence coordinators" (one of them a trainee) so that they could tell a "pilot" that he was misreading a murky image of a confused firefight eight thousand miles away or suggest that perhaps a live pilot in a plane overhead in direct communication with the ground force might have done a better job.

Unsurprisingly, the Association of Unmanned Vehicle Systems International, the increasingly potent drone lobby ("Advancing the unmanned systems and robotics community through education, advocacy and leadership," according to its mission statement) does not like to dwell on such mishaps. Now boasting 7,500 members and a board of directors well larded with defense aerospace industry stalwarts, the group lobbies for all things drone, especially their freedom to share the skies of America with traditional civilian air traffic. Among other successes, the group, by its own account, literally wrote a 2011 law mandating the Federal Aviation Authority to allow this. For the industry, law enforcement is a promising market, and so Congress obligingly appropriated money to the U.S. Border Patrol to buy six Reapers. Reviewing their operation, the Government Accountability Office found that as of 2011 these Reapers had enabled the capture of 5,103 undocumented aliens and drug smugglers at a cost of $7,054 per captive. However, some subversive border control official had arranged to rent a Cessna light aircraft that did not require a huge support team (171 people for a Reaper patrol) and equipped it with a simple infrared sensor. Performing the same duties as the Reapers, the Cessna operation yielded at least 6,500 captives at a cost of only $230 per person, 3 percent of the Reaper tally. Needless to say, the experiment was not repeated, and Congress soon appropriated more Reapers to guard the frontier.

Fortunately, as of 2014 the Border Patrol had not been required to buy and operate the most expensive drone of them all. "Northrop took billions and billions of dollars off us, and gave us a piece of junk," said a high-ranking Pentagon weapons acquisition official as we breakfasted at the Ritz-Carlton Hotel, Pentagon City (the social ground zero of the military-industrial complex). Our topic was Global Hawk, manufactured by the Northrop Grumman Corporation, the largest drone ever developed, lauded for its reach and endurance, touted as a giant step toward total situational awareness. A best-selling 2009 book on drones enthusiastically summarized its salient attributes, including the ability to "stay in the air up to 32 hours. Powered by a turbofan engine that can take it up to 65,000 feet, the stealthy Global Hawk carries synthetic aperture radar, infrared sensors, and electro-optical cameras. . . . Global Hawk can fly from San Francisco, spend a day hunting for terrorists in the entire state of Maine, and then fly back to the West Coast."

At the time of our breakfast, the $26 billion Northrop Corporation had plastered billboards situated at strategic locations, such as the Pentagon Metro station, with advertisements extolling its prowess, while Raytheon, the $30 billion defense electronics corporation responsible for its radars and other sensors, unreservedly claimed: "Day or night, on land or at sea and in all weather conditions, Raytheon's Enhanced Integrated Sensor Suite (EISS) on the Global Hawk air vehicle pinpoints stationary or moving targets with unparalleled accuracy. It transmits imagery and position information from 60,000 feet with near real-time speed and dramatic clarity—empowering warfighters to respond quickly and decisively." The fact that the cost, including research and development, had risen from an original target of $10 million to a sobering $223 million per copy did not feature in these encomiums.

"Junk is right," grumbled an air force officer who had long grappled with the aircraft's shortcomings. "On the first flight the rear access door fell off. It's made of composite plastic with adhesives instead of nuts and bolts to keep the weight down, but that glue doesn't work so well, so internal parts, fuel lines and electrical conduits, come apart in flight. That just shouldn't happen." After pausing for breath he resumed his doleful litany. "Northrop had hopes that with all the sensors on board it would replace JSTARS, but the basic aircraft was slow, underpowered, and the sensors were poor. The infrared can pick out campfires, but that's about it, and that's only when it's directly over the target, and you need the target's cooperation for that. The radar suffers from the plastic airframe twisting and flexing at high altitude, so the picture shifts with it."

Even those campfires can escape scrutiny when the weather is bad. The three Hawks stationed in Guam (flown by pilots in California) since 2010 have a primary mission to monitor North Korea's nuclear and other military initiatives. Unfortunately the rainy season lasts six months in the northern Pacific, and when fast-moving storms blow in over Guam, Global Hawk stays on the ground, unable to fly over them or, since it lacks the ability to see clouds ahead, go around them. Entire months have gone by without these massive aircraft leaving the ground.

By 2012, even the air force had had enough, announcing that the sixty-year-old U-2 spy plane, developed by the CIA for a total cost of $19 million in the mid-1950s, could fly higher and take better pictures than its purported successor and that the Global Hawk version, then under production, would be scrapped. In a 2011 report, the Pentagon's test office announced that the drone was "not operationally effective," citing such drawbacks as its inability to carry out assigned missions three-quarters of the time. The chairman of the Joint Chiefs of Staff, General Martin Dempsey, weighed in, telling Congress that Global Hawk "has fundamentally priced itself out of our ability to afford it." The White House took the same position.

It made no difference. Congress, led by House Armed Services Committee Chairman Buck McKeon and Democratic Congressman Jim Moran (whose northern Virginia district hosted the headquarters of both Northrop and Raytheon) effortlessly brushed aside these pleas, forcing the air force to keep buying the unwanted drone. No fewer than twenty-six lobbyists cited Global Hawk or surveillance issues on their required lobbying reports, including Letitia White, the longtime aide to the Predator's godfather, Congressman Jerry Lewis. Now they swung into action. This potent team was commanded by Northrop Grumman's vice president for government relations Sid Ashworth, who had spent fourteen years on the Senate Appropriations Committee staff, serving as staff director for two subcommittees, including defense. In recognition of his stellar performance in saving Northrop's profitable, if largely useless, product, *The Hill*, a widely read journal covering Congress, nominated Ashworth to a slot on its prestigious list of top lobbyists two years in a row, 2012 and 2013.

But Ashworth's greatest triumph was yet to come. On February 24, 2014, Defense Secretary Chuck Hagel announced a series of stringent cuts to the U.S. military. Among them was the entire force of A-10s, the plane that uniquely allowed pilots a clear view of what was happening on the ground. Not all programs, however, were slated for Hagel's axe. "In addition to the A-10," said the secretary, "the Air Force will also retire the 50-year-old U-2, in favor of the unmanned Global Hawk system." Sheepishly, Hagel conceded that the decision was a "close call," given previous strenuous efforts to kill the huge drone. His feeble justification was that with its "greater range and endurance," the Global Hawk makes a better high-altitude reconnaissance platform "for the future."

Northrop Grumman is one of the "primes," the too-big-to-fail contractors formed by merger and acquisition under Defense Secretary William Perry's auspices in the 1990s. Thanks to its deep coffers and a manufacturing base spread across many states and congressional districts along with those of its suppliers, the corporation's programs were always likely to survive the harshest budget cuts or the most damning evidence of technical incompetence. But the allure of manhunting surveillance technology, when lubricated by political connections, has provided similar buoyancy for smaller companies whose actual products are perhaps even less useful than Northrop's giant drone. As an example, we can look to the Sierra Nevada Corporation of Sparks, Nevada.

On January 2, 2011, the *Washington Post* reported the imminent deployment of a "revolutionary airborne surveillance system called Gorgon Stare, which will be able to transmit live video images of physical movement across an entire town." Major General James Poss, the air force's assistant deputy chief of staff for intelligence, surveillance, and reconnaissance, was quoted as claiming that with the new tool, analysts would no longer have to guess where to point the camera: "Gorgon Stare will be looking at a whole city, so there will be no way for the adversary to know what we're looking at, and we can see everything." David Deptula was no less effusive, certifying that the system offered "many orders of magnitude improvement over existing sensors on drones in Afghanistan. . . . Instead of looking at a truck or a house, you can look at an entire village or a small city" with the multiple cameras, simultaneously.

Gorgon Stare was definitely the hit of the year in intelligence-surveillance circles. That October, the U.S. Geospatial Intelligence Foundation honored Sierra Nevada with its 2011 Industry Achievement Award, given annually for "outstanding accomplishments in GEOINT tradecraft." A year later, Deptula's successor as air force intelligence chief, Lieutenant General Larry James, was still extolling the system's wide-area imaging as "very powerful in the [Afghan] battlespace" and relaying further tributes from American commanders in that country. Six months later, the general's enthusiasm was undiminished. "The combatant commanders love it," he told an interviewer. Earlier, *Air Force Times* had highlighted its utility in spotting "squirters," as people fleeing for their lives in an air attack were popularly known in the ISR community. Civil libertarians, no less impressed by the Gorgon's advertised capabilities, expressed alarm at the possibility that it might be put to use by domestic law enforcement.

First appearing in budget documents in 2008, as a response to Defense Secretary Gates' insistent request for more surveillance systems, Gorgon Stare, developed and manufactured by Sierra Nevada, essentially consisted of five "electro-optical" TV cameras for daytime and four infrared cameras for night missions. These were mounted on a pod under the right wing of a Reaper drone, while another pod under the left wing processed the images, transmitting them to recipients on the ground and storing them for later retrieval. The intent was for the cameras to provide a four-kilometer-square picture with a six-inch resolution, meaning that a scan of a town would reveal objects as small as six inches. A "chip-out" feature allowed troops on the ground to receive a segment of the overall picture. Indeed, according to its developers, the system would be able to transmit a panorama of sixty-five different pictures to different users, as opposed to the single, narrow, "soda straw" images currently available from drones. Thus a single Gorgon-carrying drone could circle over a town, effortlessly delivering images of selected areas to ground units on request. Not only could the wide area under scrutiny monitor "squirters," as discussed, it was one more attempt at the dream of being able to look back into the past to discover who planted a bomb. As Deptula himself explained, "You can review it and accomplish forensic study of the area by looking at movement and tracing activity. If you know where an improvised explosive device went off, you can 'rewind the tapes' and see where the activity was and what led to it."

There was one problem. Gorgon Stare didn't work, a fact of which the air force was perfectly well aware. In the last months of 2010, the system had been subject to an intense program of tests by a specialized air force testing unit, the 53D Wing at Eglin Air Force Base in Florida. The results were damning. The final report deemed the system "not operationally effective" and "not operationally suitable," breaking down, apart from anything else, on average, 3.7 times every sortie. Officially, Gorgon Stare generated "motion video," which turned out to be just 2 frames a second (as opposed to "full-motion video" at 24 frames a second). While it was possible to make out cars and other vehicles, it was impossible to distinguish "dismounts" (people) from bushes. One of the test team's briefing slides that I looked at compared aerial pictures of an air base. One was a Gorgon Stare infrared "full image." In other words, it showed the widest area of which it was capable. The other came from Google Earth, the free online service available to all. They were identical, revealing buildings and roads, and airfield runways, but nothing smaller and more detailed. Another slide showed a "subview," a sample of what troops in the field would get if they were to make a request to the drone overhead. It was just possible to make out the cars. People were another matter, merely the faintest of blobs and certainly indistinguishable from bushes.

The bad news continued. The wide-area images, for example, were made up of multiple smaller images taken by individual cameras and stitched together in the processor pod before being transmitted to earth. However, as the test unit reported, the imagery "is subject to gaps between stitching areas which manifests itself [sic] as a large black triangle moving throughout the image." Not surprisingly, "this causes loss of situational awareness and the inability to track activity when the 'black triangle' covers the area of interest." In addition, the system had difficulty in determining where it was and hence the precise location of any targets it might spot. True, daylight images from the pod that were downloaded when it was on the ground rather than transmitted were clear enough to allow the tracking of individuals "to their point of origin or destination, providing analysis of IED detonations." But unfortunately, said the report, "GS experiences 'dropped frames' during download—making it impossible to track moving targets over that period." The testing unit strongly recommended that Gorgon Stare not be deployed to Afghanistan.

The air force test unit was not the first informed critic to take a dim view of the vaunted surveillance device. In a withering report on the air force's request for $78.9 million to spend on Gorgon Stare in 2010, the Senate Armed Services Committee had already suggested that there did not seem to be much point for "moderate-resolution" (i.e., poor-quality) motion imagery and that increasing the camera's resolution would lead to a "dramatic reduction" in the size of the area that could be covered by one Gorgon-carrying drone, which would consequently require more drone flights, which would make the whole exercise too expensive. Adding insult to injury, the Senate report went on to point out that no one to date had "produced sufficient evidence that forensic analysis of moderate-resolution wide-area motion imagery is produc-tive enough to justify a large investment in sensors and platforms—especially in the absence of effective automated analytic tools." In plain English, this meant that the idea of using the slow motion video to "rewind the tapes" and unmask the IED layers, as suggested by Deptula, wouldn't really work, especially as the quantity of imag-ery would be too vast to be analyzed by humans and so would have to be done by computers ("effective automated analytic tools") that did not exist. The committee recommended "no funds to continue Gorgon Stare development."

These harsh verdicts made no difference whatsoever. Gorgon Stare was dispatched to Afghanistan a little over a month after the test report. Safe from prying eyes, it could now bask in uncritical plaudits from General James and others. At the end of 2011, I emailed a marine offi-cer deployed in the battleground of northern Helmand and asked if his experience justified General James' confidence in the system's ability to help the troops. After detailing the routine IED injuries inflicted on his unit in the previous four days (one double leg amputa-tion, one foot, one arm below the elbow), he went on: "I've never even heard of Gorgon Stare, let alone seen it in use. We're essentially using the same technology that men used in WWII, Korea, and Vietnam to defeat mine and booby-trap threats—the eyeball and metal detector."

How could it be that this near-useless system could survive such emphatic rejection not only from the air force's own testing professionals but from a powerful Senate committee, let alone have little impact where it was needed most? The answer would appear to lie in a classic combination of money, politics, and the ever-diminishing gap between government service and private enterprise, all turbocharged thanks to the Niagara of cash unleashed by 9/11.

In the year before 9/11, Sierra Nevada was a small aerospace company based in Sparks, Nevada, that took in $13 million in government contracts. Twelve years later, that figure had soared to $1 billion, most of it in defense work and much of that "sole source," that is, without competitive bidding. The owners, Fatih and Eren Ozmen, have long enjoyed amiable relations with politicians. For example, in 2004 they hired Dawn Gibbons, wife of then congressman Jim Gibbons, representing Nevada's 2nd District, and paid her $35,000 for consulting work. Representative Gibbons was a member of the House Armed Services Committee, in which capacity he helped steer a $2 million defense contract for a helicopter landing system to Dawn's employer. Everyone denied any connection between the two events. A 2010 Congressional Ethics Office report highlighted the close relationship between Sierra Nevada and PMA, a lobbying firm closely linked to the campaign fund-raising efforts of house members powerful in defense matters, including John Murtha of Pennsylvania and Peter Visclosky of Indiana. (PMA dissolved in 2009, following a criminal investigation and the jailing of CEO Paul Maglioccetti, a former senior staffer on the House Defense Appropriations Committee.) Nonetheless, the House Ethics Committee voted to take no action.

It seemed that Sierra Nevada's owner, Fatih Ozmen, could echo the significant statement of Neal Blue, the CEO of Predator manufacturer General Atomics: "For our size, we possess more significant political capital than you might think." In fact, there were many points of similarity between these two defense corporations, both so profitably engaged in the booming business of drones and surveillance. One of them was Big Safari, the secretive air force office that awarded and oversaw the Gorgon Stare contract. Charged with overseeing the acquisition and introduction of "special purpose" air force weapons, the office, officially known as the 645 Aeronautical Systems Group, enjoyed a reputation for its ability to cut corners and move programs swiftly without the customary bureaucratic encumbrances. Such prowess was largely due to the authority granted them to award sole-source contracts without the tiresome necessity of allowing firms to compete on price and performance.

As we have seen, Big Safari played a major role in the development and fielding of Predator, partly thanks to the intervention of former air force chief master sergeant Mike Meermans, who had spent the last five of his twenty-two-year service career working on airborne reconnaissance operations on the air staff, where he enjoyed a close friendship with the group's leadership. Following his retirement, Meermans embarked on a second career as a senior staffer on the House Intelligence Committee, when he had crafted the legislation mandating that total control of the Predator program be assigned to the air force, and that Big Safari be put in charge of its development. Given Meermans' subsequent third career as vice president for strategic planning at Sierra Nevada's Washington office, he was presumably already well informed about the company and its programs. Overall, between 2006 and 2013, Big Safari lavished no less than $3.5 billion on Sierra Nevada in sole-source contracts for which no one else was able to compete. As a source coarsely summarized the relationship to journalist Aram Roston, Big Safari and Sierra Nevada "are so close they share rubbers."

Among those deals was an $18 million contract awarded in 2011 for the Northern Command Sensor Program, a bizarre air force initiative to get a piece of the war-on-drugs action by flying surveillance planes supplied by Sierra Nevada over parts of Mexico and other regions in hopes of gathering intelligence about narco-traffickers and their operations. It is unclear whether the operation yielded any useful intelligence, but it ended tragically when one of the planes flew into a mountain in Colombia, killing three Americans and one Panamanian on board. The pilot of the twin engine Bombardier Dash-8 was blind in one eye and the plane so thoroughly laden with intelligence equipment that the FAA forbade its use for anything other than "crew training and market surveys." The altitude warning system was broken. It appeared to have been a pointless operation spawned by public-private collusion and mounted on the cheap, a telling counterpoint to the aura of glamorous mystery that envelops the world of hi-tech spy craft and the covert firms and groups that inhabit it.

# 11

# DEATH BY
# A NUMBER

September 2, 2010, was the day Mohammed Amin, a Taliban leader in the northeast Afghan province of Takhar, was supposed to die. His death would not come as a total surprise to anyone, least of all him, as the odds against his survival had definitely been lengthening. Given his position as Taliban deputy shadow governor for Takhar, Amin, an ethnic Uzbek in his forties, had strong grounds for believing that he occupied an uncoveted slot on the Joint Prioritized Effects List (JPEL), as the U.S. kill-roster was officially termed, and was therefore ripe for execution by air strike via drone, helicopter, bomber, or a Special Operations night raid whenever the opportunity arose. The recently installed U.S. commander, General David Petraeus, had expanded the list and doubled the number of such raids as one of his first acts upon arriving in Kabul. The death toll had shot up accordingly: 115 across the country in July 2010 and 394 in August. Indeed, on the very day Amin was to be killed, Petraeus told reporters that special forces operations in Afghanistan were "at absolutely the highest operational tempo," running at four times the rate ever reached in Iraq.

"Petraeus knew he was only going to be there a short time, a year or so," a close adviser to the general while he was in Afghanistan told me. "What could he do that would enable him to present good numbers to Congress in a year? The easiest way to generate good numbers was by killing people."

The renewed emphasis on high-value targeting in Afghanistan, which had already increased tenfold since Stanley McChrystal took over theater command in 2009, had a certain irony. As we have seen, the post-2001 insurgency and revival of the Taliban had to a considerable degree been caused by an obsessive hunt for Taliban and al-Qaeda leadership figures. But the surviving al-Qaeda members had decamped to Pakistan, along with the Taliban leadership. The Taliban remaining in Afghanistan had for the most part retired to private life and wished only to be left alone, resisting initial calls from Pakistani intelligence to start a jihad against the Americans.

Most Afghans were relieved to be free of their incompetent and fanatical rulers and welcomed the Americans and British. However, the dearth of genuine targets was relieved by warlords and others seeking favors from the country's new masters. Feeding the demand for targets, they fingered business rivals, tribal enemies, and other unfortunates who were duly rounded up and shipped off to the torture chambers at the Bagram base outside Kabul or the oubliette of Guantánamo. Unsurprisingly, this state of affairs, combined with the kleptocratic behavior of the U.S.-installed government, eventually provoked a fierce reaction and a revival of the Taliban. So now, to deal with this insurgency, the United States was embracing the very tactic that had generated the problem in the first place. High-value targeting had in any case become especially fashionable in senior military circles thanks to the glow of the apparent victory over al-Qaeda in Iraq, spearheaded by JSOC's industrial counterterrorism, and backed by massive troop reinforcements and a shower of cash for Sunni tribal leaders willing to change sides. In addition, the rough-and-ready methods deployed in Afghanistan in 2002 had been replaced by the systematized approach developed in Iraq. Instead of the hit-or-miss dependence on tip-offs from warlords, the JPEL was now largely reliant on the presumed cer-

tainties of technical intelligence, principally in the form of drone surveillance (i.e., "the unblinking eye"), the monitoring of phone traffic,
and the physical location of phones via their signals.

Mohammed Amin qualified for the list on at least two counts. Apart
from his Taliban leadership status, a death warrant in itself, he was
also listed as the leading member in Afghanistan of the Islamic Movement of Uzbekistan, a jihadi group centered in that neighboring country but also active in Afghanistan.

Even so, securing a place on the JPEL had not been a casual affair.
A "Joint Targeting Working Group" composed of representatives of
various operational commands and intelligence agencies met once a
week to vet the "targeting nomination packets." As of October 1, 2009,
there had been 2,058 names on the JPEL. Execution, in every sense of
the word, was primarily the responsibility of Joint Special Operations
Command, though in keeping with convention this group was operating in Afghanistan under a code name, which in this period was Task
Force 373 (as opposed to Task Force 11, as it had been known in the
days of Operation Anaconda). Even in internal classified documents,
the involvement of this roving death squad in killings around Afghanistan was deemed highly sensitive, to be concealed at all costs.

The carefully selected and highly trained task force rank and file
tended to take a cynical view of the overall utility of their operations.
"They'd come into my province, work their way down the JPEL, but
they knew and I knew that all those names on the list would be replaced
in a few months," a former U.S. official who worked closely with them
in Afghanistan told me. Then he mentioned a phrase that seems to
come up a lot in the targeted-killing business: "They called it 'mowing
the grass.'"

Further up the chain of command, there was at least the preten-
sion that the selective killing fit into an overall plan. Petraeus' "Counterinsurgency Field Manual" instructed intelligence analysts to
recommend "targets to isolate from the population, and targets to eliminate." In the cross hairs were the supposedly critical nodes in the enemy
system, which the analysts clearly regarded as akin to a corporate hierarchy helpfully subdivided into specialties such as leader, facilitator,

mayor, IED expert, shadow governor, deputy shadow governor, chief of staff, military commission member, financier, and so on.

Along with "leaders," "facilitators" were a heavily targeted category, these being variously defined either as people who provided safe houses and support, or merely influential people, village elders and landowners who had no choice but to cooperate with the Taliban. Casting doubt on the precision of the undertaking was the fact that public announcements, in the form of ISAF press releases, regarding successful operations (never mentioning the task force role) often tended to describe the same person as both a "leader" and a "facilitator."

As a deputy shadow governor, Mohammed Amin certainly qualified for a place, complete with four-digit designating number, on the Joint Prioritized Effects List. Once on the list, it remained only for the task force to locate and kill him. His movements between Pakistan and Takhar may have been furtive, but to the "unblinking eye" of ISR, that was irrelevant. All they needed was a phone number.

Just as in Iraq, where the introduction of cell phones had enabled both the insurgents, who used them to communicate and to detonate bombs, and their hunters, who used them to locate and track their quarry, cell phones have played a vital role in the Afghan war ever since they were introduced in 2002. In fact, so crucial was Afghan phone traffic to U.S. intelligence—one in every two Afghans has a cell phone—that it has been credibly reported that the NSA recorded every single conversation and stored them for five years. Just as the Constant Hawk and Gorgon Stare programs had been attempts to look into the past, Retro, as the comprehensive phone-call recording program was called, was a way of listening to the past. Collecting numbers was therefore a high priority involving such devious maneuvers as turning a blind eye to cell phones used by insurgent prisoners in the giant Pol-e-Charkhi jail on the edge of Kabul and other Taliban holding pens around the country. The Taliban, meanwhile, were not unaware of the keyhole that cell phones exposed to the enemy. In an attempt to neutralize their adversary's advantage, in 2009 they launched a campaign to destroy the system and did indeed blow up over three hundred cell towers, only to abandon the effort thanks to either popular complaint or irritation at the consequent inconvenience to themselves.

Knowing a person's cell-phone number allows anyone with access to a country's cell phone network—no problem for Special Operations in Afghanistan—to obtain the phone's International Mobile Subscriber Identity (IMSI) number. With this in hand, the phone, or more specifically its SIM card, can not only be intercepted but also tracked within a hundred meters just by triangulating signals from cell towers. But that is not close enough to fix someone in a specific car in a moving convoy, at least not in a remote region, such as the bare hills of Takhar, in northern Afghanistan. A very precise fix on a phone and therefore its owner required the device that mimics cell towers, variously known as Stingray, Triggerfish, or IMSI Catcher, which had already done McChrystal such good service in Iraq.

Sometime in early July 2010, the task force scored a breakthrough, arresting a man who revealed that he was a relative of Mohammed Amin and obligingly furnished his phone number. With this in hand, the trackers were swiftly able to locate Amin's IMSI number and thus fix at least the general location of the SIM card, assumed to be in close proximity to its owner.

In the early summer the SIM-card trackers registered that Amin was in Kabul, making and receiving calls to and from locations around the country, all of which were submitted to the exotic algorithms of social-network analysis, tracing and measuring the links of his network both as a Taliban leader and as a leader of the Uzbek Islamists. At some point the watchers noted that Amin was now calling himself Zabet Amanullah—clearly an alias, they assumed—on the phone.

Later in July, the card began moving north, out of Kabul and up to Takhar. In those wide-open spaces Amin would be that much more vulnerable to a strike, and since he was already on the list, it only remained to choose the method and place to kill him. Technically, JPEL designees are liable for kill *or* capture, but as subsequent events indicated, no one was too interested in capturing the Taliban official.

On September 2, the perfect opportunity arose. The SIM card, and therefore the phone it was in and the person carrying that phone, set out early in the morning from a district in Takhar called Khwaja Bahud-din and headed west. Streaming video from a drone showed a convoy of six cars passing through mountains and making occasional brief halts during which people apparently carrying weapons got out of the cars for a minute or so. The drone could carry an IMSI Catcher, so on video screens at JFSOC headquarters and at Hurlburt DCGS in Florida—and perhaps on multiple additional screens across the neu-ral net of ISR—the crucial SIM card signaled the car in which it was riding. Eventually the convoy rolled into an area of bare, low hills with occasional defiles.

A little after 9:00 a.m., as the first two vehicles moved out of one of these narrow passes, two fighter jets detailed for the operation began the attack. The first bomb landed beside the target vehicle, gouging a crater in the road five feet across and eighteen inches deep and flip-ping the vehicle over on its side. The watchers saw "dismounts" run from the other vehicles, turn the target vehicle right side up, and help passengers get out. A second bomb hit ten minutes after the first, this time landing directly on the target vehicle. The explosion blew apart at least seven people, leaving severed legs, arms, and other body parts strewn around the wreckage.

The planes dropped another bomb ten minutes later and another ten minutes after that. The lengthy intervals, atypical of normal bomb-ing tactics, signified the time it took for the analysts to locate the tar-get phone via the IMSI Catcher on the drone circling overhead. But the bombs were ineffective: one exploded harmlessly on the hillside, and the other, a dud, hit the road some distance away and failed to explode. Adopting a different approach after the second miss, the com-mander directing the operation ordered two helicopters, "Little Bird" MH-6s, to finish the job. Accordingly, while one circled, the other dropped down low and hovered just above the ground, allowing the crew a clear view of survivors milling around the car. "It seemed as if the helicopter pilot had a picture . . . in his hand," a survivor later recalled, surmising that he was looking for a particular target. Finally he loosed off a burst of machine gun fire that put a bullet right through the face of the man holding the phone. Then he began to move, circling around to take a closer look at the bodies and survivors from the rest of the convoy. The helicopters stayed on the scene for another hour before returning to base, leaving ten people dead at the scene. It had been a textbook targeted killing.

That same day, ISAF issued a press release on the strike, as it normally did following operations of the secret task force:

> *Kabul, Afghanistan (Sept. 2) – Coalition forces conducted a precision air strike targeting an Islamic Movement of Uzbekistan senior member assessed to be the deputy shadow governor for Takhar province this morning. . . .*
>
> *Intelligence tracked the insurgents traveling in a sedan on a series of remote roads in Rustaq district. After careful planning to ensure no civilians were present, coalition aircraft conducted a precision air strike on one sedan and later followed with direct fire from an aerial platform.*

The strike was deemed important enough for the secretary of defense himself, Robert Gates, who happened to be visiting Kabul, to call attention to it at a press conference the next day: "I can confirm that a very senior official of the Islamic Movement of Uzbekistan was the target and was killed. . . . This is an individual who was responsible for organizing and orchestrating a number of attacks here in Kabul and in northern Afghanistan."

But Mohammed Amin did not die that day. The real target had been the SIM card tracked so meticulously by "intelligence." Very unfortunately, it did not belong to Amin but to the real-life Zabet Amanullah, a man the task force analysts had confidently assumed did not exist. He had indeed existed, as a quick phone call to any of a host of provincial or Kabul officials—or even a glance at a newspaper— would have made clear. He had been campaigning for his nephew, a candidate in the upcoming Afghan parliamentary election, and he had been on his way to a rally when he was killed. The ground around his burned and twisted vehicle was littered with election posters, with slogans such as "for a better future" still legible. The dead, campaign volunteers all, included five close relatives, among them his seventy-seven-year-old uncle.

Afghans, from President Karzai on down, were well aware of these obvious facts and said so. It made no difference. The spell cast by technical intelligence, with its magical tools of IMSI Catchers and cell-phone geolocation and social-network analysis algorithms and full-motion video, was too powerful for the truth to intrude, even after a dogged and resourceful investigator laid out the truth for all to see.

Kate Clark had none of the high-tech intelligence aids, but she knew more about Afghanistan than those who did. She had arrived in Kabul in 1999, when the country was still in the iron grip of the Taliban regime. She was the BBC correspondent, and the sole Western journalist in the country. Expelled in March 2001, she returned after the regime fell at the end of that year and continued reporting for the BBC until May 2010, when she joined the in-depth research group Afghanistan Analysts Network. Clark was perfectly aware that the high-tech assassins had murdered the wrong man, or rather men, because she had known Zabet Amanullah well. She had listened to the diminutive five-foot-two-inch Uzbek's life story, which included fighting successively for the Soviet-backed Afghan regime, the anti-Soviet U.S.-backed Mujaheddin, and the Pakistani-backed Taliban prior to 2001. He also recounted his serial torture experience, first at the hands of the Soviets, then while imprisoned by the anti-Soviet and anti-Taliban commander Ahmed Shah Massoud (who kept him in a two-foot-by-two-foot-by-two-foot box for six months), and finally by ISI, the Pakistani intelligence service. These last, as he told Clark, were angry because he refused to join the reborn Taliban and go to fight the Americans. "They hung me from the ceiling by my wrists and by my ankles and beat me with chains."

Finally released by the Pakistanis in 2008, Amanullah had fled to Kabul, where he supported himself by opening a pharmacy while anxiously soliciting character references and guarantees of protection from influential figures in the capital and his home province. In the maelstrom of modern Afghan politics, alliances and enmities are always fluid. The real-life ambiguities of the relationships and connections required for survival in such a society do not necessarily conform to the neat abstractions represented in the diagrams generated by social-network analysis. So when Amanullah decided in July to leave Kabul and go north to campaign for a nephew running for Parliament against a notorious Takhar strongman, one of the people he contacted was the influential Takhar Taliban official Mohammed Amin, whose calls were duly recorded and irretrievably entered into the system by Amin's hunters.

Then came the inexplicable mix-up. Somehow, amid the swirling petabytes of America's global surveillance system, the information identifying Amanullah's SIM card, the IMSI number, was logged as belonging to Amin. From that point on, the task force had its unblinking eye on the former torture victim, nicknamed "Ant" for his short stature. Fixated on what their cell phone tracking equipment was telling them, they adopted the unshakable conviction that the Ant was in fact Amin, traveling under an alias. It was Amanullah whom they had followed north out of Kabul to Takhar, waiting and watching for the right time and place to attack. With eyes always on the telltale electronic signal, Amanullah's exuberant election rallies, the fifty-car convoy of well-wishers that escorted him to his home village, his pictures in the newspapers, his radio interviews, his daily phone calls to district police chiefs informing them of his movements—all passed the high-tech analysts by. In a feat of surreal imagination, they did not question the unlikely proposition that an important figure in the Taliban would be traveling the countryside in a highly visible convoy or that the people who got out of the cars on that last trip through the mountains "apparently carrying weapons" might in fact be carrying cameras to photograph the scenery (as indeed they were). No one seemed to notice that the man holding the phone, killed with a carefully aimed bullet in the face from the helicopter, was actually calling the police. Their electronic data told them all they wanted to know.

Rapid and outraged Afghan protests that the strike had killed innocent civilians did little to shake military confidence that they had done the right thing. "We're aware of the allegations that this strike caused civilian casualties, and we'll do our best to get to the bottom of the accusations," said Major General David Garza, deputy chief of staff for Joint Operations. "What I can say is these vehicles were nowhere near a populated area and we're confident this strike hit only the targeted vehicle after days of tracking the occupants' activity." All of the dead, as far as the command staff were concerned, were ipso facto insurgents by virtue of their keeping company with Amin, whatever he was calling himself.

Just to be absolutely sure that Mohammed Amin had not somehow infiltrated the convoy, Kate Clark tracked down and interviewed each and every survivor of the attack, not only getting their stories but also checking on who had been sitting in each seat in the six cars. Looking through Amanullah's passport, which he had left in his Kabul apartment, she saw that he had visited Delhi for a few days in late April 2010, at a time when intelligence had the Taliban leader Amin in Takhar, organizing attacks on Americans.

In December, Clark had a breakthrough. David Petraeus, the allied commander in Afghanistan who had made his name as the general that plucked victory from the jaws of defeat in Iraq, had always been assiduous in courting journalists, with great benefit to his public image. Impressed by Clark's reputation as an acute and influential observer of Afghan affairs, the general invited her to dinner. Seizing the opportunity, she brought up the Amanullah case. Petraeus was unyielding in his stated conviction that they had got the right man. As he told a TV interviewer, "Well, we didn't think. In this case, with respect, we knew. We had days and days of what's called 'the unblinking eye,' confirmed by other forms of intelligence, that informed us that this—there's no question about who this individual was."

Confident of the story as well as his proven ability to charm the press, the general actually granted Clark rare access to the mysterious unit that had organized the killing. "He basically ordered the Special Forces to be frank with me, as he was so happy that they'd got the right person," Clark told me later. Within a few days she was sitting with the notoriously unreachable Joint Special Operations Task Force as they revealed the process that had led them to target the convoy: the extraction of Amin's phone number from the relative they had held in Bagram, the correlation with the SIM card, the tracking of the SIM north to

Takhar in July, and their utter certainty that they had got the right man, even if he was calling himself by another name.

The experienced journalist was astounded at what she was hearing about the process that had led to the deliberate killing of ten people. The Special Forces refused to accept that they had mixed up two individuals, insisting that the technical evidence that they were one and the same person was "irrefutable." They freely admitted that they had not bothered to research the biography of the man they thought they were killing. Amazingly, they claimed total ignorance of Zabet Amanullah's existence. When she pointed out that Amanullah's life and death were a matter of very public record, they argued that they were not tracking a name but "targeting the telephones."

"I was incredulous," she told me. "They actually conflated the identities of two people, and they didn't do any background checks on either person. They had almost no knowledge about Amin, and they hadn't bothered to get any knowledge about Amanullah. It's quite shocking." Despite all Clark told them, the Special Operations warriors' faith in their technical intelligence remained unshaken.

The final nail in the coffin for the official story came six months after the attack. Michael Semple is an Irishman who has spent decades in Afghanistan getting to know the country intimately, speaks Dari (one of the principal languages), and, with his beard and habitual dress, can pass as an Afghan. As such, he has been able to forge contacts with many Taliban (getting himself expelled from Afghanistan by the Karzai government for his pains in 2008). In March 2011, six months after the death of Amanullah, Semple, after months of patient investigation, tracked down the real Mohammed Amin, very much alive and living in Pakistan. Amin readily confirmed many of the details unearthed by Clark, including his position as deputy shadow governor, the detention of a relative at Bagram, and the fact that Amanullah had been in telephone contact with him and other Taliban. In fact, according to Amin, the two men had spoken to each other on the phone just two days before Amanullah was killed. "There should not be any serious doubt about my identity," Amin told Semple. "I am well known and my family is well known for its role in the jihad. Anyone who knows the personalities of the jihad in Takhar will know me and that I am alive."

The meeting left Semple with the strong impression that it probably hadn't been such a good idea to put Amin on the list in the first place, classifying him as a "gray area insurgent," someone who was indeed fighting against the government and NATO but who was a "rational actor" with a plausible list of grievances who could potentially be reconciled to the Afghan government. "I did come to the conclusion that it had not been such a good idea to kill Amin and that he was much more useful alive than dead. Someone you could negotiate with," Semple told me.

Being a Taliban "rational actor" in Afghanistan in 2010 was one quick way of climbing up the Joint Prioritized Effects List, which was numbered in order of priority. Meanwhile, despite what might seem to be Semple's conclusive evidence that Mohammed Amin was alive and well, the military continued to insist they had "iron clad proof" that they had killed Amin but could not divulge what it was for fear of revealing "sensitive intelligence methods." "On September 2, coalition forces did kill the targeted individual, Mohammed Amin, also known as Zabet Amanullah," NATO spokesman Lieutenant Colonel John Dorrian told NPR in May 2011. "In this operation, multiple sources of intelligence confirm that coalition forces targeted the correct person." Naturally, like any bureaucracy, the military is loath to admit mistakes, especially the secretive Joint Special Operations Command, with its useful cloak of mystery and omniscience.

However, it is quite possible that, beyond covering their collective behinds, the people who told Dorrian what to say and those who briefed Petraeus and Defense Secretary Gates did believe that all truth was contained in the plasma screens depicting that fatal SIM card's movements. As we have seen, there is a recurrent pattern in which people become transfixed by what is on the screen, seeing what they want to see, especially when the screen—with a resolution equal to the legal definition of blindness for drivers—is representing people and events thousands of miles and several continents away. (It is not clear where, or in how many "nodes," the analysis of Amin/Amanullah's movements was made. It would certainly have been easier to ignore common sense if the fatal conclusions were being drawn at some distant point in the network.)

It had happened in Uruzgan in February 2010, when a Predator pilot in Nevada interpreted spots on a screen captured by an infrared camera fourteen thousand feet over Afghanistan as people praying, causing him to identify them as Taliban and therefore legitimate targets, while another, more open-minded observer, reviewing the same video concluded that the people in question "could just as easily be taking a piss." Following Operation Anaconda, in February 2002, Special Operations commanders on an island off Oman, a thousand miles away from the battlefield, reviewed Predator video and thankfully concluded that one of their men that they had fought to rescue from an enemy-held mountaintop had died a heroic death, whereas in fact it was another American soldier, wounded and left for dead, who had fought on alone.

Some among the military are aware of the problem and strive to resist it. A-10 attack planes, for example, are, as noted, designed to afford the pilots the best possible direct view of the ground through their canopies. They do also carry video screens on their dashboards displaying infrared or daylight images from a camera-pod under the plane's wing, but the pilots are trained to treat these as very much a secondary resource. "We call the screens 'face magnets,'" Lieutenant Colonel Billy Smith, a veteran A-10 combat pilot, told me. "They tend to suck your face into the cockpit so you don't pay attention to what's going on outside." Thus on May 26, 2012, a U.S. Air Force B-1 bomber, relying on a video image of the target (the weapons officer in a B-1 sits in an enclosed compartment with no view of the outside world), destroyed an Afghan farmer's compound in Paktia Province in the belief that it contained hostile Taliban endangering U.S. forces. Minutes before, two A-10 pilots had refused orders to bomb the same target because they had scrutinized it closely with the aid of binoculars and concluded, correctly, that it contained only a farm couple and their children. Seven people, including a ten-month-old baby, died under the B-1's multi-ton bomb load.

Neat computer-screen diagrams of Taliban or other insurgent networks based on the record of cell phone calls between their members can give a false impression of precision, making it all the easier to accept the impossible, such as the dual identity of Amin/Amanullah. The maze of ambiguous personal relationships based on shared histories, ancient enmities, and family and tribal ties in which Zabet Amanullah and Mohammed Amin moved would be impossible to reduce to a social-network chart, especially when based on imperfect intelligence. The imperfection was boosted by the policy of rounding up numbers of Afghans not because they were Taliban themselves but because they knew people who were. As Michael Semple remarked, many Afghans "have a few Taliban commander numbers saved in their mobile phone contacts" as a "survival mechanism." These phone contacts would go into the social-network database but not necessarily with any indication of what their relationships actually were. So anyone with a lot of calls to numbers associated with people already on the JPEL in their phone record was at severe risk of going on the list themselves.

The whole complex effort was strongly reminiscent of the Operational Net Assessment approach to warfare promoted by the net-centric warriors in the 1990s, the notion that thanks to sensor, computer, and communications technology, all sources of intelligence and analysis could be usefully fused into a war-winning "shared knowledge of the adversary, the environment, and ourselves," as an official manual put it. ONA was itself linked to the theories of effects-based operations (EBO), which, as we have seen, were defeated at the hands of Paul Van Riper in the Millennium Challenge war game. EBO had lost a little of its luster by the end of the decade, especially after General Mattis had banned the use of the term in his command in 2008. But the net-centric and target-list mind-set was very much alive, especially in the air force and in the rapidly expanding Special Operations Command. Stanley McChrystal himself, former chief of staff of Task Force 180, was fond of quoting (without attribution) the Rand pundit and netwar promoter John Arquilla's aphorism "it takes a network to defeat a network."

All of which leaves us with the question: What was the intended effect of the high-value-target kill/capture program in Afghanistan? Superficially, the object was straightforward and obvious: kill the enemy. Petraeus put it this way: "If you're trying to take down an insurgency, you take away its safe havens; you take away its leaders." In a slightly more detailed explanation, a lower-ranking official told me: "The intended effect was to disorganize the Taliban and put their leaders in fear, make them want to negotiate or surrender for fear of their lives. To put such a hurt on them that they would have to come to the negotiations table." Marine Major General Richard Mills evoked a bucolic note, declaring in May 2011 that the aim was to make the Taliban "go back to their old way of life and put the rifle down and pick up a spade."

The actual effects were certainly audible to anyone who heard Afghans expressing outrage at the violation of their homes by what some took to calling "the American Taliban," especially when they arrested or killed civilians with no connection to the insurgents. In August 2008, the United States had obligingly bombed a family memorial service in Azizabad, a village near Herat, on the basis of a malign tip-off from a family enemy that this gathering was a major Taliban get-together. At least ninety people were killed, including sixty children. In an infamous February 2010 incident in Gardez, south of Kabul, a JSOC raid killed seven people, including three women, a district attorney, and a police commander. In an attempt to cover up the fiasco once they realized their error, the elite commandos used their knives to cut the bullets out of the women's bodies and concocted a preposterous story about the women having been murdered by their own relatives in an "honor killing."

In the Gardez case, as in Azizabad, the botched intelligence came not from esoteric telephone intercepts and social-network analysis but from some local rival of the murdered family. The May 2012 B-1 strike in Paktia Province that deftly obliterated a family of seven was reportedly also prompted by malign intelligence from a local source. "The bottom line is we have been played like pawns in a very deliberate power-grab scheme by mafia-like warlords," an officer of great experience wrote me from Afghanistan in a bitter email in 2013 referencing such bloody mishaps. "It is like watching a gang war unfold between the Bloods, Crips, Hells Angels, Aryan Nation, etc., . . . and we are prosecuting targets in support of all four gangs. Why? Because we like prosecuting targets as a military. It briefs well. And good briefs = good reputations = good career opportunities. Also, we like people who like us."

Whether people were being killed as a result of these malign power plays or misplaced faith in technical intelligence, the United States paid a price with the civilian population. One measure of the cost to the overall U.S. war effort of the obsessive targeting of Taliban "leaders and facilitators" was unearthed by historian Gareth Porter, who noted a direct correlation between a stepped-up rate of raids in Kandahar Province in southern Afghanistan and the number of homemade road-side bombs reported by locals to the American forces. The turn-in rate had been averaging 3.5 percent between November 2009 and March 2010, according to the Joint IED Defeat Organization, which kept track of such matters. But as the Special Operations forces began their onslaught in Kandahar, the percentage of bombs voluntarily reported by locals fell like a stone to 1.5 percent and stayed at that level.

Clearly, the high-value targeting was counterproductive in terms of winning hearts and minds among the Afghan population, especially in view of the large number of innocents who were gunned down or blown apart. But the campaign did succeed in killing a large number of intended targets. Unfortunately these victims were less likely to be senior Taliban leaders, who for the most part survived in sheltered safety in Pakistan, unmolested by the CIA's drone campaign, and much more likely to be lower-level provincial and district commanders. These were indeed slaughtered in large numbers, either by air strikes of the kind that dispatched Zabet Amanullah or by ground assaults by the Navy Special Warfare Development Group (DEVGRU), formerly Seal Team 6, and other Special Operations units. In a series of media interviews in August 2010, for example, Petraeus claimed that in almost 3,000 night raids over 90 days between May and July that year, no less than 365 "insurgent leaders" had been killed or captured, 1,355 Taliban "rank and file" fighters captured, and 1,031 killed. Leaving aside the number of innocent civilians represented in those fig-ures (20 dead for every insurgent leader killed in July 2010, for example), there was clearly a high Taliban loss rate as a result of the escalating campaign. In the northern Afghanistan province of Kunduz, Task Force 373 began a sustained campaign against the Taliban in December 2009. Up until that point the enemy leadership there had been left entirely unmolested by SOF and had become used to the idea that they were invulnerable in their well-guarded compounds. But by the following fall, two successive generations of leaders had been eliminated, and the third was uneasily taking office. By October, seventeen commanders had been killed.

Special Operations had achieved similar results in Iraq, wiping out hundreds of insurgents thanks to McChrystal's "industrial counterterrorism." But, as we have seen, the *effects* of the operations were not necessarily as advertised. Rivolo's analysis of 200 high-value-target eliminations had demonstrated that dead or captured Taliban commanders were quickly replaced, almost invariably by someone more aggressive. Just as in Iraq, the insurgency did not "fold in on itself," despite claims to the contrary from U.S. headquarters. The presumed objective of the campaign was to make the Taliban less effective as a fighting force, but apart from occasional disruptions, there was little sign of this happening. Squadron Leader Keith Dear, a British military intelligence officer who later commanded the Operational Intelligence Support Group at NATO headquarters in Kabul, wrote in 2011: "the Taliban . . . today conduct attacks as complex, if not more so, than ever before, and continue to show the capability to coordinate and conduct attacks across a wide geographic area simultaneously." Meanwhile, two years of the targeted-killing campaign had cost the Taliban in many parts of Afghanistan an entire generation of leaders. In many cases, the dead men were locally born and bred, and had ties to their communities; the new commanders, however, often tended to be outsiders appointed by the leadership in Pakistan. They were also younger: Task Force 373's 2010 campaign in the north reduced the average age of commanders from thirty-five to twenty-five. A twelve-month onslaught in Helmand had similarly brought the average age down by May 2011 from thirty-five to twenty-three. "The Taliban leadership in 2011 is younger, more radical, more violent and less discriminate than in 2001, because of targeted killing," Squadron Leader Dear bluntly concluded. "This new in-country leadership has increasingly adopted Al Qaeda's terrorist tactics and have deeper links with Al Qaeda than their predecessors."

It appeared that the equation Rivolo had discerned years before with regard to the narcotics business—that targeted killing had little effect on a leadership impervious to risk—still held true in Afghanistan, as it had in Iraq. The young fighters taking command were very unlikely to "pick up a spade." Most of them had been fighting their entire adult lives. "This is Juma Khan, one of our distinguished commanders," a Taliban commander named Khalid Amin, recently promoted from foot soldier following the deaths of two predecessors, explained as he guided a visiting film crew around a Taliban cemetery in Baghlan Province in 2011. "He was killed on the front line. This is Maulvi Jabar, our district chief. He was killed with 30 others in a night raid. When he died, the enemy said the Taliban was finished here. But three months later, our Islamic emirate is still strong. We have many more fighters than back then. . . . These night raids cannot annihilate us. We want to die anyway, so those destined for martyrdom will die in the raids and the rest will continue to fight without fear."

"That's why the Special Forces guys call it 'mowing the grass,'" Matthew Hoh, who resigned his foreign-service position in Afghanistan in protest at the futility of the war, told me. "They know that the dead leaders will just be replaced."

A marine officer who served two tours in the lethally dangerous neighborhood of Sangin, in northern Helmand Province, gave me a powerful analogy during a long discussion on the drawbacks of high-value targeting. "Insurgencies are like a starfish," he said thoughtfully. "You cut off one of the legs of a starfish and within weeks it can regrow and become more resilient and be smarter about defending itself. I saw multiple Taliban commanders come in and out. The turnover rate was cyclic. So even if I kill one, it only took two weeks before the next guy came in. They didn't miss a beat. You replace one guy, chances are the guy that's coming in is more lethal, has less restraint and is more apt to make a name for himself and go above and beyond than if you had just left the first guy in there.

"The commander down here [Sangin] when I first got there had been around for years. He had become one of the water-walkers among the Taliban community, very popular amongst the people. We picked him off in an air strike with a group of ten on the other side of the Helmand River one day, standing around with their AK-47s planning their next operation. There was a good three-week period where nothing happened. It was eerie. But then we started to see some outside influence, maybe from Pakistan. The new commander was either taken from a different region and put in here, or a younger guy who was promoted and brought up to speed, he was more aggressive more radical, more ready to prove himself worthy. The amount of pressure plate IEDs [which go off when anyone steps on them] increased exponentially, to where little kids started to hit them. He wasn't even letting the population know where they were, and while that was good for us because I could leverage the population that this young immature commander was more deadly to them than he was to me, it showed me that targeting these leaders made the problem ten times worse overall."

My friend, a remarkable officer who actually managed to suppress the Taliban in his particular area by the end of his first tour in 2012, thought that making the enemy even more vicious and unpleasant than they already were was ultimately unproductive. But strange rumors, based on off-the-record conversations with military officers and Special Forces officers out in the field, were circulating that making the Taliban *even more cruel* might actually be official policy. If so, it certainly succeeded. By 2011 the Taliban were deploying eight-year-old children as involuntary suicide bombers, while in May 2014, a small group of young Taliban gunmen stormed a Kabul hotel and executed nine people in the restaurant. Three of the victims were children, including a two-year-old, shot in the face.

Among COIN (counterinsurgency) theoreticians, then ascendant in the U.S. Army, the rise of the young commanders was seen as a positive development. "That's a win for us," John Nagl, a former army officer and the coauthor of the U.S. Army's counterinsurgency manual, told me. "We want to see younger commanders take over. They have less experience, they're more inclined to mess up." In fact, young men such as Khalid Amin, who had declared "we all want to die," had a great deal of experience despite their tender years, having never known any life but war. Nor did it require a great deal of expertise to construct a $10 pressure-plate IED.

It is possible, however, that there was indeed an underlying Machiavellian element to the targeted-killing strategy: actually to encourage the already cruel Taliban to become even more vicious and barbaric. The rationale, so Special Operations officers would explain in discreet off-the-record conversations, was based on the success of the Iraq surge. The key development of that operation had been the pivot of the Sunni population, or at least their tribal leaders, from insurgency to support of the occupation forces, a development attributed to the adoption of COIN as a doctrine, not to mention the strategic genius of those who had introduced it. Hugely important in inducing the Sunnis' change of heart, along with wads of cash handed to tribal leaders, had been their revulsion at the arrogance and cruelty of al-Qaeda in the areas where it had come to dominate, such as attempts in the al-Adhamiya district of Baghdad in 2006–2007 to force each family to give up a son as an al-Qaeda recruit or the shooting of barbers for giving un-Islamic haircuts, not to mention cutting off the fingers of smokers.

The triumph of the surge, which put a welcome gloss on the overall disaster of the invasion and occupation, was still very fresh in the minds of the U.S. national security establishment, particularly the army, when attention began shifting to Afghanistan in 2008. If the increased unpopularity of al-Qaeda had led to its defeat in Iraq, so, the thinking reportedly went, what was needed in Afghanistan was a really unpopular, "radicalized" Taliban, to be generated by killing off the (slightly) more moderate field commanders. Thereby afflicted, the population would, hopefully, rally to the Americans, or at least to the government of Hamid Karzai. In other words, eliminating Taliban leaders and other supposedly key individuals across the length and breadth of Afghanistan was not merely mindless slaughter but an *effects-based operation*.

Colonel Gian Gentile, the Iraq combat veteran and former West Point history professor known for his pungent critiques of COIN and its practitioners, thought that the scheme, of which he had no personal knowledge, sounded "like the typical pop sociological/anthropological nonsense and over thinking that many army officers have gotten themselves into. It also might indicate a rabid belief that the Iraq Surge could be made to work in Afghanistan along with its techniques and methods. "It just shows you," he lamented to me in an email, "how far off the deep end the American army has gone."

Dr. Peter Lavoy is one of the little-known but dependable officials who keep the wheels of the U.S. national security machine in motion. Deemed an expert in such recondite subjects as the use of biological and nuclear weapons and asymmetric warfare, he rose steadily through the ranks of intelligence and into the wider realm of policy making. By 2008 he was national intelligence officer for South Asia in the Office of the Director of National Intelligence and as such was delegated to brief NATO allies on the U.S. intelligence assessment of the security situation in Afghanistan, which he described as "bleak," according to the record of his November 25 address that year, classified "Secret" but subsequently released by Wikileaks.

The Taliban, said Lavoy, were making significant gains. Attacks were up 40 percent in a year, largely thanks to the failure of the Afghan government to deliver any services to the rural population while the Taliban were "mediating local disputes . . . offering the population at least an elementary level of access to justice." In conclusion, he told the NATO meeting, "[T]he international community should put intense pressure on the Taliban in 2009 *in order to bring out their more violent and ideologically radical tendencies* (author's emphasis). This will alienate the population and give us an opportunity to separate the Taliban from the population."

Many greet the notion that U.S. policy makers and commanders would have been capable of thinking through second-order effects in this fashion with unbridled skepticism. Matthew Hoh, the state department official who gave up his career in protest of the Afghan war, told me that he had indeed heard about this plan but not until *after* targeted killing had the effect of radicalizing the Taliban. "I simply doubt our ability to be that prescient and competent," he told me. "I haven't seen it in other situations and I don't see it here. I think this is, by and large, people and agencies trying to take credit for an unintended consequence."

An officer serving in Afghanistan in 2014 had much the same reaction. "I don't think that it was (or currently is) a 'strategy' across the board," he wrote me. "I have yet to see one of those out here. No part of my 'welcome aboard' to Afghanistan included a history/analysis of the area . . . to include sources of instability and power players. At no time was I told 'the strategy is to isolate X, while infiltrating Y and containing Z.' Is that an effects-based strategy? Only if the effect you want is to generate chaos."

But generating chaos can be a hard habit to break.

# 12

# DRONES, BABY, DRONES!

The Richard M. Helms Award dinner, held annually at a major Washington hotel, is among the highlights of the intelligence community's social calendar. Hosted by the CIA Officers Memorial Foundation, the event raises and distributes money to aid families of officers killed in action, whose sacrifice is commemorated in the rows of stars carved into the wall of the foyer at agency headquarters in Langley, Virginia. The venue for the 2011 event, held on March 30, was the Ritz-Carlton Hotel, Pentagon City, and as usual it attracted hundreds of intelligence luminaries, current and former. Joining them were senior executives of various defense corporations—Lockheed, SAIC, Booz Allen, General Atomics, and others—who had generously sponsored tables at the event.

There was much to celebrate. President Barack Obama, who had run a quasi-antiwar liberal campaign for the White House, had embraced the assassination program and had decreed, "the CIA gets what it wants." Intelligence budgets were maintaining the steep upward curve that had started in 2001, and while all agencies were benefiting, none had done as well as the CIA. At just under $15 billion, the agency's budget had climbed by 56 percent just since 2004.

Decades earlier, Richard Helms, the CIA director for whom the event was named, would customarily refer to the defense contractors who pressured him to spend his budget on their wares as "those bastards." Such disdain for commerce in the world of spooks was now long gone, as demonstrated by the corporate sponsorship of the tables jammed into the Grand Ballroom that evening. The executives, many of whom had passed through the revolving door from government service, were there to rub shoulders with old friends and current partners. "It was totally garish," one attendee told me afterward. "It seemed like every arms manufacturer in the country had taken a table. Everyone was doing business, right and left."

In the decade since 9/11, the CIA had been regularly blighted by scandal—revelations of torture, renditions, secret "black site" prisons, bogus intelligence justifying the invasion of Iraq, ignored signs of the impending 9/11 attacks—but such unwholesome realities found no echo in this comradely gathering. Even George Tenet, the CIA director who had presided over all of the aforementioned scandals, was greeted with heartfelt affection by erstwhile colleagues as he, along with almost every other living former CIA director, stood to be introduced by Master of Ceremonies John McLaughlin, a former deputy director himself deeply complicit in the Iraq fiasco. Each, with the exception of Stansfield Turner (still bitterly resented for downsizing the agency post-Vietnam), received ringing applause, but none more than the night's honoree, former CIA director and then-current secretary of defense Robert M. Gates.

Although Gates had left the CIA eighteen years before, he was very much the father figure of the institution and a mentor to the intelligence chieftains, active and retired, who cheered him so fervently that night at the Ritz-Carlton. He had climbed through the ranks of the national security bureaucracy with a ruthless determination all too evident to those around him. Ray McGovern, his supervisor in his first agency post, as an analyst with the intelligence directorate's soviet foreign policy branch, recalls writing in an efficiency report that the young man's "evident and all-consuming ambition is a disruptive influence in the branch." There had come a brief check on his rise to power when his involvement in the Iran-Contra imbroglio cratered an initial attempt to win confirmation as CIA director, but success came a few years later, in 1991, despite vehement protests from former colleagues over his persistent willingness to sacrifice analytic objectivity to the political convenience of his masters.

Gates' successful 1991 confirmation as CIA chief owed much, so colleagues assessed, to diligent work behind the scenes on the part of the Senate Intelligence Committee's staff director, George Tenet. In 1993, Tenet moved on to be director for intelligence programs on the Clinton White House national security staff, in which capacity he came to know and esteem John Brennan, a midlevel and hitherto undistinguished CIA analyst assigned to brief White House staffers. Tenet liked Brennan so much that when he himself moved to the CIA as deputy director in 1995, he had the briefer appointed station chief in Riyadh, an important position normally reserved for someone with actual operational experience. In this sensitive post Brennan worked tirelessly to avoid irritating his Saudi hosts, showing reluctance, for example, to press them for Osama bin Laden's biographical details when asked to do so by the bin Laden unit back at headquarters.

Brennan returned to Washington in 1999 under Tenet's patronage, initially as his chief of staff and then as CIA executive director, and by 2003 he had transitioned to the burgeoning field of intelligence fusion bureaucracy. The notion that the way to avert miscommunication between intelligence bureaucracies was to create yet more layers of bureaucracy was popular in Washington in the aftermath of 9/11. One concrete expression of this trend was the Terrorist Threat Integration Center, known as T-TIC and then renamed the National Counterterrorism Center a year later. Brennan was the first head of T-TIC, distinguishing himself in catering to the abiding paranoia of the times. On one occasion, notorious within the community, he circulated an urgent report that al-Qaeda was encrypting targeting information for terrorist attacks in the broadcasts of the al-Jazeera TV network, thereby generating an "orange" alert and the cancellation of dozens of international flights. The initiative was greeted with malicious amusement over at the CIA's own Counterterrorism Center, whose chief at the time, José Rodríguez, later opined that Brennan had been trying to build up his profile with higher authority. "Brennan was a major factor in keeping [the al-Jazeera/al-Qaeda story] alive. We thought it was ridiculous," he told a reporter. "My own view is he saw this, he took this, as a way to have relevance, to take something to the White House." Tellingly, an Obama White House spokesman later excused Brennan's behavior on the grounds that though he had circulated the report, he hadn't believed it himself.

Exiting government service in 2005, Brennan spent the next three years heading The Analysis Corporation, an obscure but profitable intelligence contractor engaged in preparing terrorist watch lists for the government, work for which he was paid $763,000 in 2008. Among the useful relationships he had cultivated over the years was well-connected Democrat Anthony Lake, a former national security adviser to Bill Clinton, who recommended him to presidential candidate Barack Obama. Meeting for the first time shortly after Obama's election victory, the pair bonded immediately, with Obama "finishing Brennan's sentences," by one account. Among their points of wholehearted agreement was the merit of a surgical approach to terrorist threats, the "need to target the metastasizing disease without destroying the surrounding tissue," as Brennan put it, for which drones and their Hellfire missiles seemed the ideal tools. Obama was initially balked in his desire to make Brennan CIA director because of the latter's all-too-close association with the agency's torture program, so instead the new president made him his assistant for counterterrorism and homeland security, with an office down the hall from the Oval Office. Two years into the administration, everyone in the Ritz-Carlton ballroom knew that the bulky Irishman was the most powerful man in U.S. intelligence as the custodian of the president's kill list, on which the chief executive and former constitutional law professor insisted on reserving the last word, making his final selections for execution at regularly scheduled Tuesday afternoon meetings. "You know, our president has his brutal side," a CIA source cognizant of Obama's involvement observed to me at the time.

Now, along with the other six hundred diners at the Helms dinner, Brennan listened attentively as Gates rose to accept the coveted award for "exemplary service to the nation and the Central Intelligence Agency." After paying due tribute to previous honorees as well as his pride in being part of the CIA "family," Gates spoke movingly of a recent and particularly tragic instance of CIA sacrifice, the seven men and women killed by a suicide bomber at an agency base, Forward Operating Base Chapman, in Khost, Afghanistan, in 2009. All present bowed their heads in silent tribute.

Gates then moved on to a more upbeat topic. When first he arrived at the Pentagon in 2007, he said, he had found deep-rooted resistance to "new technology" among "flyboys with silk scarves" still wedded to venerable traditions of fighter-plane combat. But all that, he informed his rapt audience, had changed. Factories were working "day and night, day and night," to turn out the vital weapons for the fight against terrorism. "So from now on," he concluded, his voice rising, "the watchword is: drones, baby, drones!"

The applause was long and loud.

Far away in a town in northwest Pakistan, two craters in a bus depot, some ruined buildings scorched by fire, and several dozen fresh graves in the neighborhood gave concrete illustration to Gates' theme. Two weeks before, the leading lights of the district of Datta Khel, a scattered community on the edge of hills running to the Afghan border a few miles away, had met in a *jirga*, a community meeting to settle a thorny issue concerning mineral rights. A tribal elder, Malik Dawood, had recently bought the rights to harvest a large tract of oak trees. But while doing this he had noticed that the land contained chromite, used in making stainless steel and chrome and about the only natural resource in this poverty-stricken region, where annual income averages $250. Now he was in dispute with the owner of the land over his right to mine it. As is the custom in Pashtun culture, the dispute would be hashed out in two days of discussion among the local elders, most of whom were appointed and paid by the Pakistani government, which endorsed and supported the jirga system. Although the ominous buzz of drones was always in the air, the men had been confident enough of their innocent intent to notify the local army commander, Brigadier Abdullah Dogar, about the meeting well ahead of time. However, the land in question was in an area controlled by the Pakistani Taliban, who could therefore enforce whatever decision was reached at the jirga, and so four of them had been invited to the meeting.

Some of the tribesmen making their way on the morning of March 17, 2011, to the Nomada bus depot, an open space next to the bazaar in Datta Khel where the meeting was to be held, might have been dimly aware of events the day before in a courtroom in Lahore, several hundred miles to the east. None of them could have known about a related argument being waged over secure communications between the U.S. embassy in Islamabad and CIA headquarters in Langley, Virginia. But the consequences of that argument would cost most of them their lives.

In Lahore, a burly American named Raymond Davis had been brought to trial for shooting and killing two men the previous January. Davis, a former Special Forces soldier inhabiting the murky world of public/private intelligence that had metastasized since 9/11, was under contract by the CIA (under diplomatic cover) to spy on the Pakistani government–sponsored Lashkar-e-Taiba terrorist group in Lahore, in which capacity he had gunned down the two men under circumstances that remain obscure. The killing had generated outrage across Pakistan, exacerbated as far as the government and the powerful military ISI spy agency were concerned by CIA Director Leon Panetta's straightforward lies regarding his agency's connection to Davis. Davis had seemed ripe for the gallows until a quiet deal negotiated by U.S. Ambassador Cameron Munter had secured "forgiveness" by his victims' relatives in a dramatic courtroom scene, in return for CIA payments totaling $2.34 million in *diyat*, blood money.

The CIA, already bitter at the Pakistanis for keeping Davis in prison for seven weeks, hated having to agree to the deal. Now, with their man safely out of the country, the agency was determined to demonstrate their anger by launching a convincing drone strike. The man they selected to kill was Sherabat Khan Wazir, a commander in what Pakistani intelligence deemed the "good" Taliban because they focused their energies on fighting the Americans across the border in Afghanistan, while maintaining cordial relations with the government and military in Islamabad. Targeting an important Pakistani ally would be satisfactory payback for the humiliation of Davis' incarceration, not to mention the $2.34 million. "It was in retaliation for Davis," a U.S. diplomat told AP reporter Kathy Gannon. "The CIA was angry."

Ambassador Munter thought this was a terrible idea and said so in an urgent cable to the State Department in Washington, which relayed his plea to CIA Director Leon Panetta. Panetta, a career politician and part-time walnut farmer appointed CIA chief by Obama in 2009, had become instantly partisan on behalf of the institution. "He embraced [the institution] with both arms," an official with whom he worked closely told me. Panetta straightforwardly rejected Munter's advice. Brennan, the ultimate controlling authority for CIA strikes, did not intervene.

So, when Sherabat climbed into a car with three of his followers on the morning of March 17 and set off for the jirga, he was under the scrutiny of at least two CIA drones. It would have been feasible to strike the car while en route, and indeed this was a routine drone strike tactic. Just six days earlier, for example, there had been two separate attacks on two cars, one of which had employed another favored CIA drone tactic, the "double tap," in which a second missile is reserved for rescuers, and had killed eight people. But the targeters at Langley and the pilots in Nevada (CIA drones are flown by air force personnel at Creech Air Force Base) held off. They were awaiting a more lucrative target—the crowd of men converging on the bus depot to which the car was headed. After all, it was an established point of drone-strike doctrine that any "military aged male" (from thirteen up) in the company of terrorists could themselves be deemed a terrorist in the absence of explicit intelligence to the contrary.

Finally, sometime after 10:00 a.m., the Taliban contingent arrived, and the meeting began. About forty-five men were sitting in two circles twenty feet apart. They must have made an inviting target, for the two impact craters left in the rocky ground of the bus parking lot from the Hellfire missiles that began landing around 10:45 appear to have been in the center of those circles. The blasts were especially lethal, thanks to the pieces of rock flung up by the blasts. Given the sixty-foot blast radius of a Hellfire, it is hard to see how anyone at the meeting could have survived. One gray-haired elder, Ahmed Jan, who was thrown twenty feet and knocked unconscious, later recalled the hissing sound the first missile had made as it zeroed in. A local man who arrived at the scene a few minutes after the blasts described later how "the tribal elders killed in the blast could not be identified because there were body parts strewn about. The smell was awful." The buildings bordering the area continued to burn for two days.

Subsequent investigations by journalists and human rights organizations indicate that forty-four people, one of them possibly a child, died in the strike. There was an immediate and unusually furious reaction from Pakistani leaders. General Ashfaq Kayani, the all-powerful army chief, announced that the jirga had been "carelessly and callously targeted with complete disregard to human life." The country's foreign office called it "not only unacceptable but also a flagrant violation of all humanitarian rules and norms," while the local governor called the dead "martyrs." The particular vehemence of the protests led some on the American side to believe that they had killed more than just elders and a few Taliban. "From the body language [of senior Pakistani commanders] I concluded there had been ISI people at that meeting," one official told me.

The United States, however, was and remains adamant that every single one of the victims deserved his fate. As one U.S. government official explained, the group targeted was heavily armed, some of its members were connected to al-Qaeda, and all 'acted in a manner consistent with AQ [al-Qaeda]-linked militants.'" "These guys were terrorists, not the local men's glee club," another declared confidently. But researchers for the Stanford and New York University Law School, after conducting in-depth interviews with witnesses, survivors, and family members, concluded that the victims had indeed been mostly civilians. A separate probe by the Associated Press came to the same conclusion, putting the number of dead at forty-four.

Drone partisans customarily hail the surgical precision of these weapons. But in terms of effects this strike was not surgical at all, cutting a wide and indiscriminate swath through local society. Most of the dead men were on the Pakistani government payroll as designated tribal leaders or auxiliary policemen. Their salaries supported extended families. Malik Daud Khan, for example, the man who convened the jirga, was an official liaison between the government and all the tribes of North Waziristan. His pay, considered adequate for a "decent family," supported not only his six sons but also the sons of his brothers. Another petty official, Ismail Khan, left behind a family of eight, only two of which were sons old enough to find work of any kind. Although the positions held by the dead men were now of course vacant, they were reserved, as officials in the region explained, for elders with "experience and years of wisdom," which their sons could not supply.

It had been the 202nd drone strike of the Obama presidency, the 248th (outside of Afghanistan) by the CIA since an agency-directed missile had hit a car in Marib, Yemen, on November 3, 2002, and killed six people, one of whom was an American. Much had changed since those early days, most fundamentally the acceptance by Americans that their premier intelligence agency's principal occupation had become assassination.

Allegedly, the CIA had entered reluctantly into the business. When presented with the tool of a Hellfire-armed Predator, George Tenet is said to have demurred, telling a National Security Council meeting that it would be a "terrible mistake" for the director of Central Intelligence to fire such a weapon and that it would happen only "over his dead body." Tenet, a deft bureaucratic politician, may have had in mind the political earthquake that hit the agency following the assassination program revelations of the 1970s. In any event, his rejection did not last long. "He was the Director of Central Intelligence, he could have refused to use it," a former senior agency official pointed out to me. "And if they had ordered him to do it, he could have quit."

Of course, Tenet did not quit. Soon, visiting dignitaries from friendly allied intelligence agencies were being treated to exclusive viewings of lethal drone strikes in Afghanistan at CIA headquarters. In the early years, when the strikes were almost entirely against targets in Afghanistan, the line between CIA and military operations was blurred. Thus it was a CIA-controlled Predator that the JSOC Task Force commanders in Oman used to try and run the firefight on Takur Gar Mountain during Operation Anaconda. This was in part due to the fact that two separate arms of the agency were vying for control of the new weapon. One was the Counterterrorism Center. The other was the Special Activities Division, the agency's paramilitary arm, whose personnel were largely drawn from the army or other of the military services. The division did not necessarily rank high in status among other elements of the intelligence community. "[They were] generally people who washed out from the military," sniffed one former senior official. "Knuckle-draggers," carped another. With such views circulating, it was not surprising that the Counterterrorism Center (CTC) emerged from the tussle with exclusive control of the Predator fleet.

Now that they owned the remote-killing weapon system, the agency had to gain waivers from target countries in order to use it. In 2004, when the CIA sought Pakistani permission to launch drone strikes in Pakistan, the price was the head of a militant young tribal strongman in Waziristan named Nek Muhammed Wazir who had infuriated the Pakistani military by repeatedly breaking truce agreements and humiliating forces sent to capture him—an early stage in the slow-burning Pashtun insurgency against Islamabad. Easily located thanks to his penchant for giving radio interviews via satellite phone, he was duly dispatched with a Hellfire on June 18, 2004, along with a number of fellow militants and two youths, aged sixteen and ten. By agreement, the Pakistanis took credit for the strike. Thereafter, the CIA was cleared to seek out victims but with restrictions. Only precisely identified high-value targets were to be hit, and there were to be no civilian casualties.

Compared to what was to come, strikes in the early years in Pakistan were few and far between, a mere eleven between 2004 and the beginning of 2008. Nor was the tally of high-value targets impressive: one in 2004 (Nek Muhammed), two the following year, and two the year after that. There were none in 2007. Civilians, on the other hand, fared less well, with as many as 121 civilians, 82 of whom were accounted for in a single misconceived attack in 2006 on a madrassa, a religious school, in the tribal areas of northwest Pakistan. In keeping with agreed procedure, both U.S. and Pakistani spokesmen lied briskly, denying any American involvement. "It was completely done by the Pakistani military," a U.S. military spokesman told reporters in Kabul, while a Pakistani Foreign Office spokesman claimed, "It is something that we have done and we have been doing for peace and security in our own region." Within a week, a suicide bomber struck at a Pakistani police barracks near Islamabad, killing 42 and wounding 20. It was a lesson to the Pakistani government that collusion with drone strikes could bring unpleasant aftereffects.

Meanwhile, despite the low-rate campaign, back at home the CIA was bolstering the assassination bureaucracy embedded in the Counterterrorism Center. As noted, the center, despite its lamentable performance prior to 9/11, had emerged from the disaster as "the most powerful institution in the country." Cofer Black, its director at the time of the attacks, had endeared himself to President Bush with macho boasts that the attackers would soon "have flies crawling across their eyeballs" as he supervised the CIA's descent into torture and rendition. His peers at the agency, concluding that Cofer was "out of control," as one recalled to me, hoped that appointing José Rodríguez, deemed to be "more responsible," as his deputy would compel some restraint on the theatrical Black. But Rodríguez, who took over as director when Black departed in 2002, was soon exhibiting the same behavior as Black, later becoming notorious as the principal apologist for torture. "Is Cofer some sort of vampire?" asked an exasperated senior official at the time. "Does he bite people and then they become like him?" Rodríguez was in turn succeeded in 2004 by a more polished agency veteran, Robert Grenier, who might be deemed an exception to the pattern since he was fired in 2006, reportedly for his opposition to prevailing policies on torture and rendition. But his opposition to torture was qualified. As he later wrote, ". . . the fact is that I supported continued use of harsh interrogation methods—notably excluding waterboarding" and cited "the clear effectiveness of our interrogation program." (He was writing as part of a concerted campaign by former senior officials to denounce and discredit the Senate Intelligence Committee's investigation of the CIA torture program.) "Grenier was never really against torture," one of his former colleagues remarked to me. "He just didn't think it was being done the right way."

The rapid turnover ended with Grenier's successor. Appointed in 2006, Mike D'Andrea stayed in the post for an unprecedented nine years. Unlike previous occupants, he chose to remain officially anonymous, meaning that the American public could not know who was assassinating people in their name. Notoriously harsh on subordinates, D'Andrea lived a monkish existence, rarely leaving his office, even to sleep (he kept a foldaway bed there), except to smoke in the courtyard. He retained the Shia faith adopted on his marriage to a Shia during an overseas posting earlier in his career. "As I understand it, she was pretty relaxed about the rules on alcohol and so on," a former colleague recalled. "But he takes them more seriously than she ever did."

By common agreement among insiders, he was the unrelenting champion of the drone assassination program, successfully quashing any and all attempts to restrain it. His immense power rested in large part on his skills as a political operator, which enabled him to survive attempts by various CIA directors under whom he served to dismiss him. "They've tried several times," a former senior agency official who worked with D'Andrea told me. "But each time he goes to his allies in the White House and Capitol Hill, and it stops."

"I've had a lot of run-ins with the CIA; most of their people are pretty reasonable to deal with," a former State Department official told me. "But not that guy. He's scary."

At a time when America's drone war generated ever-mounting comment and condemnation, very few people outside the innermost circles of the counterterrorist bureaucracy understood that the war was being directed by this strange, devout recluse, his influence indirectly reflected in headlines and graveyards far from Washington.

By 2011 the Counterterrorism Center accounted for 10 percent of the agency's entire workforce and occupied a large portion of available floor space at CIA headquarters, including a whole department assigned specifically to Pakistan and Afghanistan. (For public consumption, Alec Station, the unit set up in 1996 to hunt Osama bin Laden, was abolished in 2006. In fact, it was merely renamed but still dedicated to the pursuit of the number-one target.)

Most significantly, one in every five of the agency's intelligence analysts was now a targeter. Setting this development in stone in 2006, the agency designated targeting as a distinct career track, meaning that employees could garner raises and promotions without ever leaving the targeting field. This specialty had originally been conceived as devoted to the recruitment of agents. "There was an acronym we used," a former agency official who helped develop the program told me. "'SPADR,' which stood for Spot, Assess, Develop, Recruit. We spent years getting the bureaucracy to approve it as a career track, and it came in just in time when we needed people to spot targets for strikes. It was the same skills. We're not thinking about bloodthirsty butchers," he cautioned, "these were ordinary people, soccer moms, who would come in to work on their vacations because they felt they were 'saving lives.'"

The budget for this inexorably expanding machine was a closely held secret, but by comparison, the FBI's spending for counterterrorist operations in 2010 was $3.1 billion. Naturally, a multibillion-dollar budget needed more than two or three strikes a year in end results, but with irksome restrictions on hitting only clearly identified high-value targets, not to mention avoiding civilians, this would be hard to achieve. So it was in July 2008 that CIA Director Michael Hayden, a former air force intelligence general who came to the agency after heading NSA, went to the White House to make the case for a little loosening of the rules, as forcefully demanded by D'Andrea, the powerful counterterror chief. With him went his deputy, Stephen Kappes.

The pair knew just which buttons to press. Al-Qaeda, they told President Bush and his senior national security staff, had regrouped and was massing in the lawless frontier of northwest Pakistan. Despite the isolation of their lair, the "network" was weaving plots to strike across the globe. "After the next attack," warned Hayden, "knowing what we know now, there's no explaining it if we don't do something." Recounting his triumph afterward, the spy chief explained how he and Kappes "kept building and building the case of the safe havens. They were coming at us. They were a threat to the homeland." In other words, as in every war since World War II—Korea, Vietnam, Iraq, Serbia—the target list had to be expanded, after which victory would be assured.

It was an easy sell. Bush rapidly agreed that henceforth the CIA could launch attacks with only the briefest warning to the Pakistanis. But Bush also gave his assent to an astonishingly far-reaching change. Henceforth, it would no longer be necessary to identify the target. Merely looking like a terrorist would be sufficient to trigger a strike. From now on, people could be killed on the basis of their behavior, as detected by various sensors: the unblinking eyes of the Predators and Reapers or the ears of the phone-monitoring networks of the NSA. Thus the notorious "signature strike" based on "patterns of life" was officially sanctified.

Forty years earlier, when Hayden had been a very junior air force officer, the targeters of Task Force Alpha had relied on sensors scattered throughout the Laotian jungles to detect patterns, such as a sequence of engine noises and slight earth movements that denoted an enemy truck convoy or urine smells and scattered conversations that might indicate a column of troops. After four decades the theater had shifted from dense jungle to the barren hills of the northwest frontier, but the concept was the same: a belief that enemy behavior was so well understood that the targeters knew what to look for, such as the unique features of an al-Qaeda convoy or a terrorist meeting or a particular pattern of phone calls. Once a telltale pattern was detected, the target could be destroyed without further investigation. As with the Predator pilot who thought that washing and praying at dawn was a sure Taliban giveaway, the accuracy of the pattern was all-important. Among the elements that could combine for a lethal signature was a man's mode of urinating. Someone informed the targeters that while Pashtun men urinate standing up, Arab men squat. This then became a means of identifying Arab al-Qaeda otherwise indistinguishable from their Pashtun colleagues and was duly incorporated in the targeting algorithms.

The immediate effects of Hayden's successful solicitation were dramatic. Drone strikes on the frontier took off, with thirty-two in the second half of 2009 alone. Then, as of January 20, 2009, a new commander in the drone wars appeared. Though the idealistic youths who had campaigned so hard for him in his presidential run may not have noticed, Barack Obama had quietly signaled early in his campaign that his view on high-value targeting was entirely orthodox. "It was a terrible mistake to fail to act when we had a chance to take out an al-Qaeda leadership meeting in 2005," he told a Washington think-tank audience in August 2007, referring to a planned SEAL commando raid on an alleged high-level enemy meeting in Waziristan, aborted at the last minute by Donald Rumsfeld. Interestingly, these bellicose remarks were guided by Richard Clarke, the Clinton-era "terror czar" who had lobbied forcefully for the development of the lethal Predator drone. Those national security insiders who took solace in the candidate's militant stance would not be disappointed.

On January 23, 2009, just three days after Obama was inaugurated, two separate drone strikes in North and South Waziristan authorized by the new president and relayed via John Brennan killed up to twenty-five people, including possibly as many as twenty civilians. Neither strike hit its intended high-value targets. The second killed a local elder and member of a progovernment peace committee named Malik Gukistan Khan along with four members of his family. Khan's brother later told human rights researchers from Columbia Law School, "We did nothing, have no connection to militants at all. Our family supported the government . . . no one has accepted responsibility for this incident so far." Some in Washington took a cynical view of the CIA's eagerness to involve the new president in a strike. "He's been blooded, just like you would a hunting dog," a former White House official remarked to me at the time. Afterward, when Hayden and Kappes explained the concept of a signature strike—targeting people who look like terrorists—to the chief executive, Obama reportedly snapped,

"That's not good enough for me." But he authorized them to continue all the same.

The strikes not only continued, they doubled and redoubled. There were 52 in all of 2009 and 128 in 2010. According to a rare outside observer, the *New York Times* journalist David Rhode, held hostage in North Waziristan between November 2008 and June 2009, life became "hell on earth." After 7 months in captivity, he recalled the terror of life under drones: "From the ground, it is impossible to determine who or what they are tracking as they circle overhead. The buzz of a distant propeller is a constant reminder of imminent death. Drones fire missiles that travel faster than the speed of sound. A drone's victim never hears the missile that kills him."

Under the onslaught, patterns of life began to change. People, for example, tried not to gather in large groups, fearful of displaying a potentially lethal signature. Following the attack on the jirga at Datta Khel, this form of community activity, integral to tribal culture, fell into disuse. Wedding parties, one of the few forms of social entertainment permitted in this straitlaced society, also disappeared. A relative of one of the March 17 victims later described how "We do not come out of our villages because it's very dangerous to go out anywhere. . . . In past we used to participate in activities like wedding gatherings [and] different kinds of jirgas, different kinds of funerals. . . . We used to go to different houses for condolences, and there were all kinds of activities in the past and we used to participate. But now it's a risk to go to any place or participate in any activities."

Back in Washington, the administration maintained stoutly that civilian casualties were nonexistent or minimal (though of course death by drone for a military-aged male brought involuntary posthumous enlistment, according to U.S. methodology, as a "militant"). No remotely objective tabulation of the civilian death count in the Obama years has suggested that the drones were killing more civilians than al-Qaeda or Taliban members, but the ordinary inhabitants in the kill zone of the tribal territories clearly understood that the strikes were not precise, that anyone could unwittingly display the wrong signature. Had the drones struck only "deserving" targets, innocents would have known that and gone happily to their neighbors' weddings and funerals without fear.

Drone partisans naturally hailed the universal precision of their weapons. As David Deptula said to me, "We can now hit any target anywhere in the world, any time, any weather, day or night." Strikes were certainly a perfect instrument of effects-based operations in removing the terrorists of various descriptions who lurked in the midst of tribal society. But the effects of hundreds of strikes, concentrated in an area the size of Maryland, were anything but precise. In fact, they devastated the life of the society as comprehensively as if it had been subjected to a World War II–style carpet bombing but in ways that would be invisible to distant spectators peering at their Predator feeds. Thus the "double-tap" tactic of reserving a second missile for rescuers converging to help victims of an initial strike put a crimp on the generosity of ordinary citizens, not to mention the Red Cross, which ordered its people to stay away from a house or car hit by drones for at least *six hours*. The sole survivor of Obama's first strike, a youth named Faheem Qureshi, felt that he survived only because he was able to walk out of the burning house on his own; none of his neighbors would have dared approach. Similarly, because there have been strikes on funerals, people are wary of funeral processions and other ceremonies of collective grieving. In a further general effect on the population at large, the cost of travel and shipping goods soared as truck and taxi drivers grew fearful of the risks of being hit on the road.

Meanwhile, the increased rate of drone strikes inside Pakistan from mid-2008 was not due solely to the advent of signature strikes. The growing scale of the Tehrik-i-Taliban—the Pakistani Taliban known as TTP—insurgency against the government in Islamabad encouraged the Pakistanis to solicit further U.S. help in eliminating their domestic enemies. In return, they were prepared to assist in targeting what they considered "good" Taliban groups that reserved their energies for attacking Americans in Afghanistan. At the same time, by dint of unstinting effort and large amounts of cash, the CIA had recruited agents among the tribal populations of Waziristan to assist them in nominating and locating targets. Combining traditional spy craft with modern technology, at least some of these agents were equipped with a geolocation device (really just a SIM card with a transmitter) that could be used by a drone for targeting purposes. Clearly, whoever possessed one of these devices held the power of life and death over anyone they chose. They could plant it in the home of an al-Qaeda terrorist or that of a neighbor with whom they were on bad terms. The drones need not discriminate. However many of the devices were actually deployed, their existence naturally induced paranoia among a population fearful that an argument over a broken fence or the price of a sheep might bring a missile down on their heads.

Quite apart from such neighborly differences, the empowerment of local agents to call in a strike put a powerful weapon in the hands of two rival tribes in Waziristan, the Mehsud and the Wazirs. The Mehsud, hailing from South Waziristan and so ferocious even by local standards that the British had dubbed them "wolves," fell into open warfare with the Pakistani state and pursued an unbridled campaign of bombings, shootings, and beheadings across the country in the name of the TTP. Meanwhile, their rivals, the Wazirs, in North Waziristan, were at peace with the Pakistani government and were primarily concerned with assisting their tribal brethren fighting the Americans across the border in Afghanistan. Thus the CIA targeters were less interested in the Mehsud, until, that is, a routine NSA phone intercept in May 2009 picked up someone discussing the fact that Baitullah Mehsud, the vicious, semiliterate, but capable thug who had created and led the TTP, had a nuclear weapon. When another conversation on the topic of Islamic doctrine regarding the use of such weapons surfaced, Washington went into (secret) convulsions. Even when it was concluded that the device was merely a "dirty bomb"—radioactive nuclear waste wrapped around explosives—the level of hysteria remained high. "We got played all the time," a former CIA operations officer told me. "All the other side had to do was to have a conversation on the phone talking in some kind of mysterious code about an upcoming 'wedding party' and we'd go on red alert."

Naturally, the Pakistani government was happy to encourage the newfound U.S. antipathy toward Baitullah Mehsud, who only two months before had attacked the Sri Lankan cricket team and a police academy in Lahore in retaliation, he announced, "for U.S. missile strikes off drones inside the Pakistan territory." A crafty initial attempt on June 23, 2009, to kill Mehsud by first killing a subordinate in the expectation he would attend the funeral, which was duly struck with three missiles, proved disappointing. Some sixty people were killed, including a number of children, but not Baitullah Mehsud. In August a second attempt that caught him on his roof having his feet massaged by his young wife proved more successful. Obama called the targeter to congratulate her.

Baitullah's successor as leader of the Pakistani Taliban was his charismatic and more capable cousin Hakimullah. Baitullah had been nurturing a Jordanian jihadi doctor and blogger named Humam Balawi, who had convinced Jordanian intelligence, and by extension the CIA, that he was a double agent prepared to spy on al-Qaeda, whereas his true loyalties remained fervently jihadist. The CIA at the highest levels, especially "Mike," was so excited by the possibility of finally having an agent inside the terrorist group, that the news was hurried all the way to the Oval Office. Their focus fixed on head-hunting rather than intelligence, the agency's most fervent desire was that Balawi would lead them to a really high-value target, Ayman al-Zawahiri, number two on the list after Osama bin Laden, whom they could thereupon locate and kill.

As related in Joby Warrick's gripping account of the Balawi affair, Baitullah had cunningly bolstered Balawi's credentials by having him notify the agency that the Taliban leader would be traveling in a particular car on a specific day. In reality the driver of the car, duly destroyed by a drone-launched missile, was a sacrificial lamb deployed by Mehsud to convince the Americans that Balawi was on the level. The scheme worked; excitement in Washington over this potentially priceless asset grew more fevered. Balawi was now tasked by Hakimullah, along with various al-Qaeda leaders lurking in the area, to manipulate the CIA into inviting him to meet them at their heavily guarded base at Khost, just inside the Afghan border, a way station for collecting human intelligence used to target drone strikes. Tragically, the plan succeeded. All normal security procedures were waived, and on

December 30, 2009, Balawi was welcomed to the base by a throng of CIA officers and contract employees, led by base commander Jennifer Matthews, a veteran of the CTC's Alec Station who had spent the intervening years trying to live down the unit's pre-9/11 errors. Unfortunately, Balawi was wearing a suicide vest packed with thirty pounds of C4 explosive provided by his real masters, which he detonated on arrival, immolating seven CIA personnel in a massive explosion.

The Mehsud clan and their al-Qaeda allies had extracted a bloody revenge for relatives and comrades blown apart by drones. The Khost attack was, by any standard, a very successful high-value targeting operation. Hakimullah proudly claimed credit for avenging cousin Baitullah, posting a video online of himself conferring with Balawi shortly before the bombing. But now they, too, would discover the inevitable result of a high-value target elimination as they themselves were subjected to a hail of Hellfires: eleven strikes over the next three weeks, killing at least sixty-two people. One attack in particular generated the highest hopes at Langley and the White House: a phone intercept had located Hakimullah Mehsud himself at an abandoned madrassa that was immediately attacked. Celebrations followed initial reports that Hakimullah had been struck down, but the intelligence was false. The Taliban leader had survived. A second attempt the following year also failed.

Whatever higher purpose they may have had in mind, and notwithstanding their futuristic apparatus of remote split operations, streaming infrared videos, and social-network analytics, the CIA's drone warriors were now embroiled in an old-fashioned tribal blood feud. In fact, given reports that the rival Mehsud and Wazir tribes were settling scores by identifying each other to the CIA as terrorist targets, the agency was being employed in more than one such feud. "It was like inmate politics," one official in close touch with the drone program commented to me, "gangs settling scores in the prison yard with knives."

The intense fusillade of drone-launched missiles continued, roughly 1 every 3 days in 2010 (117 overall), but drone strikes declined to half that rate in the following year. Confusingly, although the majority of strikes were now aimed at Pakistan's allies, the so-called good Taliban at peace with Islamabad while at war in Afghanistan, ISI (Pakistani military intelligence) claimed to a Western journalist in the spring of 2010 that they were supplying the targeting information for *all* drone strikes. In this Machiavellian environment, ISI, intent on regaining the control of Afghanistan it had lost in 2001, was playing a devious game. "Hitting the Haqqanis and other groups that were allied with Pakistan helped ISI keep them under control," a former adviser to the U.S. military commanders in Kabul pointed out to me. "They could tell them 'do what we want in Afghanistan, or we'll have the Americans drone you.'" Ahmed Wali Karzai, the Afghan president's brother, laid out the facts of life to a U.S. official in February 2010, according to a classified cable published by Wikileaks, telling him that "some Afghan (Taliban) commanders . . . are told by the Pakistanis that they must continue to fight or they will be turned over to the coalition."

On November 1, 2013, after another failed attempt, the CIA finally caught up with Hakimullah Mehsud, dispatching him with a drone strike. Though this was satisfying revenge for Khost, the killing also sabotaged nascent peace negotiations between the Pakistani Taliban and the Pakistani government, which had been due to start the following day. Among other "second-order effects," the killing increased the power of Mehsud's tribal rivals, the Haqqanis, the group that was busy spearheading the insurgency and killing Americans in eastern Afghanistan. It also goes without saying that the killing of Hakimullah yet again verified the rule that elimination of a high-value target leads to someone worse, since the next leader of the Pakistani Taliban was none other than Maulana Fazlullah, known locally as "Mullah Radio" for his use of that medium when pronouncing beheadings for sundry infractions of sharia law such as polio vaccinations. Fazlullah, furthermore, had commissioned the infamous shooting of fifteen-year-old schoolgirl Malala Yousafzai in response to her campaign for female education. Unfortunately, apart from his psychopathic zealotry, Fazlullah proved to be a capable and efficient commander, orchestrating further mayhem across Pakistan in revenge, he said, for Pakistani complicity in the U.S. strike on Hakimullah.

Amid the mayhem, President Obama still gamely insisted that the strikes had been "very precise precision [*sic*] strikes against al-Qaeda and their affiliates." Defense Secretary Leon Panetta echoed the sentiment, calling the drone strikes "the most precise campaign in the history of warfare." Two months after the strike on the Datta Khel jirga that killed over thirty civilians, John Brennan insisted that there had not been "a single collateral [civilian] death because of the exceptional precision of the capabilities we've been able to develop."

Sooner or later, U.S. officials and diplomats toiling to implement what they believed was American policy came to realize that there was really only one issue at stake: the domestic U.S. political fortunes of the Obama administration. "'No bombs on my watch,' that's all they wanted to be able to say," explained one former Obama White House official to me. "Drones were a cheap, politically painless way of dealing with that. No one even talked about it very much." Cameron Munter, ambassador to Pakistan from 2010 to 2012, recalled to me how, during visits to the region by a top White House official, an ardent drone champion, he would try and explain how there might be some political drawbacks in the drone campaign for the U.S. vis-à-vis Pakistan. "[The official] would look at me with a mixture of sympathy and pity, as if to say 'I understand U.S. domestic politics and you don't.'"

John Brennan did like to put a "strategic" gloss on the undertaking, explaining at meetings, according to the former White House official, how al-Qaeda was "like a table, and when you cut off the legs of a table, the table falls." Michael Morrell, the CIA's deputy and sometime acting director, on the other hand, appeared less interested in the theory of high-value targeting. Instead, he tended to wax emotional about the need to use the drones to help American troops fighting on the other side of the border. "He had religion on this," recalled the former official.

Despite Brennan's theorizing about table legs, the hard-and-fast arithmetic of the northwest frontier, as revealed in leaked intelligence numbers, suggested that the strikes, whomever they hit, were having little effect on the al-Qaeda leadership. In the years 2006 to 2008 and the 12 months from September 2010, a mere 6 senior al-Qaeda leaders were struck. Of the 482 people listed in the leaked assessments as killed, 265—over half—were categorized as "non–al-Qaeda," Afghan Taliban, Pakistani Taliban, and unknowns. Just under half of the total strikes were aimed at these non–al-Qaeda targets. The Haqqani network, Pakistan's friends fighting the Americans, got hit with 15 strikes, while their enemy, the TTP, who were generally fighting the Pakistanis, suffered 9 strikes. No one was quite sure how many civilians had died in the middle of all this or who should even be counted as a civilian. By 2012, for example, the CIA had clearance to treat armed men traveling by truck toward Pakistan, in a country where a gun is an article of clothing, as a "pattern of life" worthy of a lethal strike, the dead being counted as "militants." Nor could some civilian deaths ever be counted, given that Pashtun men consider it inappropriate for outsiders even to know of the existence, let alone the names, of women in their strictly segregated households. So near neighbors might not know how many women and female children could be lying under the rubble of a strike, doomed to be forever anonymous.

It is worth bearing in mind that Pakistan, in the form of its ISI intelligence agency, was the dominant influence on the Afghan Taliban, its proxies in the campaign to reacquire Pakistan's control of Afghanistan lost in 2001. The majority of CIA strikes in Pakistan were aimed not at the remaining senior al-Qaeda leadership lurking in Waziristan, who in any case had little capability to threaten U.S. interests, but at the Taliban, who were fighting and killing Americans in Afghanistan. However, drone strikes in Pakistan required the cooperation of the Pakistanis, not merely their permission to bomb their country without being shot down but also their intelligence help in finding targets.

Strikes on the Pakistani Taliban waging their war against the Pakistani state, largely stemming from the CIA's urge to settle scores in its feud, meanwhile engendered retaliatory attacks inside Pakistan. As security deteriorated in the politically fragile but nuclear-armed country, the danger that the militant Islamists might actually gain power and control of a nuclear arsenal became more real. Given that this was Washington's very worst nightmare, the CIA may not exactly have been acting in the U.S. national interest. "The drone campaign only makes sense," a former civilian adviser to the U.S. military command in Kabul remarked to me as we discussed this surreal scenario, "if you assume that the entire objective of the operation so far as the CIA was concerned was to continue the drone strikes. The operation became an end in itself." Given the burgeoning intelligence budgets, this was of course an entirely logical position from the agency's point of view.

Ironically, after years of experience in managing a remote-killing campaign that depended on questionable intelligence, involved allies who were themselves in an equivocal relationship with the targets, and caused extensive collateral damage while traumatizing an entire society, Washington moved to duplicate the effort elsewhere.

▸▸▸

The November 3, 2002, killing of Qa'id Salim Sinan al-Harithi, a leader of al-Qaeda in Yemen (and one of the reputed masterminds of the attack on the USS *Cole*), in Marib, a district about a hundred miles east of Yemen's capital Sana'a, by a drone-fired missile was notable on several accounts. It was the first assassination by drone in a country with which the United States was not at war (unlike the Afghan hits). In those more innocent days this was cause for shock to many people, including Asma Jahangir, the UN special rapporteur on extrajudicial, summary, or arbitrary executions, who thought the development "truly disturbing." Officially, the killing was entirely the work of the Yemeni government, but Deputy Defense Secretary Paul Wolfowitz bragged on CNN about a "very successful tactical operation" by the CIA. The strike also broke new ground, in that it was the first remote-control summary execution without trial of an American citizen. Kamal Derwish, from Buffalo, New York, Harithi's assistant, was riding in the car with him when the missile hit. In addition, coming a year and a half before the CIA obliged the Pakistanis by killing Nek Muhammed Wazir, it may also have been the first time a drone strike was put in service of local political machinations.

According to a cable later published by Wikileaks, Edmund Hull, the U.S. ambassador to Yemen, told a visiting human rights delegation that "the action was taken in full cooperation with the ROYG

[Republic of Yemen Government], against known al-Qaida operatives after previous attempts to apprehend the terrorists left eighteen Yemenis dead." That statement was true as far as it went, and Ambassador Hull may have sincerely believed that the Yemeni government had suffered heavy casualties while making a good-faith effort to arrest Harethi. But Yemenis versed in the labyrinthine and devious politics of their country knew better.

Ali Abdullah Saleh, Yemen's cunning and corrupt dictator since 1978, had long had an alliance of convenience with Yemeni Jihadis, a group nurtured by the Saudis and the CIA in the anti-Soviet Afghan war of the 1980s. They had provided crucial support for his crushing of South Yemeni independence in 1994, and remained an important if unacknowledged element of his ruling coalition, enjoying support and funds from Saudi Arabia. For example, Majeed al-Zindani, an extremist Yemeni cleric who had been Osama bin Laden's spiritual mentor and who exercised enormous influence in Yemen, including but not limited to supervision of the Yemeni school syllabus, had long enjoyed Saleh's favor and protection. (He has also laid claims to some striking scientific breakthroughs, including the discovery of cures for hepatitis and AIDS using "natural herbal compounds.") Though placed on the State Department's list of Designated Global Terrorists in 2004, Zindani lived openly in Sana'a as head of Imam University, which was founded with Yemeni government and Saudi financial support. Imam U. was the alma mater of, among others, the "American Taliban" John Walker Lindh. Anwar al-Awlaki, the Islamist cleric destined to be the second American citizen killed by a drone, was also on its faculty for a period. Zindani was a cofounder of the Islah party, the Islamist group headed by the tribal leader Sheikh Abdullah al-Ahmar, the second most powerful man in the country. These allies, and others of like mind, were key, in Saleh's view, to maintaining his grip on power and fending off the threat of secession by South Yemen, an independent Marxist state until 1990.

On the other hand, it was also important for Saleh to retain the support of Washington, which was anxious to see the al-Qaeda members in Yemen either in their graves or at least under lock and key.

Saleh's challenge therefore was to cooperate with the United States while avoiding any serious confrontation with al-Qaeda and thus remain in power and enlarge his already colossal fortune. (According to an eyewitness, Saleh, who was distrustful of banks, kept a large portion of his money in cash—hundreds of millions of dollars—stacked on pallets secreted in the basement of his palace.) When he had first seized power in a 1978 coup that followed several other short-lived coups, the expatriate community in Sana'a had held a sweepstake on how long he would last. The winning ticket had been "at least six weeks." Saleh's endurance was a tribute to his unscrupulous mastery of Yemeni tribal politics in all their infinite complexity.

On December 18, 2001, a force of Yemeni soldiers approached al-Hosun, a village in Marib Province, the reputed lair of al-Harithi, the al-Qaeda leader. But before they got anywhere near their target, the troops came under a hail of gunfire. Eighteen were killed and several wounded, the rest being surrounded and effectively held hostage until negotiations with local tribal sheikhs secured their release. Well-informed political sources in Sana'a told me on several occasions that there was more to the story than that, as is usually the case in Yemen. "Neither the military expedition nor the claim that they could not get al-Harithi can be taken at face value," I was told. "Saleh dispatched the military mission to al-Huson, and Shaykh al-Ahmar (Saleh's ally) sent his men to ambush the soldiers. When the soldiers got to al-Huson, they met no resistance at all. As they exited the town, there was a massive attack from the sand dunes just outside." Thus, by this account, Saleh could convincingly demonstrate to Washington that the wanted terrorists, despite his tireless efforts, were well out of his reach.

Following the successful al-Harithi strike, the skies of Yemen were quiet for several years. From Saleh's point of view they became perhaps a little too quiet, as a lull in al-Qaeda activity led to a cut in U.S. aid and irksome lectures from visiting officials about democracy and human rights. However, a reinvigoration of the jihadi group following a spectacular jailbreak in 2006 soon led to renewed attention and aid from Washington. Everyone in Sana'a assumed the escape had high-level clearance, part of Saleh's ongoing policy of making himself necessary to the United States while not directly antagonizing al-Qaeda. "They were supposed to have used forks to dig through sixty-centimeter-thick reinforced concrete," joked one local to me. "Imagine what they could have done with knives!" Nevertheless, with the unveiling of al-Qaeda in the Arabian Peninsula, a merger of Yemeni and Saudi groups in January 2009, Yemen attained the status of a terrorist hotbed with consequent prominence on the Washington radar screen. Ruled by a kleptocracy, mired in poverty, weak, and unimportant enough to be everybody's plaything, Yemenis were about to experience the full weight of twenty-first-century U.S. counterterrorism. Adding to their woes was the fact that manhunting rights in their country would be shared by two U.S. targeted-killing agencies, the CIA and the Joint Special Operations Command. While JSOC flew its drones out of the leased French base in Djibouti, across the Red Sea, the CIA built a special base in Saudi Arabia, close by the Yemeni border.

As drone strikes by one or the other of these agencies ramped up, from two in 2009 to four in 2010, ten in 2011, to forty-one in 2012, ordinary Yemenis would experience a lesson in drone warfare all too often lost on far-off officials who authorize the killings: though it may appear that drones offer a remote, sanitized mode of warfare, to their victims they are very much a local affair, a fact that was forcefully impressed on Jaber al-Shabwani, the deputy governor of Marib Province, in May 2010.

Given the closely woven texture of Yemeni family and tribal connections, it should have come as no surprise that al-Shabwani was a cousin of Ayed al-Shabwani, a prominent local al-Qaeda leader. Jaber was also a business partner of a Saleh relative who held a very important position in the security services and with whom he was now in dispute over a matter of $9 million owed him by the Saleh relative. On May 24, Jaber al-Shabwani, accompanied by his uncle, two of his sons, and several bodyguards, went to meet his cousin in hopes of getting him to lay down his arms. A few minutes into the meeting came the distant but unmistakable sound of a drone, whereupon the al-Qaeda

Shabwani made a rapid departure. The deputy governor stayed put on the reasonable but mistaken assumption that no one would want to target him. He was wrong. The exploding missile, most likely targeted at his cell phone, killed him, his uncle, and two of his bodyguards, and injured his sons. In Washington, the realization dawned that someone (in this case, the Joint Special Operations Command) had fed the targeters very incorrect information that, according to one report, "may have been intended to result in Mr. Shabwani's death." Obama gave his influential adviser, General James "Hoss" Cartwright, a "chest thumping," by the latter's account, angrily asking, "How could this happen?" Brennan, meanwhile, was "pissed," and demanding to know why a deputy governor was meeting with al-Qaeda. If anyone in Washington knew about the $9 million, they kept it to themselves.

This mistargeted killing had more far-reaching consequences than most, since Shabwani's father, Sheikh Ali al-Shabwani, led members of his tribe in blowing up a section of the vital trans-Yemen oil pipeline in retaliation, leading to millions of dollars in lost revenue for the treasury. Chastened, Washington suspended drone operations in Yemen for a year. Supposedly, when operations resumed, the CIA was playing a greater role and strikes were no longer quite so reliant on Saleh and his cronies for targeting intelligence. But Yemenis may not have noticed the difference, since people were still picked off either in error or as collateral damage. In many cases, security forces could easily have arrested the victims instead of having them summarily incinerated by Hellfire.

Anwar al-Awlaki, for example, billed for a time as "the most dangerous man in the world," was publicly nominated to the CIA's kill list in April 2011. Awlaki had already retreated to the heartland of his tribe, the Awalik. It was easy to believe that the fugitive was hidden in the desert fastness, but in fact, as *Guardian* reporter Ghaith Abdul-Ahad discovered when he visited the tribe's ruling Sultan, although everyone in the neighborhood knew where the notorious preacher was living, no one seemed interested in arresting him. "The government haven't asked us to hand him in," Sultan Fareed bin Babaker told the reporter. "If they do then we will think about it. But no one has asked us."

A few weeks before this conversation took place, a pair of Justice Department lawyers in Washington had obligingly provided the Obama administration with a secret legal justification for summarily executing Awlaki, accepting as a premise that he posed an "imminent" threat and that his capture was "infeasible." The July 16, 2010, memorandum, which the *New York Times* later described as "a slapdash pastiche of legal theories . . . clearly tailored to the desired result," invoked, among other precedents, a 2006 Israeli court decision on targeted killing. The Israeli Supreme Court did indeed rule in December 2006 that "targeted preventions" would be legal in certain cases, when absolutely necessary to prevent a "ticking bomb" scenario but not otherwise. However, as revealed by Anat Kamm, an Israeli whistle-blower who copied documents while serving in the IDF, the Israeli military routinely disregarded the judgment when making targeting decisions. Kamm was sentenced to four and a half years in prison for her action.

Awlaki was finally killed by a CIA drone in September 2011 and his son, Abdul Rahman, by a JSOC drone two weeks later. The boy died because he and seven others happened to be having dinner at a restaurant where a high-value al-Qaeda target, Ibrahim al-Banna, was thought to be eating, it evidently being the targeters' assumption that any fellow diners were guilty by culinary association.

Anwar al-Awlaki had been a prime target thanks to his connection to two failed attempts to explode bombs on American planes, not to mention his mentoring of Nidal Malik Hasan, the army psychiatrist accused of killing thirteen people at Fort Hood, Texas, in November 2009. But although the direct threat to "the homeland" apparently receded with his elimination, the pace of U.S. attacks on Yemeni targets only increased. In 2011, President Saleh, faced with massive protests against his misrule, withdrew his forces from the southern province of Abyan, a center of southern separatism in which al-Qaeda had gained a strong foothold. To those who knew him, this was a typical Saleh ploy. As Abdul Ghani al-Iryani, a well-known political analyst in Sana'a, stated flatly at the time: "The regime decided to hand over this territory to [al-Qaeda] to underline the risk of terrorism in the eyes of the west. That didn't really work, except that it created a very dangerous situation for the population. So, the regime hands over the land, the territory, to the extremists and then starts bombing them with all kinds of weapons." The hapless inhabitants of this miserably poor enclave found themselves lumped in with al-Qaeda under a rain of bombs and Hellfire missiles unleashed by the United States but for which the Yemeni government, corrupt, repressive, hated, was happy to take responsibility.

Saleh's Abyan ploy did not save his presidency, although he did get to keep all that neatly stacked cash in the basement. His replacement, Abd Rubbah Mansour Hadi, continued many of the same policies, including, at least for a while, wholehearted endorsement of the drone strikes. Many of those being hunted were no doubt al-Qaeda officials in good standing, even if their international impact was limited, but the targeting of people who could easily have been arrested persisted. Al-Qaeda member Hamid al-Radmi, for example, was incinerated in his car in central Yemen in April 2013 by three missiles even though he was in frequent contact with security and political officials as a mediator. Adnan al-Qadhi, a colonel in an elite army unit who was clearly sympathetic to al-Qaeda, was killed although he lived and moved openly in a village on the edge of Sana'a that was home to many of the country's ruling elite. "They could have picked him up any time, but he was a relative of Ali Mohsen [a very important commander]. It would have been too embarrassing to arrest a relative," one Sanani explained to me, "so Ali Mohsen said 'let the Americans kill him.'"

Inevitably, collateral victims accumulated; the driver and his cousin whose taxi passengers were two targeted al-Qaeda members or the twelve passengers in a minibus, including three children and a pregnant woman, on their way home from market in the central highland town of Rada'a in September 2012, burned so badly their bodies were unrecognizable, or the anti–al-Qaeda preacher, Salim bin Ali Jaber, killed in August 2012 along with his cousin, village policeman

Walid bin Ali Jaber, while arguing with three targeted suspects. "If Salim and Walid are al-Qaeda," chanted infuriated villagers as they marched through the village four days after the strike, "then we are all al-Qaeda."

The villagers also chanted, "Obama, this is wrong," a point with which the president should have agreed, at least after May 23, 2013, when the White House issued "U.S. Policy Standards and Procedures for the Use of Force in Counterterrorism Operations Outside the United States and Areas of Active Hostilities." This document stated clearly and unequivocally: "[L]ethal force will be used only to prevent or stop attacks on U.S. persons, and even then, only when capture is not feasible." Moreover, "the United States will use lethal force only against a target that poses a continuing, imminent threat to U.S. persons," and only when there was a "near certainty that non-combatants will not be killed or injured."

It all depended on what was meant by "imminent." Over fifteen days in the summer of 2013 the United States hit Yemen with nine strikes, killing as many as forty-nine people, including up to seven civilians, three of whom were children. Officials told the *New York Times* that intelligence of a possible terrorist threat (in the form of an intercepted dispatch from al-Qaeda leader Ayman Zawahiri instructing his lieutenant in Yemen, Nasir al Wuhayshi, to "do something") had "expanded the scope of people we could go after" and that none of those killed in the stepped-up strikes were "household names." Rather, they were "rising stars" who could become future leaders. An unnamed official was quoted as explaining: "Before, we couldn't necessarily go after a driver for the organization; it'd have to be an operations director. Now that driver becomes fair game because he's providing direct support to the plot."

Clearly, things had come a very long way since George Bush had begun crossing out names in the list he kept in his desk drawer. A well-funded bureaucratic mechanism to service the "disposition matrix," as the kill list had been euphemistically relabeled, was centered at the National Counterterrorism Center, whose 500-strong staff was charged with, among other things, collating the various lists crafted by the CIA and JSOC and others. (As noted, the president liked to have the very last word. "Turns out I'm really good at killing people," he remarked the day Awlaki died. "Didn't know that was gonna be a strong suit of mine.") John Brennan, who moved from the White House to take formal command of the CIA in 2013, was credited with having overseen the crafting of this elaborate and complex system, a monument to the principle of "precise precision" while nominating people far away for execution. In reality, this arrangement illustrated how faithfully twenty-first-century assassination practices followed the hoary traditions of strategic bombing, in which "targeting committees" had long labored to discern "critical nodes," remorselessly expanding target lists in the process.

In April 2014, Western media took notice of an al-Qaeda rally—a party to welcome twenty-nine fellow jihadis who had broken out of jail in Sana'a in February—that had taken place somewhere in Yemen the month before. As shown in an al-Qaeda video, many hundreds of armed, chanting, cheerful-looking fighters paraded through a canyon and stood in long lines to greet a smiling Nasir al-Wuhayshi. No one appeared concerned that they might be under surveillance by the "unblinking eye." Coincidentally or not, this striking demonstration of jihadi insouciance was immediately followed, once the video reached a wider audience, by multiple drone strikes in several southern provinces. As many as sixty-five people, including at least three children, died over three days.

Despite the intensity of the attacks, no one in authority was able to name a single one of the victims, nor were there any official leaks or even hints that the attacks were aimed at foiling any threat, imminent or otherwise, to "U.S. persons." The White House off-loaded the chore of commenting on the strikes to the Yemeni government, which duly followed orders in claiming responsibility. Reports from Sana'a indicated that the Yemeni regime had been hoping to persuade the United States to limit the strikes that provided al-Qaeda with such an effective recruiting tool, but such pleas from a feeble client regime could easily be brushed aside.

In any event, there were fresh opportunities beckoning for drone warfare, not just traditional operations in benighted regions of the third world, such as North Africa, but against more formidable enemies. This in turn offered new challenges and the alluring prospect of enhanced budgets.

# 13

# ONE BIG ROBOT

"We want to be everywhere, know everything, and we want to predict what happens next," declared an earnest Lieutenant General Joseph Votel, commander of JSOC, the Joint Special Operations Command, in April 2014. Twenty years after promoters of the revolution in military affairs first promised a world of networked and omniscient precision, the dream lived on. Votel was addressing "GeoInt," the well-funded annual Florida jamboree that brings together surveillance-industry executives with their intelligence agency customers for a week of mutually profitable confabulation. The general's words drew respectful attention, for the night-raiding JSOC was one of the few entities relatively secure from the famine eating into budgets and revenues across the U.S. defense establishment. While most public defense forums echoed with lamentations of the "painful choices" engendered by the legally mandated cuts in defense spending known as sequestration, Special Operations Command (SOCOM), of which JSOC is a key and especially secretive component, had seen its upwardly curving budget survive almost undisturbed.

Incoming Obama administration officials inspecting the national security system bequeathed them by the Bush-Cheney team in 2009 told me at the time that "Special Operations are out of control," and the intervening years had done little to change the picture. Operating in at least 134 countries, empowered to kill people without recourse to higher authority, endowed with "unique acquisition authority" to spend money with a minimum of congressional oversight, the "point of the spear," as the special operators liked to refer to themselves, had grown from a 1980 force of 11,600 specialists focused on strengthening third world allies into 2013's 66,000-person machine. From a mere $2.3 billion in 2001, the command, which extracts its budget directly from Congress, had garnered $9.3 billion in 2008, $10.3 billion in 2011, and was looking for $9.9 billion in 2015, the slight decline due to the drawdown of Afghan war operations. Such generosity to the heavily publicized "secret" warriors that had cut down bin Laden, Zarqawi, and others had endowed SOCOM with a prosperous sheen. Streams of congressional delegations invited to visit the headquarters in Tampa, Florida, marveled at the gleaming modern buildings and lavish accoutrements. "They have professional lighting engineers for the displays they put on to show us what they are doing around the world," one awestruck house staffer told me on his return.

Unquestioning largesse had generated the inevitable result. "When SEAL Team 6 operators are sent on 'training' missions to Alaska to go hunting on the government's dime, you know you have budgets that are both too fat and lack oversight," one member of the elite force told a reporter. "If [SOCOM Commander Admiral William] McRaven is concerned with his budget, he should start with fighting the wartime tradition of fiscal abuse that has gone unchecked since 9/11 in the SOF community. Our love affair with special operations has caused the DOD to turn a blind eye on very questionable fiscal practices." Nevertheless, there was little sign that the high-tech assassins were falling out of favor, though Congress did raise some questions about a scheme for a "National Capital Region Headquarters" with a $10 million annual budget as well as an $80 million project, championed by McRaven, to develop an "Iron Man" battle suit for the commandos. TALOS, the battery-powered "tactical-assault light operator suit," featured full-body bulletproof protection as well as muscle-boosting components, embedded computers, night vision, and video sensors for "increased situational awareness" (with a slick, expensive, gamelike video to promote the project). Among other items on a Special Operations wish list for Advancement of Technologies in Equipment for Use by U.S. Special Operations Forces issued shortly after Votel's address, was a "Concealable/Take Down Urban Sniper Rifle" folded into a small 12-by-20-inch suitcase, guided bullets, and tiny missiles as well as "neutraceutical and/or pharmacological enhancements to increase neuroperformance."

Another McRaven initiative, that of building a $15 million "regional SOF coordination center" in Colombia, ran into concerted opposition from the other services, who complained to Congress. Special Operations has been heavily engaged in Colombia since the Clinton era in combating the venerable FARC Marxist guerrilla insurgency. In recent years this campaign has been promoted as *the* textbook example of high-value targeting powered by precise electronic intelligence, a strategy that had clearly failed in Afghanistan but was hailed as having enjoyed great success in Colombia.

Conducted in conjunction with the CIA, the ongoing operation followed the traditional pattern of the recent Asian wars. Targeted leaders of FARC were tracked by NSA via their cell phones or covertly planted tracking devices. Once located, they were struck, not by drone-fired missiles but by 500-pound GPS-guided bombs dropped from Vietnam-era light A-37 bombers provided to Colombia by the United States. According to American and Colombian officials who briefed the *Washington Post* on their success, the campaign eliminated at least two dozen high-value rebel leaders, causing "mass desertions" and "chaos and dysfunction" within the organization. Such results would seem to validate the whole concept of high-value-people targeting and indeed are celebrated as such by JSOC and the CIA.

But the reality was a little different. True to form, almost all the dead leaders were speedily replaced, often by younger, more able, or more brutal men. Mono Jojoy, for example, an aging senior leader who had risen through the ranks, was killed in September 2010; the Colombian president hailed his death as the "hardest blow" ever suffered by the rebel group. Yet he was almost immediately replaced by "El Médico," Alberto Parra, an able younger leader who was an educated and astute doctor. Other high-level hits, except those in regions, such as the Caribbean coast, where FARC had already been shredded by government-sponsored paramilitary death squads, had produced the same result. Paul Reyes, a senior leader killed in a cross-border operation in 2008, was similarly replaced, in three days, by another experienced commander, a former university professor with the nom de guerre Joaquín Gómez. "You can see that their command and control stayed intact," Adam Isacson, a specialist on the topic at the Washington Office on Latin America, pointed out to me. "They've had two ceasefires in recent years and made them stick; if command had broken down you'd have had groups going rogue and that didn't happen." In May 2014, in seeming rejection of long-standing U.S. policy, the Colombian government announced it had agreed in peace talks with FARC to work together in combating the cocaine trade, an initiative endorsed by the electorate with the re-election of President Santos the following month.

Notwithstanding the claimed victory in Colombia and the glamour associated with the Special Operations "brand," opinion polls have for years suggested that a majority of Americans firmly believe the United States should be "less active" in world affairs. Nevertheless, in 2014 Votel stressed that he still saw his mission as global: "Since we can no longer draw a box on a map and say that's where the problem is, we must be everywhere, in the sense that we must be able to find the threat anywhere on the planet."

A decade or so earlier, he might have lapsed into the acronym-laden jargon associated with effects-based operations, but now JSOC's youthful-looking three-star general, who would shortly be nominated to a fourth star and to succeed McRaven as overall head of Special Operations Command, contented himself with the simple desire, expressed with a straight face, to "know everything." Pursuit of this goal would require "wide area persistent surveillance" and "precision geolocation." The former was a reference to a system that might live up to the undelivered promises of Gorgon Stare, Sierra Nevada's attempt to monitor entire cities with one sensor, while the latter referred to a computerized version of the phone-tracking IMSI Catcher that had mistakenly drawn the missiles down on Zabet Amanullah in the middle of his election campaign tour. Along with a desire to "see through clouds," Votel also expressed the need to "bring the data from all disciplines of intelligence together in near real time so that we can know everything."

Three days after this speech, Votel's CIA partners in the drone war unleashed a hail of drone-launched missiles across southern Yemen, killing some sixty-five people. Yemeni journalist Farea al-Muslimi succinctly described the effect of such strikes in a tweet following the attacks: "Dear America," he wrote, "there is an infinite support in Yemen for the army in its current battles against #Aqap [al-Qaeda in the Arabian Peninsula]. Plz don't ruin tht by launching #Drone."

Given that weeks later no government official in the United States or Yemen had been able to name a single one of the intended victims of what Muslimi called a "tsunami" of strikes, it appeared that neither Votel's command nor the CIA targeters could yet "know everything." Even the facts Votel said he knew may have been incorrect. On December 12 of the previous year, a JSOC drone strike near Rada'a in central Yemen had hit a tribal wedding party, killing twelve people and injuring fifteen, including the bride. The alleged target, a "midlevel operative" named Shawqui Ali Ahmed al-Badani, deemed to have been involved in a mysterious plot that had sparked a shutdown of nineteen U.S. embassies and a torrent of strikes the previous August, was not among the victims.

The resulting outcry was sufficiently vehement to generate official investigations, one commissioned by Votel and another, on White House orders, by the CIA's Counterterrorism Center. Contradicting a detailed Human Rights Watch on-the-ground investigation that drew on many interviews with survivors, concluding that probably all and certainly most of the victims were civilians, both official enquiries duly reported that mostly "militants" had been killed. Officials shown the drone-feed video of the attack were later quoted as saying it showed that the trucks that were hit contained armed men. However, in an implicit reminder that any Yemeni tribesman considers himself undressed without a gun, the Yemeni government not only apologized for the attack, calling it a "mistake," but also presented 101 Kalashnikov rifles in compensation to leaders of the victims' tribe. Meanwhile a convenient leak suggested that the CIA had informed JSOC before the strike that the "spy agency did not have confidence in the underlying intelligence" and that afterward, CIA analysts had assessed that "some of the victims may have been villagers, not militants." The timing could not have been better (at least from the agency's point of view), given JSOC's low-intensity campaign to take over all CIA drone operations. In fact following the wedding-party fiasco, JSOC drone operations in Yemen were suspended, at least temporarily.

Despite this setback, Votel, as his remarks to the intelligence-industry gathering indicated, affirmed his faith in remote sensing and the need to "leverage technology" to help analysts "predict what's going to happen next." This was entirely in line with official high-tech pro-curement orthodoxy, maintained with undeviating vigor for at least the half century since General Westmoreland had promised that "enemy forces will be located, tracked and targeted almost instanta-neously through the use of data links, computer assisted intelligence evaluation, and automated fire control."

One exception to the rule of high tech had been the introduction of the A-10 attack plane, optimized for "close air support" of troops on the ground and hence detested by the air force hierarchy as detract-ing from their preferred mission of long-range bombing independent of ground action. Recurring efforts by successive air force chiefs to dis-card the A-10 had been stymied by imminent combat or congressio-nal opposition.

In 2014, the Air Force mounted its most determined effort yet, announcing the abolition of the A-10 force on the excuse that budget cutting left it no other option. Henceforth, all aerial strikes would be inflicted via video screens, not just with drones but also with bombers and fighters that flew too high and fast to assess targets with the naked eye, instead relying on the screens linked to the sensors in their targeting pods.

In the face of the air force edict, many rose in defense of the plane, notably soldiers whose lives had been saved by its timely interventions when they were badly outnumbered or ambushed. Special Operations troops had particular reason to be grateful in this regard. Yet from Fort Bragg, their home base, there was only silence. Strict orders, so I was informed, had gone out from Votel's headquarters that no one in his force was to say a word in defense of the A-10. A leadership wedded to $80 million armored suits inspired by a comic-book fantasy was clearly not interested in anyone saving lives by looking at the real world close-up.

Fifteen years earlier, in his speech at the Citadel outlining his vision for America's defense, George W. Bush had promised that "when direct threats to America are discovered, I know that the best defense can be a strong and swift offense—including the use of Special Operations Forces and long-range strike capabilities . . . we must be able to strike from across the world with pinpoint accuracy—with long-range aircraft and perhaps with unmanned systems." In 2012, Barack Obama, in a speech at the Pentagon outlining *his* defense vision, had declared that "as we reduce the overall defense budget, we will protect, and in some cases increase, our investments in special operations forces, in new technologies like ISR and unmanned systems . . ."

In the decade and a half between these visionary statements, American forces had been embroiled in two long and bloody wars costing unimaginable sums of money. The wars were publicly justified by the urgent need to crush al-Qaeda, which at the outset occupied a few training camps in Afghanistan on the sufferance of the Taliban government. As of the summer of 2014, jihadi manpower had grown faster than SOCOM's, and the area controlled by al-Qaeda and its equally militant jihadi spin-offs in western Iraq and eastern Syria alone was equal in size to Great Britain or the state of Utah, with other territories across North Africa and beyond falling into its sway. Abu Bakr al-Baghdadi, the leader of the formidable ISIS (as he had renamed al-Qaeda in Iraq),

was the more effective successor to previous leaders whose eliminations, starting with Abu Musab al-Zarqawi, had been serially hailed
by U.S. officials as "devastating blows" to the group.

Yet the doctrine propounded by Bush and restated by Obama was
more strongly in force than ever. At the end of the Bush tenure, SOCOM
was operating in sixty countries. Five years later, Special Operations
had an ongoing presence in over twice as many countries and basked
in the approval of politicians, media, and the public. Reaper drones
were still rolling off the General Atomics production lines. Though the
public was repeatedly assured that the wars were ending as U.S. troops
withdrew from Afghanistan, the administration was working hard to
preserve a residual force of some ten thousand men in that country—
principally, it seemed, to secure a drone base to attack Pakistan's
Taliban along with remnants of the original al-Qaeda leadership—
apparently a crucial need since Pakistan's eviction of U.S. drone bases
in 2012.

Meanwhile, as central Asian target lists shrank, army engineers
were busily constructing an archipelago of bases for drones and Special Operations across Africa. In 2014, Niger, for example, was host-
ing drones at the airport outside Niamey, its capital, as were Ethiopia,
the Seychelles, and Djibouti. Djibouti indeed was the centerpiece of
ambitious plans for coverage of both the continent and southern Arabia, affirmed in 2014 by a thirty-year $2 billion lease for an expanded
Camp Lemonnier, the former French Foreign Legion base on the edge
of the country's main airport. The camp, home to the JSOC drones targeting Yemen (so many crashed into the nearby city on takeoff and
landing that they had to be moved to a desert facility a few miles away),
already featured a $220 million Special Operations compound,
along with a $25 million fitness center, forerunners of a $1.4 billion
decade-long expansion planned for the base.

Even less visibly, the U.S. Air Force was maintaining and expanding its global network of "unmanned aircraft systems operations center support," also known as "reach-back sites," electronic nerve centers
in the elaborate communications system that make "striking across

the world with pinpoint accuracy" possible. (Other countries may buy or build drones, but none have the global command and control system that make worldwide strikes possible.) Thus while Ramstein Air Force Base in Germany hosted "EUR-1," relaying communications and video feeds between the United States and its drones operating in the Middle East and Central Asia, the Pentagon was spending millions of dollars constructing a new site, EUR-2, in Italy to handle expanding drone operations in Africa. PAC-1 at Kadena Air Force Base in Japan dealt with the drones flying over east Asia, while yet another new site, PAC-2, was planned for somewhere in the Pacific to focus on drone flights over the South China Sea. As General Votel liked to empha-size, the threat could be "anywhere on the planet." Most of the drones linked to this system would be General Atomics Reapers. As of 2014 the air force planned to have 346 of these in service by 2021, of which more than 80 would likely be under CIA control. As the proliferating bases across Africa made clear, Reapers targeting lightly armed tribes-men and insurgents still had a promising future. That future was nec-essarily restricted to countries unable or unwilling to contest foreign airstrikes on their territory, since Reapers or Predators were liable to be shot down by anyone with any antiaircraft weapon more powerful than a machine gun, let alone an air force.

Clearly, there was no guarantee that the United States would enjoy the same lopsided advantage in future wars, especially if they were against developed states in the former Communist bloc. This was why, sometime around the end of the first decade of the century, a new acro-nym entered military jargon, A2/AD, which stands for antiaccess/area denial, and in plain English means strong defenses against U.S. incur-sions by air, sea, or land. Thus in "Air Sea Battle," a 2013 defense depart-ment document promoting combined air and sea power as the best way to attack China, the authors define A2/AD capabilities as "those which challenge and threaten the ability of U.S. and allied forces to both get to the fight and to fight effectively once there. Notably, an adversary can often use the same capability for both A2 and AD." Once this concept, which could apply equally well to locks on the doors of a house, had been suitably dressed up with the impenetrable acronym, it quickly became the favorite peg on which to hang expensive new weapon system development programs.

One early example of such a program was a mysterious delta-winged jet-powered unmanned aircraft first spotted by outsiders at Kandahar Airport in Afghanistan in 2007 and eventually revealed to be the RQ-170, a "stealth" drone designed to operate over unfriendly territory while remaining invisible to defenders' radar. It was not an attack drone carrying bombs and missiles like the Reaper or Predator but one dedicated to surveillance with TV and infrared cameras as well as radar. Designed and built by Lockheed Martin, its status as a "black," that is, secret, program guaranteed that its costs and performance would remain cloaked from public scrutiny, as was its very existence until it made its debut on the runway at Kandahar Airport and was promptly nicknamed "the Beast of Kandahar." As we shall see, the Beast was by no means invisible or invulnerable to ground defenses, but it did represent an all-important feature of post-Reaper/Predator drone development: the advantage of being expensive.

Thanks to Predator and Reaper, General Atomics had flourished in the post-9/11 era, scooping up just over $2 billion from the Pentagon in 2013. But that was a mere 0.68 percent of U.S. defense contracts that year, a pittance compared with the $37 billion raked in by Lockheed Martin, the leading contractor. Despite the fact that its products had sold so well and were the topic of worldwide discussion, the San Diego–based firm ranked only twenty-first in the league table of U.S. defense firms. Furthermore, despite the prominent role played by the attack drones in the recent and ongoing wars, there had been no sign that the "prime" contractors, the five giant firms that had emerged from the mergers of the early 1990s, had made any attempts to break into that market. The reason was easy to discern: the drones were too cheap. For the twelve Reapers the air force planned to buy in 2015, for example, the service requested $240 million, or $20 million per copy. Boeing's F/A-18 "Growler" electronic warfare plane, by contrast, weighed in at $67 million each, while Lockheed was happily extracting $106 million for the C-130J transport plane, an upgraded version of a 50-year-old design, not to mention the Bell Boeing V-22 troop transport, which clocked in at $119 million per. Clearly, with such rich pickings available elsewhere, the primes were not going to be too interested in crashing General Atomics' market.

Such lack of interest would inevitably evaporate if drones were worth real money. It was no accident that while Reapers could be had for $20 million apiece, Global Hawk, a new, much larger, higher-flying drone offering the "wide-area persistent surveillance" so desired by General Votel, cost at least $300 million a copy and was built by Northrop Grumman, number four in the contractors' rankings. As discussed in Chapter 10, Global Hawk has turned out to be functionally inadequate, given its inability to fly in bad weather and the tendency of its plastic airframe to twist and even disintegrate in flight. Nevertheless, with the lobbying power of a major contractor behind it, the program entered into that happy state where no reported failing—or even an effort by the air force to discard it—could drive a stake through its heart.

As noted, Lockheed's RQ-170 drone, of which twenty were built, had its price tag mercifully obscured by its "black" status, but a calculation based on estimates of the secret drone's weight, conservatively estimated the cost at $140.1 million, most likely rising to $200 million if the costs of the stealth features were included.

Following on the heels of the Beast was the even more secret RQ-180, which, like the Beast, was due to be operated jointly by the air force and the CIA. Apparently the same size as Global Hawk but conceived in hopes of being entirely stealthy, its cost would almost certainly soar past the latter's already staggering $300 million price tag. Like the Hawk and the Beast, it was to be designed purely for surveillance. A drone designed to carry out strikes with bombs and missiles, defend itself against attackers, conduct electronic warfare, refuel in midair, *and* take off and land on an aircraft carrier would quite certainly be a far more ambitious and therefore costly undertaking. So in 2013 the U.S. Navy dangled a prospective $3.7 billion contract as inducement for corporations to develop something that could do just that. The program followed claims of success for the Unmanned Combat Air System Demonstrator, a seven-year program launched in 2006 to show that a drone could indeed take off and land on a carrier. That feat was ultimately accomplished at an overall cost of $1.7 billion for two Northrop Grumman delta-winged X-47B prototypes, flown from the USS *George H. W. Bush* on a July day when the sea off Virginia was very, very calm.

Back in the distant days of the Carter administration, high-tech apostle William Perry, occupying the powerful post of director of defense research and engineering, had begun pouring huge money into stealth. The money spigot has stayed open ever since, although the actual results in combat have fallen short of expectations (and public boasts). The F-117, the first stealth bomber, had in fact proven visible enough to enemy radars in the 1991 Gulf War to require escort by fleets of radar-jamming aircraft, while in the 1998 Kosovo conflict, the Serbs had managed to use elderly Soviet SAM radars to locate and shoot down one F-117 and severely damage another. Nevertheless, stealth continued to be deemed essential to any scheme for using drones, or any other aircraft, in the face of determined enemy air defenses such as the dreaded A2/AD so frequently invoked in official discussions of future weapons systems. The incorporation of stealth features—exotic plastic and glue coatings to absorb radar waves and special airframe shaping to deflect them—makes drones and planes not only less airworthy and less maneuverable but also enormously costly, which means, given the cost-plus business model of the defense industry, they could be enormously profitable. Drones, once hailed for their cheapness, were inevitably becoming more expensive than the manned planes they were supposed to replace.

Given their cost, these superdrones will inevitably be few in number and will require a more elaborate "reach-back" communications network with an ever-more voracious appetite for bandwidth (the amount of data that can be transmitted over a communications link). Already, a single Global Hawk drone requires five times as much bandwidth as that used by the *entire* U.S. military during the 1991 Gulf War, an amount that will only increase. With this Niagara of information pouring across the heavens from satellite to ground stations and up to satellites again comes the certainty that someone will at some point listen in and may well be capable of inserting their own commands to the machine.

In 2009, Shia insurgents in Iraq used SkyGrabber software, priced at $29.95 on the Internet, to capture and download Predator video feeds for use in their own battle planning. More spectacularly, in December 2011, an RQ-170 Beast overflying Iran landed comparatively undamaged. Initial denials by U.S. authorities of Iranian claims that they had captured the drone were silenced when the Iranian Revolutionary Guard put it on display. Like all drones, the machine relied on GPS for navigation, the network of satellites that had made remote drone operations possible in the first place. But GPS signals are extraordinarily weak, the equivalent of a car headlight shining 12,000 miles away, because the size of the satellite limits the power output. This makes it comparatively easy to jam or interfere with the signals, which is what the Iranians claim to have done.

As an Iranian engineer explained to *Christian Science Monitor* reporter Scott Peterson, the Iranian electronic-warfare specialists had the benefit of their experience working on the remains of several simpler U.S. Navy Scan Eagle drones they had retrieved earlier. To get control of the CIA's drone, they first jammed its communication links to the pilots back in Nevada. "By putting noise [jamming] on the communications, you force the bird into autopilot," explained the engineer. "This is where the bird loses its brain." Once that happened, the aircraft was preprogrammed to return to its Kandahar base, navigating by GPS. But at this point the Iranians made their second intervention, feeding false signals that mimicked the weaker GPS transmissions, and gradually guided the aircraft toward an Iranian landing site. As an electronic-warfare commander explained to an Iranian news agency, "[A]ll the movements of these [enemy drones]" were being watched, and "obstructing" their work was "always on our agenda." The landing site was carefully chosen, as the engineer explained, because it was at almost exactly the same altitude as Kandahar. So, when the drone "thought" it was at its home base, it duly landed. However there was an altitude difference of a few feet. Landing heavily, the aircraft damaged its undercarriage and one wing.

Despite energetic attempts by U.S. officials to discredit the Iranian claims, there is no reason to doubt the story, especially as their feat was later duplicated by a University of Texas professor, Todd Humphreys, in repeated public experiments in which he took control of nonmilitary drones and, on one occasion, a large yacht in the Mediterranean.

The difficulties of controlling future superdrones in the face of Iranian or perhaps Chinese electronic warriors inevitably generated speculation about the onset of "autonomous" systems capable of conducting a mission without human intervention and without command links vulnerable to hacking. Indeed, the navy's demonstrator drone that managed two carrier landings (out of four attempts) in a flat, calm sea in July 2013 was autonomous, flying only under the direction of its onboard computers. The challenge of landing on a pitching, rolling deck, something that requires intense training for humans to accomplish, has yet to be faced. Nevertheless, the supposed imminence of robotic systems endowed with the ability and power to make lethal decisions has become a recurring topic of concern among human rights activists, complete with TED talks about the near-term probability that "autonomous military robots will take decision making out of the hands of humans and thus take the human out of war, which would change warfare entirely." In November 2012, Human Rights Watch called for a "preemptive ban on the development, production, and use of fully autonomous weapons." Naturally, in view of the money to be made, interested parties have been eager to bolster the notion that such systems are a practical possibility. As David Deptula said of drone video analysis: "Making this automatic is an absolute must." The Office of Naval Research has even funded a joint project by several major universities to "devise computer algorithms that will imbue autonomous robots with moral competence—the ability to tell right from wrong." This was clearly destined to be a multiyear contract, since, as one sympathetic commentator noted, "[S]cientifically speaking, we still don't know what morality in humans actually is."

Early experiments appeared to confirm that autonomous drones, ethical or otherwise, might be just around the corner. An experiment involving two small drones with computers that process images from onboard cameras reportedly managed to locate and identify a brightly colored tarp spread out in an open field. "The demonstration laid the groundwork for scientific advances that would allow drones to search for a human target and then make an identification based on facial-recognition or other software," explained the *Washington Post* confidently. "Once a match was made, a drone could launch a missile to kill the target."

Picking out a brightly colored object with sharp edges against a plain background is in the grand tradition of budget-generating Pentagon tests. (Infrared systems are usually tested in the early morning, for example, so that the warm target-object shows up nicely against the ground, still cool from the night air.) In the real world, where edges are not sharp and shades of gray are hard to differentiate, not to mention the shifting silhouette of a human face, life becomes a lot more difficult, especially if the target is taking steps to stay out of sight. (According to an al-Qaeda tip sheet discovered in Mali, Osama bin Laden had advised his followers to "hide under thick trees" as one of several sensible suggestions for evading drones.) Given the difficulty humans face in making correct decisions on the basis of ambiguous electro-optical and infrared images of what may or may not be an enemy (is that a squatting Pashtun?), not to mention the ongoing and oft-lamented failure to get computers to analyze surveillance video, such anxiety might be premature. Exponentially increasing computer processing power has kept alive the dream of artificial intelligence, founded on the belief that the brain operates just like a computer through a series of on-off switches and that therefore a computer is capable of performing like a human brain. But it has become clearer that the brain does not operate in any such fashion but rather, as Berkeley philosopher Hubert Dreyfus has long maintained, on intuitive reactions based on accumulated expertise and intuition, not on the mechanistic process, characteristically evoked by Votel, of "connecting the dots."

In one sense, however, the system is already "autonomous." On the eve of World War II, air force planners identified the few targets they needed to destroy to bring Germany to its knees. The plan did not work, targeting committees met, their target lists expanded, the enemy adapted to each list change, and the war dragged on for year after bloody year. Nevertheless, the same strategy was followed in Korea, Vietnam, and Iraq, each time with more elaborate technology. Ultimately the technology offered the promise of destroying not just the physical objects—power plants, factories, communications, roads, and bridges—that sustained the enemy but also selected individuals, duly listed in order of importance, who controlled the enemy war effort. By 2014, with Afghanistan sinking back into chaos and the jihadis' black flag waving over ever-larger stretches of the globe under the aegis of a leader, Abu Bakr al-Baghdadi, more capable and successful than his targeted predecessors, it was clear that this latest variation of the strategy had also failed. Michael Flynn, formerly McChrystal's intelligence officer in the hunt for Zarqawi who had gone on to command the Defense Intelligence Agency, ruefully admitted as much as he prepared to leave office, telling an interviewer, "We kept decapitating the leadership of these groups, and more leaders would just appear from the ranks to take their place."

Flynn's insight made no difference. President Obama, claiming success in assassination campaigns in Pakistan, Yemen, and Somalia (where a recently assassinated leader had been immediately replaced), pronounced that this newest threat would be met with the same strategy. Predators, Reapers, and Global Hawks accordingly scoured the desert wastes of Iraq and Syria, beaming uncountable petabytes of video back up the kill chain. Among the recipients were four hundred members of the Massachusetts National Guard sitting in darkened rooms at a base on Cape Cod, gazing hour after hour at blurry images in search of "patterns of life" that might denote the elusive enemy. "None of them are on the ground, and none of them are in the theater of operations," said their local congressman proudly, "but they are contributing from here, conducting essential frontline functions."

As David Deptula promised that "with a more intense campaign" victory would come quickly, enemy leaders switched off their cell phones and faded from view. Pentagon officials demanded more spending. Wall Street analysts hailed the prospect of "sure-bet paydays" for drone builders and other weapons makers. The system rolled on autonomously—one big robot mowing the grass, forever.

# AFTERWORD TO THE 2016 EDITION

With the rise of the Islamic State of Iraq and Syria (ISIS) in 2014, the U.S. faced its most formidable jihadist enemy yet. After gaining Washington's attention by capturing Mosul, Iraq's second largest city, in June of 2014, the group went on to overrun most of Sunni Iraq and half of Syria. Such a dramatic resurrection of Zarqawi's al-Qaeda in Iraq, supposedly laid low by the surveillance drones and assassination squads of the Joint Special Operations Command years before, might have prompted a radical rethink of the remote-control/high-value targeting strategy pursued by the U.S. since 2001. Yet as the jihadis established their well-armed, highly organized state and steadily conquered new territory, the U.S. responded with the same methods employed in earlier phases of the post-9/11 wars.

To a greater extent than most people realized, Operation Inherent Resolve, the campaign to "degrade and destroy" ISIS, was a drone war. With the exception of a few Special Operations troops, American soldiers and airmen never saw the enemy except as images on video screens—if then. This was not immediately evident to the outside world, since official bulletins generally referred only to "air strikes" against the enemy, without detailing how they were carried out. In fact, a year into the campaign, in June 2015, the U.S. and its allies had aimed more than 3,800 airstrikes at the enemy. Of these, 875 had been inflicted by Reaper and Predator drones dropping guided bombs and missiles themselves. However, according to Colonel Julian Cheater, a senior officer at Creech Air Force Base in Nevada—home base to the majority of drone crews—many of the remaining strikes also directly involved drones. In a process known as "buddy-lasing," a drone operator "acquired" the target and directed a laser beam at it. A manned bomber then released a bomb that homed in on the spot "illuminated" by the beam. The bomber most in need of this service was the B-1, originally developed to deliver nuclear strikes on the Soviet Union and equipped with a notoriously poor video display, which flew about a third of the total number of manned bomber missions. Even when planes were capable of "lasing" targets by themselves, drones were the preeminent means for spotting potential targets.

This, of course, was all very much to the taste of a military high command addicted to top-down control. "The level of centralized execution, bureaucracy, and politics is staggering," emailed an attack pilot deployed on the anti-ISIS operation. "In most cases, unless a general officer can look at a video picture from a [drone] over a satellite link, I cannot get authority to engage. . . . It's not uncommon to wait several hours overhead a suspected target for someone to make a decision to engage or not."

Given the near impossibility of independent reporting from behind ISIS lines, opportunities to assess how well the war was really going were rare, but one such came when drones were deployed on a humanitarian mission to relieve tens of thousands of Yazidis trapped on the barren slopes of Mount Sinjar in Iraq without food or water in August 2014. In response to media coverage of the crisis, the U.S. dispatched transport planes to drop necessary supplies by parachute. President Obama was quick to report that this was successfully accomplished. Col. Cheater later proudly announced that drones had been key to the operation, pinpointing the Yazidis and tracking the parachutes so that "the supplies reached the people who needed it (sic)."

Those with a direct view of events told a very different story. "They must have been the shittiest drones in the shop!" exclaimed one American journalist who had spent several days on the summit of Mt. Sinjar in the relevant period, when I told him of Cheater's claim. "I never saw a single parachute. Everyone complained that the aid never reached them." Others reported that at least half of the drone-guided parachuted supplies fell in areas that were unreachable. It was thanks mainly to intervention on the ground by fighters of the Marxist

Kurdish YPG militia that some of the Yazidis were rescued and guided to safety. Others were not so lucky; months later, Yazidi slave girls were reportedly being offered as prizes in a Koran-reading contest in the ISIS capital of Raqqa.

Such unpleasant realities did not affect the sunny optimism customarily displayed by high officials directing U.S. policy. "Fifty percent of [ISIS] top commanders have been eliminated," boasted Secretary of State John Kerry in January 2015. In early June, Deputy Secretary of State Antony Blinken announced that the strikes had killed "more than 10,000" of the enemy, up from the 6,000 kills claimed by the general commanding the operation six months earlier. Seeking to disguise the steady growth of territory controlled by ISIS, the Pentagon for a while simply omitted western Syria, where ISIS had made significant advances, from its published maps of the conflict region.

Elsewhere, CIA and Special Operations targeters stuck to their familiar routines, picking off designated high-value al-Qaeda targets in Yemen, Somalia (where JSOC operated a drone base), Libya, and beyond. In Yemen, the cruel futility of such operations was highlighted by the fact that the U.S. assisted Saudi Arabia in its bombing campaign against al-Qaeda's Houthi enemies, laying waste to much of the poverty-stricken country, even while the Saudis themselves carefully avoided hitting al-Qaeda–held strongholds.

Fifteen years after 9/11, the all-too-evident bankruptcy of remote-control war as a strategy had little effect where it counted—on the bottom line. Taxpayer dollars continued to flow in the direction of anyone promising esoteric applications of concepts that had beguiled Pentagon weapons buyers since the days when the Jasons had dreamed up Operation Igloo White to wire the Ho Chi Minh Trail (see Chapter 2, "Wiring the Jungle.") In June 2015, for example, Deputy Defense Secretary Robert Work revealed a recent demonstration of large numbers of "micro-UAVs capable of autonomous swarming behaviors . . . designed in part to display military advantage over China and Russia." Future plans for swarmers included "Sea Mob," a fleet of drone boats capable of "cooperative swarming behaviors." The Naval Research Laboratory meanwhile unveiled the Close-In Covert Autonomous

Disposable Aircraft (CICADA), a hand-sized device that could be dropped behind enemy lines to collect intelligence. "You equip these with a microphone or a seismic detector, drop them on that road, and it will tell you 'I heard a truck or a car travel along that road.' You know how fast and which direction they're traveling," explained one of the developers excitedly, clearly ignorant of the multibillion-dollar fiasco of Igloo White forty-five years before, in which the very same concept had been combat-tested for five years and utterly failed.

Such ignorance of the long, failure-strewn pursuit of a system that could "know everything" was necessary to keep taxpayers beguiled with fables such as drone swarms reacting autonomously to infinitely variable real-life circumstances. Yazidis expiring from thirst on a distant mountaintop or consigned to the ISIS slave markets might have had something to say about it, but such people belonged only at the very far end of the kill chain, and no one listened to them.

Andrew Cockburn
July 2015

# NOTES

**1 | Remember, Kill Chain**

1  In a cold February dawn in 2010: The description of events in this chapter is drawn from U.S. Central Command, "AR16-6 Investigation, 21 February 2010, U.S. Air-to-Ground Engagement in the vicinity of Shahidi Hassas, Uruzgan District, Afghanistan." https://www.aclu.org/drone-foia-department-defense-uruzgan-investigation-documents. The report was originally released following an FOIA request by *Los Angeles Times* reporter David S. Cloud.

**2 | Wiring the Jungle**

17  Asked who the enemy was: Personal investigation by Leslie Cockburn, who led an ABC News team to the area in 1994.

18  The scheme had been conceived far away: Anne Finkbeiner, *The Jasons: The Secret History of Science's Postwar Elite* (New York: Viking Penguin, 2006), p. 92.

19  On the eve of World War II: Charles R. Griffith, *The Quest, Haywood Hansell and American Strategic Bombing in World War II* (Maxwell AFB, Alabama: Air University Press, 1999), p. 70.

20  Early in 1966 air force planners believed they had identified the "critical node": Bernard C. Nalty, *The War Against Trucks* (Washington, DC: U.S. Air Force, Air Force History and Museums Program, 2005), p. 7.

21  To process the data Garwin, the IBM scientist: Finkbeiner, op. cit., p. 100.

21  Ensconced in Santa Barbara: Ibid., p. 97.

21  Their preferred choices: Ibid., pp. 100–101.

23  "On the battlefield of the future": The full text is carried in the appendix of Paul Dickson's amazingly percipient book, *The Electronic Battlefield* (Bloomington, IN: University of Indiana Press, 1976).

23  Marshall Harrison, a former high school teacher: Marshall Harrison, *A Lonely Kind of War, Forward Air Controller Vietnam* (Bloomington, IN: Xlibris Corp., 2010), pp. 106–107.

23  "Just as it is almost impossible . . .": Dickson, op. cit., p. 22.

24  "after analyzing various names of insects and birds": Thomas P. Ehrhard, *Air Force UAVs: The Secret History* (Washington, DC: Mitchell Institute, 2010), fn. 159, p. 66.

24  In World War II the U.S. Navy had brought about the death: Jack Olsen, *Aphrodite, Desperate Mission* (New York: G. P. Putnam's Sons, 1970), p. 224.

25  Come the Vietnam War, they were adapted for reconnaissance: Ehrhard, op. cit., p. 20.

25  The raids were therefore conducted in deepest secrecy: Department of Defense, "Report on Selected Air and Ground Operations in Cambodia and Laos, Sept. 10, 1973." http://www.dod.mil/pubs/foi/International _security_affairs/vietnam_and_southeast_asiaDocuments/27.pdf. Accessible via Google.

26  Back in Santa Barbara, the Jasons had entertained: Finkbeiner, op. cit., p. 101.

26  "We spent seven days trying to arrive at a solution": James Zumwalt, *Bare Feet, Iron Will—Stories from the Other Side of Vietnam's Battlefields* (Chantilly, VA: Fortis Publishing Co., 2010), p. 258.

26  Otherwise the Vietnamese ran herds of cattle down the trail: Vietnamese language Wikipedia page on Igloo White (auto-translated). http://vi .wikipedia.org/wiki/Chi%E1%BA%BFn_d%E1%BB%8Bch_Igloo_White #cite_note-ReferenceA-2. Accessed April 19, 2013.

26  The electronic barrier cost almost $2 billion to set up and roughly $1 billion a year to operate: Nalty, op. cit., p. 283; Edgar C. Doleman, *Tools of War* (Boston: Boston Publishing Co., 1984), p. 151.

26  The funds for the secret operation were so artfully hidden: Dickson, op. cit., p. 101.

27  "This process," an official U.S. Air Force historian tartly noted: Nalty, op. cit., p. 110.

27  As the same air force historian pointed out: Ibid., p. 296.

27  When General Lucius Clay, commander of the Pacific Air Force: Ibid., p. 302.

27  A CIA analyst's suggestion: George W. Allen, *None So Blind, A Personal Account of the Intelligence Failure in Vietnam* (New York: Ivor R. Dee, 2001), p. 271.

28  At a public meeting in Boston of the antiwar Winter Soldier movement: Fred Branfman, "Guide to the Laos Automated War Archive," Testimony by former U.S. Air Force member Eric Herter (grandson of former secretary of state Christian Herter), November 22, 2009. http://fredbranfman .wordpress.com/.

29   "They knew what they were doing when they sent John": Interview with Tom Christie, Washington, DC, May 8, 2013.

29   "John" was Colonel John Boyd, a legendary fighter pilot: General information about Boyd derived from interviews over many years with, among others, John Boyd, Pierre Sprey, Franklin Spinney, and Tom Christie. For best published source on Boyd, see Roger Coram, *Boyd, the Fighter Pilot Who Changed the Art of War* (Boston: Little Brown, 2002).

29   His superiors had already used him: Interview with Pierre Sprey, Washington, DC, March 17, 2013.

29   Packs of wild dogs roamed unmolested: Coram, op. cit., pp. 268–69.

30   One suggestion actively touted by an air force research base: Nalty, op. cit., p. 279.

30   "They sent me to close it down": Interview with John Boyd, Washington, DC, 1989.

30   Rivolo watched in amazement: Interview, Rex Rivolo, Washington, DC, February 10, 2011.

31   Task Force Alpha was finally switched off: Nalty, op. cit., p. 279.

## 3 | Turning People into Nodes

32   "Don't knock the war that feeds you": Interview with A. Ernest Fitzgerald, former management systems deputy, Office of the Assistant Secretary of the Air Force for Financial Management and Comptroller, Washington, DC, January 2001. The slogan was also featured on a badge worn by aerospace workers around the U.S. during the Vietnam War. See also "Oral History of Edward S. Davidson," SIGMICRO online newsletter, http://newsletter.sigmicro.org/sigmicro-oral-history-transcripts/Ed-Davidson-Transcipt.pdf. Accessed July 19, 2014.

32   Money authorized for buying weapons: The defense budget authority in 1975 was approximately $17 billion for procurement and $9 billion for research, development, test, and evaluation, for a total of $26 billion. http://fraser.stlouisfed.org/docs/publications/usbudget/bus_1977.pdf., p. 330. The defense budget authority in 1978 was approximately $30 billion for procurement and $11 billion for research, development, test, and evaluation, for a total of $41 billion. *The Budget of the United States Government for Fiscal Year 1977* (Washington, DC: U.S. Government Printing Office, 1977), p. 537. http://fraser.stlouisfed.org/docs/publications/usbudget/bus_1980.pdf.

32   In 1976, McDonnell Douglas, then the largest contractor: John Finney, "Not Enough Profits for the Defense Industry?" *New York Times,* January 9, 1977.

33   Intelligence reappraisals of Soviet intentions: Raymond Garthoff,

"Estimating Soviet Military Intentions and Capabilities," ch. 5 in *Watching the Bear, Essays on CIA's Analysis of the Soviet Union* (Washington, DC: CIA Center for the Study of Intelligence, 2007). https://www.cia .gov/library/center-for-the-study-of-intelligence/csi-publications/ books-and-monographs/watching-the-bear-essays-on-cias-analysis-of -the-soviet-union/article05.html.

33  The new barrier fostered by the Pentagon's DARPA: General Accounting Office, "Decisions to Be Made in Charting Future of DOD's Assault Breaker," January 28, 1981, p. 1. http://www.gao.gov/assets/140/132235.pdf. Accessed February 23, 2013.

33  Instead of the sensors: Carlo Kopp, "Precision-Guided Munitions, The New Breed," Air Power Australia, 1984. http://www.ausairpower.net/TE -Assault-Breaker.html. Accessed January 15, 2013.

35  "The objective of our precision guided weapon systems": Robert R. Tomes, *U.S. Defense Strategy from Vietnam to Operation Iraqi Freedom* (Florence, KY: Taylor & Francis, 2006), p. 67.

35  The General Accounting Office, the watchdog agency that monitors: GAO, "Decisions to Be Made," op. cit., p. 9.

35  "Precision weapons, smart shells, electronic reconnaissance systems": Michael Sterling, "Soviet Reactions to Nato's Emerging Technologies for Deep Attack," A Rand Note Prepared for the U.S. Air Force, Santa Monica, 1985. http://www.rand.org/content/dam/rand/pubs/notes/2009 /N2294.pdf.

36  When, for example, the navy's development of invulnerable ballistic-missile submarines: Fred Kaplan, *Wizards of Armageddon* (New York: Simon & Schuster, 1982), pp. 233ff.

36  At the beginning of World War II: Don Sherman, "The Secret Weapon," *Air & Space Magazine* (February/March 1995).

37  On an infamous raid: "Factsheet: The Norden M-9 Bombsight," The National Museum of the U.S. Air Force, Dayton, OH. Posted August 16, 2010.

37  The device was still being used to drop sensors: Nalty, op. cit., p. 27.

37  In December 1968, John Foster told an interviewer: John S. Foster Jr., Transcript of Oral History Interview II by Dorothy Pierce, December 12, 1968, p. 6. http://www.lbjlibrary.net/assets/documents/archives/oral_histories /foster_j/Foster2.PDF.

37  Though hailed as a momentous event: David Evans, "Sorting Out the Sorties," *Chicago Tribune*, February 8, 1991.

38  Intimations that something new: Richard H. Van Atta et al., "Transformation and Transition: DARPA's Role in Fostering an Emerging Revolution in Military Affairs, vol. 2: Detailed Assessments" (Washington, DC: Institute for Defense Analyses, 2003).

39  Pierre Sprey, a mathematical prodigy: Interview with Pierre Sprey, Washington, DC, October 19, 2013.

41  In reality, an actual Soviet invasion: Jason Vest, "The New Marshall Plan," InTheseTimes.com, April 2, 2001. http://inthesetimes.com/issue/25/09/vest2509.html.

41  Warden, deeply immersed: Interview with John Warden, Washington, DC, June 1991.

42  As for targets, he had developed what he called the "five rings" theory: Colonel John A. Warden III, "The Enemy as a System," *Airpower Journal* (Spring 1995).

42  Saddam's name was erased: Rick Atkinson, *Crusade: The Untold Story of the Gulf War* (New York: Houghton Mifflin, 1993), p. 64.

43  Under "Expected results": Ibid., p. 61.

43  Earlier in 1990, he had coined the air force's new motto: Fred Kaplan, *The Insurgents* (New York, Simon & Schuster, 2012), p. 49.

44  As Lockheed publicists reported: Report to the Ranking Minority Member, Committee on Commerce, House of Representatives, "Operation Desert Storm, Evaluation of the Air Campaign," Washington, DC, General Accounting Office GAO/NSIAD-97-1341997, June 1997, p. 26.

44  Writing soon after the war, Perry celebrated: William J. Perry, "Desert Storm and Deterrence," *Foreign Affairs* 70, no. 4 (Fall 1991): pp. 66–82.

44  Andrew Marshall was quick to catch the wave: Barry D. Watts, "The Maturing Revolution in Military Affairs," Washington, DC, Center for Strategic and Budgetary Assessments, 2011, p. 2.

45  Deptula . . . took to print: David A. Deptula, *Firing for Effect: Change in the Nature of Warfare*, Defense and Airpower Series (Arlington, VA: Aerospace Education Foundation, 1995).

45  "saved my ass": Communication from the late Colonel Robert Brown, USAF.

46  a diligent three-year investigation: General Accounting Office: Operation Desert Storm, Evaluation of the Air Campaign, GSO/NSIAD-97-134.

47  Catchphrases such as "system of systems": Admiral William A. Owen, "The Emerging U.S. System-of-Systems," *Strategic Forum* 63 (February 1996), Washington, DC, National Defense University. http://www.dtic.mil/cgi-bin/GetTRDoc?AD=ADA394313.

47  "If we are able to view a strategic battlefield: Senate Budget Committee, Hearing on National Defense Budget in the New Century, February 12, 2001.

47  Other high-ranking officers talked wistfully: Pelham G. Boyer, Robert

S. Wood, eds., *Strategic Transformation and Naval Power in the 21st Century* (Newport, RI: Naval War College Press, 1998), p. 229.

47 The Pentium III microprocessor: Information supplied by Dr. Herb Lin, National Research Council, March 1, 2013.

48 This inherent problem was apparently lost on Cebrowski: Vice-Admiral Arthur K. Cebrowski and John A. Garstka, "Net-Centric Warfare, Its Origin and Future," *Proceedings Magazine*, U.S. Naval Institute, January 1998.

48 Two Rand Corporation researchers: John Arquilla and David Ronfeldt, eds., *In Athena's Camp: Preparing for Conflict in the Information Age* (Santa Monica, CA: Rand Corporation, 1997).

48 Their report, "Transforming Defense: National Security in the 21st Century": Report of the National Defense Panel, "Power Projection," December 1997. http://www.dod.gov/pubs/foi/administration_and_Management/other/902.pdf.

48 Paul Van Riper, for example: Lieutenant General Paul Van Riper, Testimony before Procurement Subcommittee and Research and Development Subcommittee of the House National Security Committee, March 20, 1997.

49 Nor did Van Riper think much of air power enthusiasts in general: Text of "From Douhet to Deptula," kindly supplied to the author by Paul Van Riper.

49 A Vietnam combat veteran: Interview with Paul Van Riper, Quantico, VA, March 19, 2013.

49 In 1973, in his final session of congressional testimony: Testimony of John S. Foster, Hearings on Cost Escalation in Defense Procurement Contracts and Military Posture, House Armed Services Committee, April 12, 1973.

50 Even so, Boeing and other defense corporations: Ehrhard, op. cit., p. 20.

50 Perry helped speed the process along: Ibid., p. 20.

### 4 | Predator Politics

51 The Predator drone was originally designed: Thomas Ehrhard, op. cit., fn. 170, p. 67.

51 After falling out with his employer: Richard Whittle, "The Man Who Invented the Predator," *Air & Space Magazine*, April 2013.

52 Code-named Amber: Ehrhard, op. cit., p. 20.

52 However, just as Karem's company: David Axe, *Shadow Wars: Chasing Conflict in an Era of Peace* (Washington, DC: Potomac Books, 2013), p. 5.

52 Coincidentally, its initial project: Triga History, http://triga-world.net/history.html.

52  After parting company with parent General Dynamics: Matt Potter, "General Atomics—Color It Blue," *San Diego Reader*, July 12, 2001.

53  As Neal later told an interviewer: Di Freeze, "Linden Blue: From Disease-Resistant Bananas to UAVs," *Airport Journals*, Englewood, CO, October 2005. http://airportjournals.com/2005/10/page/4/.

53  Furious residents blocked the scheme: Mick O'Malley and Ben Cubby, "Digging Dirt with a Sledgehammer," *Sidney Morning Herald*, July 31, 2009.

53  The brothers also bought the decrepit Sequoyah uranium-processing facility: Chris Kraul, "GA Tech to Buy Kerr-McGee's Uranium Plant," *Los Angeles Times*, November 21, 1987.

53  Undeterred, General Atomics kept operating the leaky facility: Keith Schneider, "Troubled Factory Is to Be Shut in Oklahoma," *New York Times*, November 25, 1992.

53  An investigation found: Ibid.

54  To that end they set up a defense programs group: Dan Berger, "Haig, Vessey, to Help Guide New GA," *San Diego Union-Tribune*, February 13, 1986.

54  Cassidy, described by subordinates as "not beloved, but admired": Alan Richman, "Now Hear This: An Admiral Goes Down with His Ashtray," *People Magazine*, June 17, 1985. http://www.people.com/people/archive/article/0,,20091015,00.html.

54  But the Predator, as the device was called, repeatedly crashed: Steve LaRue, "S.D. Firm's Unmanned Plane Tested," *San Diego Union-Tribune*, December 2, 1988.

54  Karem's design suddenly became a CIA program: Ehrhart, op. cit., p. 67, note 178.

55  Almost half the 268 Predators: Craig Whitlock, "When Drones Fall from the Sky," *Washington Post*, June 20, 2014.

55  "The problem is that nobody is comfortable with predator": Ibid.

56  Familiar to anyone with a smartphone: Daniel Parry, "Father of GPS and Pioneer of Satellite Telemetry and Timing Inducted into National Inventors Hall of Fame," *Naval Research Laboratory News*, March 31, 2010.

56  Thanks mainly to exponential increases in the amount of data: "Global Bandwidth, Feast or Famine?" *Network*, October 1, 2000. http://www.globalsecurity.org/space/systems/bandwidth.htm.

57  Two of these prototypes disappeared during the 1995 missions: Ehrhart, op. cit., p. 50.

58  In October 1994, when General Ronald Fogleman: Ehrhart, op. cit., p. 51.

58    In April 1996, William Perry, by now defense secretary: Richard Whittle, *Predator's Big Safari* (Washington, DC: Mitchell Institute Press, 2011), p. 10.

59    As Neal Blue, who contributed $100,000: Barry M. Horstman, "Some Knew Where George Was and Sent Lots of Money for Him," *Los Angeles Times*, January 25, 1988.

59    "For our size, we possess": Gopal Ratnam, "Predator Maker Spreads Wings: General Atomics Expands into Sensors, Lasers, Launchers," *Defense News*, May 2, 2005.

59    As originally written: Melvin Goodman, *National Insecurity* (San Francisco, City Lights Books, 2013), p. 31.

59    "We must provide the resources": Dan Morgan, "House Approves $289 Billion for Defense in 367 to 58 Vote," *Washington Post*, July 20, 2000.

59    In 2005 Lewis took command of the full appropriations committee and in 2006 was nominated: Citizens for Responsibility and Ethics in Washington, "Beyond Delay, The 20 Most Corrupt Members of Congress (and Five to Watch)," Washington, DC, 2006, p. 67. http://www.crewsmostcorrupt.org/mostcorrupt/entry/most-corrupt-2006.

60    "The chairman [Lewis] is too modest": Hearing of the Defense Subcommittee of the House Appropriations Committee on U.S. Army Posture and Acquisition Programs, March 12, 2003.

60    Thus it was that Lewis, in his capacity as vice chairman: Whittle, op. cit., p. 11.

60    The three-month war on behalf of the insurgency: "Fellow Military Leaders May Prove to be Clark's Toughest Hurdle," *InsideDefense.com*, September 13, 2003.

60    Also hit were businesses belonging to President Milošević's friends: Julian H. Tolbert, Major, USAF, "Crony Attack Strategic Attack's Silver Bullet?" Thesis presented to the School of Advanced Air and Space Studies, Air University, Maxwell Air Force Base, Alabama, Air University Press, November 2006.

60    As Deptula, by now a brigadier general: Abe Jackson, "America's Airman, David Deptula and the Airpower Moment," School of Advanced Air and Space Studies, Air University, Maxwell Air Force Base, Air University Press, June 2011.

61    As General Michael Jackson, commander of the British contingent, said afterward: Andrew Gilligan, "'Russia, Not Bombs, Brought End to War in Kosovo' Says Jackson," *Daily Telegraph*, August 1, 1999.

61    Nevertheless General Henry Shelton, chairman of the Joint Chiefs of Staff: John Barry, "The Kosovo Cover-up," *Newsweek*, May 15, 2000.

62  As U.S. Army Colonel Douglas MacGregor: Email to author, April 14, 2012.

62  They had put dummy tanks on display: Associated Press, "NATO Attack on Yugoslavia Gave Iraq Good Lessons," *Toronto Globe and Mail*, November 20, 2002.

62  Richard Armitage . . . wrote the speech: Eric Schmidt, "A Longtime Friend of Powell's Is Tapped to Be His Deputy," *New York Times*, February 13, 2001.

62  "Our forces in the next century must be agile, lethal, readily deployable": George W. Bush, "A Period of Consequences," Speech delivered at The Citadel, Charleston, SC, September 23, 1999. http://www3.citadel.edu/pao /addresses/pres_bush.html.

63  So Slobodan Milošević's personal residence was duly destroyed: BBC News, "Milosevic House Destroyed by NATO," April 22, 1999.

63  As one officer told a reporter: James W. Canan, "Seeing More, and Risking Less, with UAVs," *Aerospace America*, Aerospace Industries Association, Washington, DC, October 1999, p. 26.

63  Jumper himself excitedly reported to Congress: General John Jumper, Testimony to House Armed Services Military Readiness Subcommittee, October 26, 1999.

64  Apart from that one incident hailed by Jumper: Interview with James G. "Snake" Clark, Director, Intelligence, Surveillance and Reconnaissance Innovation, Deputy Chief of Staff for ISR, U.S. Air Force Headquarters, Washington, DC, October 13, 2013.

64  In a significant step along the road to remotely controlling the battle: Department of Defense, Report to Congress, "Kosovo/Operation Allied Force After-Action Report," January 2000, p. 124.

64  Meanwhile, thanks to the same expansion in communications bandwidth: Ibid., p. 26.

64  The general and his micromanaging habits: Interview with former senior U.S. Air Force officer, Washington, DC, February 2013.

67  Even as the smoke of the Balkan battlefields cleared: Interview with Tom Christie, Washington, DC, May 8, 2013.

68  The tests, carried out over nine days: Director, Operational Test & Evaluation, "Report on the Predator Medium Altitude Endurance Unmanned Aerial Vehicle," Department of Defense, Washington, DC, October 3, 2001.

68  Overall, Predator could find less than a third of its targets: Ibid., p. 20.

68  National Imagery Interpretation Rating Scale: Ibid., p. 3.

68  29 percent: Ibid., p. 20.

69 The infrared camera: Ibid., p. 18.

69 One or another component: Ibid., p. 40.

69 In Vietnam, troops fighting on the ground: Harrison, op. cit., p. 109.

69 "The air force had had this idea . . .": Interview, Pentagon official, Washington, DC, April 19, 2013.

70 Just as the muddy pictures from Kosovo: Interview with "Snake" Clark, op. cit.

70 Yet, the closer one looks at those pictures: "Missed Opportunities," *NBC Nightly News*, March 17, 2004. http://www.nbcnews.com/id/4540958/ns /nbc_nightly_news_with_brian_williams/t/osama-bin-laden-missed -opportunities/#.Uf7BSmR-xU4.

71 As George Tenet later told the 9/11 commission: "CIA Director Says Terrorist Threat Warnings Made in 1997; Tenet Says His Warnings, Intelligence Reports Heard," U.S. State Department, Washington File, March 24, 2004.

71 The cover letter of Christie's report: Accessible at pogoarchives.org/m/ dp/dp-predator.pdf.

72 Three years later she would be sentenced: Leslie Wayne, "Ex-Pentagon Official Gets 9 Months for Conspiring to Favor Boeing," *New York Times*, October 2, 2004.

72 "What the fuck is this?": Interview with Tom Christie, Washington, DC, May 8, 2013.

72 In December 2001, President Bush returned to the Citadel: "President Bush Addresses the Corps," Speech delivered at The Citadel, Charleston, SC, December 11, 2001. http://www3.citadel.edu/pao/addresses/presbush 01.html.

### 5 | It's Not Assassination If We Do It

73 "As long as Hitler continues": Dennis Rigden, *Kill the Fuhrer: Section X and Operation Foxley* (Stroud, Gloucestershire, UK: The History Press, 1999), Kindle ed., 2011, location 1196.

74 Although Heydrich, one of the cruelest of the Nazi bosses, did die from wounds: Robert Gerwarth, *Hitler's Hangman: The Life of Heydrich* (New Haven: Yale University Press, 2011), pp. 280–87.

74 "grave divergence of views": Rigden, op. cit., location 1287.

75 "It would be disastrous if the world . . .": Rigden, op. cit., location 1170.

76 In any event, SOE was in reality a surprisingly ineffective operation: Jean Overton Fuller, *The German Penetration of SOE: France 1941–44* (London, UK: William Kimber, 1975), passim.

76 The biographer of OSS Director William Donovan summarized:

Anthony Cave-Brown, *William Donovan, The Last Hero* (New York: Times Books, 1982), p. 236.

76 Sadly, the intelligence turned out to be entirely bogus: Cave-Brown, op. cit., p. 701.

77 Clarke's colorful style and views: Forrest Pogue, interview with Carter Clarke, July 6, 1959, tape 99. Transcript kindly supplied by the George C. Marshall Foundation, 1600 VMI Parade, Lexington, VA.

78 So McCormack was asked to come down from New York: Memorandum by McCormack to Clarke on problems, origins, and functions of the Special Branch M.I.S., April 15, 1943, Records of the National Security Agency, National Archives Record Group 457.

78 Thus in 1944 Clarke was dispatched: "Carter W. Clarke Dies at 90; An Army Intelligence Officer," *New York Times*, September 7, 1987.

78 Dewey had learned of this: Telephone interview with Carter Clarke, September 1983.

79 American commanders saw an opportunity for revenge: Don Davis, *Lightning Strike, The Secret Mission to Kill Admiral Yamamoto and Avenge Pearl Harbor* (New York, St. Martin's Griffin, 2006), pp. 53, 232.

80 "I remember when we got the news of Hiroshima": Interview with Edward Huddleston, San Francisco, December 1984.

81 Donovan and others assumed that the leaker: Jennet Conant, "Swashbuckling Spymaster," *New York Times*, February 11, 2011.

81 Even when the agency did take a successful technical intelligence initiative: Dino Brugioni, *Eyes in the Sky: Eisenhower, the CIA, and Cold War Aerial Espionage* (Annapolis, MD: Naval Institute Press, 2010), p. 101.

81 Even more secretly, and dangerously: Fred Kaplan, *Wizards of Armageddon* (New York: Simon & Schuster, 1982), p. 134.

82 "following in the footsteps of the OSS": Tim Weiner, *Legacy of Ashes* (New York: Doubleday, 2007), p. 55.

82 Yet in both cases, as one historian: Ibid., p. 80.

83 Starting in 1952, according to internal agency documents: Kate Doyle and Peter Kornbluh, eds., "CIA and Assassination, The Guatemala Documents," The National Security Archive Electronic Briefing Book, no. 4, doc. 1. http://www.gwu.edu/~nsarchiv/NSAEBB/NSAEBB4/.

83 To aid in training the specialists: Ibid., doc. 2.

83 On the other hand, human rights groups estimate: Ibid., introduction.

84 According to Castro's longtime bodyguard: Duncan Campbell, "638 Ways to Kill Castro," *The Guardian*, August 3, 2006.

84 As Richard Bissell, the CIA's deputy director for plans later testified: Weiner, op. cit., p. 215.

84  "I want him destroyed, don't you understand?": Stephen Dorrill, *MI6, Inside the Covert World of Her Majesty's Secret Intelligence Service* (New York: The Free Press, 2002), p. 613.

85  In Laos, for example: Leslie and Andrew Cockburn, producers, "Guns, Drugs and the CIA," PBS *Frontline*, WGBH Boston, transmitted May 17, 1988.

85  "So I sent them a head-count": Interview with Tony Po, Udorn Thani, Thailand, November 1987.

85  Officially termed the Viet Cong Infrastructure Information System: Doug Valentine, *The Phoenix Program* (Bloomington, IN: iUniverse, 2000), p. 258.

86  Before long the list had grown to 6,000: William Rousseau and Austin Long, *The Phoenix Program and Contemporary Counterinsurgency* (Santa Monica, CA: The Rand Corp., 2009), p. 9.

86  In August of the following year, Robert "Blowtorch" Komer: Valentine, op. cit., p. 250.

86  "Sure we got involved in assassinations": Valentine, op. cit., p. 311.

86  Thus in 1969 the *New York Times*: Terence Smith, "C.I.A.-Planned Drive on Officials of Vietcong Is Said to Be Failing; U.S. Sources Say Suspects Are Often Freed by Local Vietnamese Authorities," *New York Times*, August 19, 1969.

86  By 1971 euphemism had been cast aside: Felix Belair Jr., "U.S. Aide Defends Pacification Program in Vietnam Despite Killings of Civilians," *New York Times*, July 20, 1971.

87  "a program for the assassination of civilian leaders": Valentine, op. cit., p. 321.

87  Alternatively, the program met with wholehearted approval: Mark Moyar, *Phoenix and the Birds of Prey, Counterinsurgency and Counterterrorism in Vietnam* (Annapolis, MD: Naval Institute Press, 1997), p. 167.

87  Though large numbers of people were indeed being killed: Nick Turse, *Kill Anything That Moves* (New York: Henry Holt, 2013), p. 190.

87  As he told author Nick Turse: Ibid., p. 190.

87  Unsurprisingly, it was well penetrated: Sam Adams, *War of Numbers* (Hanover, NH: Steerforth Press, 1994), pp. 178–79.

87  Vincent Okamoto, later a distinguished Los Angeles Superior Court Judge: Christian Appy, *Patriots: The Vietnam War Remembered from All Sides* (New York: Penguin Books, 2004), p. 321.

88  In 2004, for example, David Kilcullen: David Kilcullen, "Countering Global Insurgency," *Small Wars Journal*, November 30, 2004. smallwarsjournal.com/documents/kilcullen.pdf.

88 "Sam, this may sound strange . . .": Adams, op. cit., p. 168.

89 The ban, first pronounced by President Gerald Ford: President Gerald R. Ford's Executive Order 11905: United States Foreign Intelligence Activities, February 18, 1976. http://www.ford.utexas.edu/library/speeches/760110e .asp#SEC. 5.

90 Administration officials later explained to the *Washington Post*: "Covert Hit Teams Might Evade Presidential Ban," *Washington Post*, February 12, 1984.

90 So, in 1986, President Reagan sent a fleet of F-111 bombers: Seymour Hersh, "Target Qaddafi," *New York Times*, February 22, 1987.

90 W. Hays Parks, a military lawyer working for the army's judge advocate general: W. Hays Parks, Memorandum on Executive Order 12333 and Assassination, Department of the Army, Office of the Judge Advocate General, November 2, 1989. Posted by John F. Kennedy School of Government, Harvard University. http://www.hks.harvard.edu/cchrp/Use %20of%20Force/October%202002/Parks_final.pdf.

91 As Parks later explained to me: Telephone interview, January 25, 2014.

91 According to an authoritative account of the affair: Seymour Hersh, "Target Gaddafi," op. cit.

## 6 | Kingpins and Maniacs

93 "That was a good time": Interview with Rex Rivolo, Chantilly, VA, December 19, 2013.

94 By the late 1980s, Rivolo, always enthusiastic about a new project: Jim Detjen, "Mapmaker Hopes to Chart Milky Way Star System," *Miami Herald,* November 19, 1988.

95 Early on, he concluded that the V-22 was dangerously unstable: Interview with Barry Crane, Williamsburg, VA, December 18, 2013.

95 In 1993 the Clinton administration awarded the post to Brian Sheridan: Vanessa Mizell, "New at the Top: Brian Sheridan's Interest in International Security Started Early in Life," *Washington Post*, February 13, 2011.

96 The ultimate solution appeared simple and obvious: Edward J. Epstein, *Agency of Fear* (London, UK: Verso, 1990), p. 144.

97 Among these major traffickers: Andrew and Leslie Cockburn, "On the Trail of Medellín's Drug Lord," *Vanity Fair*, December 1992.

97 At one point there were seventeen of these surveillance aircraft simultaneously in the air: Mark Bowden, *Killing Pablo* (New York: Penguin, 2002), p. 154.

98 "We used Cali": Interview, Washington, DC, February 2010.

98 In a revealing address to a 1992 meeting of DEA veterans: Robert Bonner (one of several speakers), "The Kingpin Strategy, Did It Work and Is

It Still Relevant?" DEA Museum Lecture Series, September 12, 2012. http://www.deamuseum.org/education/transcripts/091212-DEA-Kingpin-transcript.pdf.

99  No less threateningly, the CIA had been anxious not to lose out: Ronald Chepesiuk, *Drug Lords, The Rise and Fall of the Cali Cartel* (Preston, UK: Milo Books, 2005), p. 99.

99  The new unit pursued identical targets: Testimony of DEA Acting Administrator Donnie R. Marshall, DEA Oversight Hearing, House Judiciary Committee, Subcommittee on Crime, July 29, 1999.

99  "DEA and CIA were butting heads": Interview with Robert Bonner, Los Angeles, January 28, 2013.

100  The agency budget, always the surest token: Drug Enforcement Administration website, "DEA Staffing and Budget." http://www.justice.gov/dea/about/history/staffing.shtml.

100  The DEA, he discovered, put enormous effort: Dr. Barry D. Crane, Dr. A. Rex Rivolo, and Dr. Gary C. Comfort, "An Empirical Examination of Counterdrug Interdiction Program Effectiveness," Institute for Defense Analysis, Washington, DC, January 1997, p. II-2. http://www.dtic.mil/dtic/tr/fulltext/u2/a320737.pdf.

100  The implications were considerable: Ibid., p. II-20.

101  Far from impeding the flow of cocaine onto the streets and up the nostrils of America: Ibid., pp. IV-3, IV-4.

102  Deep in the jungles of southern Colombia: Alan Weisman, "The Cocaine Conundrum," *Los Angeles Times Magazine*, September 24, 1995.

103  This was more than just a hunch: IDA, "Deterrence Effects and Peru's Force-Down/Shoot-Down Policy: Lessons Learned for Counter-Cocaine Interdiction Operations," Paper P-3472, Washington, DC, 2000.

105  The formula for the U.S.-sponsored eradication spray: Steve Kroft, "Good Intentions, Bad Results; Health Effects on Colombian Citizens from Pesticide Spraying by U.S. Planes to Kill Coca Plants," CBS News, *60 Minutes*, January 13, 2002.

106  They show the median price of a gram of cocaine: UN Office on Drugs and Crime, "Illicit Drug Markets," Bulletin on Narcotics, vol. LVI, nos. 1 and 2, 2004. http://www.unodc.org/unodc/secured/wdr/Cocaine_Heroin_Prices.pdf.

106  As later reported by the *Washington Post*'s Dana Priest: Dana Priest, "US Role at a Crossroads in Mexico's Intelligence War on the Cartels," *Washington Post*, April 27, 2013.

106  However, when Enrique Nieto replaced Calderón as president in December 2012: NPR, "Mexico's New President Changes Drug-Trafficking Tactics," January 1, 2013.

107 "It led to the seconds-in-command . . .": "Mexico's War on Cartels Made Drug Crisis Worse, Says New Government," *The Guardian*, December 19, 2012.

108 "These were people who had done nothing else but look at Russia and Eastern Europe for forty years": Interview, Washington, DC, December 4, 2013.

109 Scheuer himself paints a different picture: Telephone interview, February 12, 2014.

109 It should come as no surprise: National Commission on Terrorist Attacks Upon the United States, "The 9/11 Commission Report," July 22, 2004, p. 184.

110 Coincidentally the CIA already had on the payroll a team: James Bamford, *A Pretext for War: 9/11, Iraq, and the Abuse of America's Intelligence Agencies* (New York: Doubleday, 2004), pp. 184–88.

110 Even when the White House did authorize a cruise missile strike: Interview with Michael Scheuer.

110 In retrospect, of course, this sporadic and ill-planned pursuit of: Chris Wallace, Interview with Bill Clinton, Fox News *Sunday*, September 22, 2006.

111 He even earned a word of commendation from the man himself: Mary Louise Kelly and Melissa Block, "CIA Chief Says al-Qaida Is Plotting Attack on U.S.," NPR, September 7, 2007.

111 Black had spent much of his career in the agency's Africa Division: Craig Whitney, "A Onetime Backer Accuses Savimbi," *New York Times*, March 12, 1989.

111 The bloody attacks on the U.S. embassies in Kenya and Tanzania on August 7, 1998: John Mintz, "Panel Cites U.S. Failures on Security for Embassies," *Washington Post*, January 8, 1999.

112 Amazingly, a pair of FBI agents: WGBH Boston, "The Spy Factory," PBS *Nova*, February 3, 2009.

112 The accusation drew a heated denial from CIA Director Tenet, Cofer Black, and Richard Blee: "Joint Statement on Richard Clark Allegations," posted on Georgejtenet.net, August 11, 2011. http://www.georgejtenet.com /latest-statements/joint-statement-on-richard-clarke-allegations -august-11-2011/2011.

113 Shaikh, who later recalled the pair as being "nice but not what you call extroverted people": Kelly Thornton, "Hijackers Who Lived Here: 'Nice,' 'Dull,' " *San Diego Union*, September 16, 2001.

113 Settling into their new home: Consortium News, "NSA Insiders Reveal What Went Wrong," memo from former senior NSA officials Thomas Drake and William Binney, January 7, 2014. http://consortiumnews.com /2014/01/07/nsa-insiders-reveal-what-went-wrong/.

114 President Obama himself, in defending the massive domestic "metadata" phone records program: President Obama, "Remarks by the President on Review of Signals Intelligence," U.S. Department of Justice, Washington, DC, January 17, 2014. http://www.whitehouse.gov/the-press -office/2014/01/17/remarks-president-review-signals-intelligence.

114 As it was, the pair was left unmolested: Consortium News, Former NSA officials' memo, op. cit.

114 Late in the evening of 9/11: Interview, Maclean, VA, June 26, 2014.

114 "On the morning of September 11, 2001, the Counterterrorism Center was a collection of rejects and cast-offs": Interview, Washington, DC, March 28, 2014.

115 On the day he signed the document, Bush spoke with reporters at the Pentagon: ABC News, "Bush: Bin Laden Wanted Dead or Alive," September 17, 2001. http://abcnews.go.com/US/story?id=92483.

115 Reporting on the presidential "kill list": "Threats and Responses: Hunt for Al Qaeda; Bush Has Widened Authority of CIA to Kill Terrorists," *New York Times,* December 15, 2002.

116 fully 20 percent of all CIA analysts: Greg Miller and Julie Tate, "CIA Focus Shifts to Killing Targets," *Washington Post,* September 1, 2011.

116 For many years the preferred Hebrew term for assassination: Gideon Alon, "Rubinstein Expressed Support for the Assassinations, Added That the Term 'Killings' Tarnishes Israel's Name and That They Should Be Named 'Targeted Prevention,'" *Haaretz,* November 29, 2001. http://www .haaretz.co.il/misc/1.752603. Trans. by Noga Malkin.

116 "the sexiest trend in counterterrorism: Ben Kaspit, "The Polish Poet and the Art of Prevention," *Maariv,* June 10, 2005. Trans. by Noga Malkin.

117 'barrel of terror': Patrick Tyler, *Fortress Israel* (New York: Farrar, Straus & Giroux, 2012), pp. 456–57.

117 "If you do something for long enough,": Jeff Halper, "Globalizing Gaza" Counterpunch.org., August 18, 2014. http://www.counterpunch.org/2014 /08/18/globalizing-gaza/. Accessed August 20, 2014.

117 Immediately following his retirement: Avi Dicter, Daniel L. Byman, *Israel's Lessons for Fighting Terrorism and their Implications for the United States.* Washington, DC. Saban Center for Middle East Policy at the Brookings Institution, Analysis Paper no. 8. March 2006.

## 7 | Legally Blind

118 "I felt a familiar rush of adrenaline": Tommy Franks, Malcolm McConnell, *American Soldier* (New York: William Morrow, 2005), pp. 291ff; Interview with David Deptula, Washington, DC, February 14, 2013.

119 a former day care center: Dana Priest and William Arkin, *Top Secret America* (Boston: Little Brown, 2011), p. 204.

120 According to the Mullah's driver: Anand Gopal, *No Good Men Among the Living* (New York: Metropolitan Books, 2014), p. 14.

121 Tirin Kot: Gopal, op. cit., p. 28ff.

121 Bin Laden himself had slipped the net with relative ease: Peter Bergen, *Manhunt: The Ten-Year Search for Bin Laden from 9/11 to Abbottabad* (New York: Broadway Books, 2013), p. 54.

121 Less fortunate was Mohammed Atef: Richard Whittle, *Predator. The Secret Origins of the Drone Revolution* (New York: Henry Holt, 2014), pp. 276–79.

121 but was swiftly replaced as military commander: BBC News "al-Qaeda's New Military Chief," December 21, 2001.

123 "to capture or kill as many Al Qaeda as we could": Yaniv Barzilai, *102 Days of War* (Washington, DC: Potomac Books, 2014), p. 45.

123 Abdul Rahim al-Janko: Gopal, op. cit., pp. 145–46.

123 "the Joint Special Operations Task Force (i.e., Task Force 11) had become frustrated": Colonel Andrew N. Milani, *Pitfalls of Technology: A Case Study of the Battle on Takur Ghar Mountain* (Carlisle, PA: U.S. Army War College, 2009), p. 1.

123 One such was Saifur Rahman Mansoor: Rahimullah Yusufzai, "Battle Creates a New Taliban Legend," *Time*, May 7, 2002.

123 he opened negotiations with the authorities in Kabul: Gopal, op. cit., p. 133.

124 A surge in cell-phone traffic: Sean Naylor, *Not a Good Day to Die* (New York: Berkley, 2006), p. 37.

124 "Unfortunately . . . the enemy thought so too": Milani, op. cit., p. 12.

124 the pictures showed no sign of any human presence: Ibid., p. 8.

125 These were exactly the kind of telltale signs: Harrison, op. cit., p. 107.

125 But in the sudden jolt of the takeoff: Milani, op. cit., p. 13.

125 This was a means of revealing location: Milani, op. cit., p. 17.

126 They felt they had "total situational awareness": Malcolm Macpherson, *Roberts Ridge* (New York: Presidio Press, 2005), pp. 68–71.

126 "Get off the Net": Naylor, op. cit., location 6620.

126 $1 million a day: Dana Preist, op. cit., p. 246.

126 legal definition of blindness: http://police.laws.com/illegal/legally-blind.

126 To make matters worse, the people operating this drone: Macpherson, op. cit., p. 68.

127 Technical Sergeant John Chapman . . . who was left for dead: Milani, op. cit., p. 21.

128 rain of bombs: Sean Naylor, Operation Anaconda, MIT Security Studies program seminar, March 22, 2006.

128 "Go get 'em": David Wood, "Inside Command Post in Hunt for Bin Laden," *Seattle Times*, March 8, 2002.

129 when Scott "Soup" Campbell arrived on the scene, he found chaos:

Telephone interview with Campbell, January 10, 2014; Lawrence Lessard, Interview with Lieutenant Colonel Scott "Soup" Campbell, Combat Studies Institute, Fort Leavenworth, Kansas, pt. 3, May 15, 2009.

131  But he lived to fight on many more days: Rahimullah Yusufzai, "Battle Creates a New Taliban Legend," *Time*, March 7, 2002.

131  He finally died in a battle: Bill Roggio, "Taliban Leader Killed in Clash in South Waziristan," *Long War Journal*, January 13, 2008. http://www.longwarjournal.org/archives/2008/01/taliban_commander_ki.php.

132  At his crowded memorial service: Milani, op. cit., p. 34.

132  "enmeshed in a network of preconceptions": Milani, op. cit., p. 30.

## 8 | Kill Them! Prevail!

133  Three years in the planning, budgeted at $250 million: Sean Naylor, "War Games Rigged," *Army Times*, August 16, 2002.

134  But Van Riper was a twofold enemy: Telephone interview with Paul Van Riper, September 6, 2006.

136  This happy state being achieved: Harlan K. Ullman and James P. Wade, *Shock and Awe: Achieving Rapid Dominance* (Washington, DC: National Defense University, 1996), XXIV.

137  According to a postwar Pentagon assessment: BBC News, "Russia Denies Iraq Secrets Claim," March 25, 2006. http://news.bbc.co.uk/2/hi/middle_east/4843394.stm.

137  "We were sure we'd got him": Interview with former DIA analyst, Alexandria, VA, February 18, 2014.

138  "I really didn't care": Julian Borger, "2 pm: Saddam Is Spotted. 2:48 pm: Pilots Get Their Orders. 3pm: 60ft Crater at Target," *The Guardian*, April 9, 2003.

138  According to the former Defense Intelligence Agency analyst Marc Garlasco: "Bombing Afghanistan," CBS *60 Minutes*, October 25, 2007.

139  But there was a flaw: the Thuraya's GPS system was not so precise in fixing its position: Human Rights Watch Report, "Off Target: The Conduct of the War and Civilian Casualties in Iraq," December 12, 2003. http://www.hrw.org/reports/2003/usa1203/usa1203.pdf.

139  "Our number was thirty": CBS *60 Minutes*, "Bombing Afghanistan," op. cit.

139  In no case had it been refused: Michael Gordon, "After the War, Preliminaries, U.S. Air Raids in '02 Prepared for War in Iraq," *New York Times*, July 20, 2003.

139  "if you lop the head off a snake": John Burns, "The Capture of Saddam Hussein," *New York Times*, December 15, 2003.

140  "Kill them! Prevail!": Lieutenant General Ricardo Sanchez, *Wiser in Battle: A Soldier's Story* (New York: HarperCollins, 2008), pp. 149–50.

140  "producing desired futures": Major Robert Herndon et al., "Effects Based Operations in Afghanistan: The CJTF-180 Method of Orchestrating Effects to Achieve Objectives," *Field Artillery*, January–February 2004.

141  whose head Zarqawi sawed off with a carving knife for the benefit of the camera: CBS News, "CIA: Top Terrorist Executed Berg," May 13, 2004.

142  To guarantee his high-value status as the cause of all ills: Thomas E. Ricks, "Military Plays Up Role of Zarqawi," *Washington Post*, April 10, 2006.

142  "[I]t was mentioned every morning": Mark Urban, *Task Force Black: The Explosive True Story of the Secret Special Forces War in Iraq* (New York: St. Martin's Press, 2011), p. 80.

143  again being held in "tiny" dog kennels: Ibid., p. 67.

143  Tellingly, McChrystal, at that time and since, liked to repeat the mantra: e.g., Stanley McChrystal, "It Takes a Network," *Foreign Policy*, February 22, 2011.

143  Arquilla served as a Pentagon adviser: John Arquilla (autobiography), "John Arquilla, Professor and Director," Naval Postgraduate School website, posted September 20, 2011. http://www.nps.edu/About/News/Faculty/NPSExpert/John-Arquilla.html.

144  NSA, under the ambitious command of General Keith Alexander: Ellen Nakashima and Joby Warrick, "For NSA Chief, Terrorist Threat Drives Passion to 'Collect It All,'" Observers Say," *Washington Post*, July 13, 2013.

144  That was where a classified technology developed by NSA: Dr. Christopher Soghoian, American Civil Liberties Union, "Testimony Before the LIBE Committee Inquiry on Electronic Mass Surveillance of EU Citizens," December 18, 2013. https://www.aclu.org/sites/default/files/assets/libe-testimony-csoghoian.pdf.

145  *What resembles "LITTLE BOY"* . . .: Jeremy Scahill and Glenn Greenwald: "The NSA's Role in the U.S. Assassination Program," *The Intercept*, February 10, 2014. https://firstlook.org/theintercept/article/2014/02/10/the-nsas-secret-role/.

146  "It is not enough to have several eyes on a target": M. T. Flynn, et al., "SOF Best Practices," National Defense University, Institute for National Strategic Studies, Fort Lesley J. McNair, Washington, DC, 2008. www.dtic.mil/cgi-bin/GetTRDoc?AD=ADA516799.

146  "industrial counterterrorism": Mark Urban, op. cit., p. 91.

146  Reminiscing years later about happy days at Balad: Stanley McChrystal, *My Share of the Task* (New York: Penguin, 2013), p. 165.

146  apart from discreet references by privileged insiders: e.g., Bob Woodward, "The War Within," CBS News, *60 Minutes*, September 7, 2008.

147  "By hollowing out its midsection": McChrystal, op. cit., p. 162.

147  A leading pioneer had been the mathematician and social scientist Valdis

Krebs: Valdis Krebs, "Case Study: Connecting the 9/11 Hijackers," *War 2.0: National Security and the Science of Networks.* http://national securityzone.org/war2-0/case-studies/september-11-hijackers/.

147 "shaping" the enemy network": Paulo Shakarian, Jeffrey Nielsen, and Anthony N. Johnson, "Shaping Operations to Attack Robust Terror Networks," U.S. Military Academy, 2012.

148 "185 separate Attack the Network efforts": House Committee on Armed Services, Subcommitee on Oversight and Investigations, The Joint Improvised Explosive Defeat Organization, "DoD's Fight Against IEDs Today and Tomorrow," November 2008, p. 23.

148 "The illusion that they fragment": Keith Patrick Dear, "Beheading the Hydra? Does Killing Terrorist or Insurgent Leaders Work?" RAF Department of Defense Studies, 2011. http://www.tandfonline.com/doi/pdf/10 .1080/14702436.2013.845383.

148 U.S. Army Field Manual, FM3-24, published to rapturous public acclaim: U.S. Army/Marine Corps, "Counterinsurgency," Department of the Army, December 2006, pp. 131–32. http://usacac.army.mil/cac2 /Repository/Materials/COIN-FM3-24.pdf.

149 I asked a JSOC veteran who had worked closely with McChrystal in Iraq: Interview, San Francisco, CA, January 2013.

149 At the subsequent press briefing the military displayed a twice-life-size matte photo-portrait: Philip Kennicott, "A Chilling Portrait, Unsuitably Framed," *Washington Post,* June 9, 2006.

149 *Newsweek*, in its cover story: Evan Thomas, "Death of a Terrorist," *Newsweek*, June 19, 2006.

150 Suicide bombers were put to work: Michael Gordon and Bernard Trainor, *The Endgame* (New York: New Pantheon, 2012), pp. 230–31.

## 9 | Killing Effects

151 Built by a Jordanian company, the $200,000 Seeker looked like a helicopter: Daniel Moore et al., "Integrated Air-Ground Operations at the Platoon Level: An Operational Assessment Using Rugged, Low Cost, Fixed-wing Manned Aircraft," IDA Paper P-4054, Institute for Defense Analysis, Washington, DC, August 2005.

153 A strongly worded after-action report: William C. Schneck, "After Action Report Somalia," Countermine Directorate, U.S. Army Belvoir Research, Development and Engineering Center, Ft. Belvoir, VA, p. 27.

153 Called for a Manhattan Project: Rick Atkinson, "Left of Boom," *Washington Post*, September 30, 2007.

154 EDO revenues soared: http://www.faireconomy.org/reports/2006 /ExecutiveExcess2006.pdf.

154 Brandon Bryant, a "stick monkey": Matthew Power, "Confessions of a Drone Warrior," *GQ*, October 23, 2013.

155 In September 2007 the giant defense contractor ITT: Defense Industry Daily Staff, "ITT Corp. Acquires EDO in $1.7B Deal," *Defense Industry Daily*, September 18, 2007.

155 systems such as Compass Call Nova: Colonel Bill Grimes, *History of Big Safari* (Richmond, BC, Canada: Archway Publishing, 2014), p. 288.

155 Rex Rivolo got an invitation to go to Iraq: Interview with Rex Rivolo, Chantilly, VA, December 19, 2013.

159 Stigmergic systems use simple environmental signals: R. Beckers, O. E. Holland, and J. L. Deneubourg, "From Local Actions to Global Tasks: Stigmergy and Collective Robotics," *Artificial Life* 4, 1994, pp. 181–89.

160 (JIEDDO) . . . the new bureaucracy rapidly swelled to more than 3,000 people: Statement of Deputy Secretary of Defense Gordon England Before House Budget Committee 31, July 2007.

161 sniffer dogs . . . and "Fido": Rick Atkinson, "Left of Boom," *Washington Post*, September 30, 2007.

162 Gates writes movingly: Robert Gates, *Duty: Memoirs of a Secretary at War* (New York: Knopf, 2013), pp. 120–24.

162 An exhaustive analysis of the number of killed and wounded: Interview with former Department of Defense official, Washington, DC, April 19, 2013.

163 "On Rigor in Science": Jorge Luis Borges, *A Universal History of Infamy*, trans. by Norman Thomas de Giovanni (London: Penguin, 1975).

163 Constant Hawk, billed $84 million for 2007, while the air force's offering, Angel Fire, received $55 million: "Electronic Weapons: Constant Hawk Versus Angel Fire Deathmatch," Strategy Page, October 12, 2007. https://www.strategypage.com/htmw/htecm/20071012.aspx.

163 "detect any movement of any object as small as a cockroach": Jim DeBrosse, "Gotcha Radar Aims to Help Troops See in Any Conditions," *Dayton Daily News*, August 30, 2009.

163 Defense Secretary Gates, for example, was beguiled by Task Force ODIN's videos: Gates, op. cit., p. 126.

164 "no detectable effect": Interview with Rex Rivolo, Washington, DC, February 10, 2011.

165 May 5, 2006, report on the shooting of Allah Harboni: War diaries, BN HVI KILLED BY 3-187 IVO IVO SAMARRA: 1 AIF KIA, 0 CF INJ/DAMAGE 2006-05-08 02:10:00, Wikileaks. https://wardiaries.wikileaks.org/id/70F15038-6A38-4257-8495-1E09F15B677B/.

165 Be Happy Day as an initiative to raise morale: Interview with former military intelligence officer, Los Angeles, CA, September 19, 2012.

166 "Conclusion: HVI Strategy, our principal strategy in Iraq, is counter-productive": Interview with Rex Rivolo, Washington, DC, February 10, 2011.

167 "When you mow the grass": Interview, Washington, DC, March 19, 2007.

## 10 | A Piece of Junk

168 Billy Mitchell ... bombing and sinking a number of surrendered Ger-men warships: Navy Department Library, "The Naval Bombing Experi-ments, Bombing Operations." http://www.history.navy.mil/library/online/navybomb2.htm. Accessed February 13, 2014.

169 In essence, the DCGS is the repository of the oceans of data: U.S. Air Force Fact Sheet, "Air Force Distributed Common Ground System," August 31, 2009. http://www.af.mil/AboutUs/FactSheets/Display/tabid/224/Article/104525/air-force-distributed-common-ground-system.aspx. Accessed January 30, 2014.

170 Further monies are being garnered: http://www.dtic.mil/descriptivesum/Y2013/AirForce/stamped/0305208F_7_PB_2013.pdf.

170 An admiring air force biographer: Abe Jackson, "America's Airman, David Deptula and the Airpower Moment," School of Advanced Air and Space Studies, Air University, Maxwell Air Force Base, Air University Press, June 2011, p. 53.

170 Deptula's "vision": Ibid., p. 55.

171 "ten minutes of F-16 time": Lieutenant General D. A. Deptula, remarks, Air Force Strategy and Transformation Breakfast, Capitol Hill, Wash-ington, DC, April 27, 2007.

171 Indeed, at this time Deptula was also leading a push: Megan Scully, "Pen-tagon Rejects Air Force Bid to Control UAV Programs," *Government Executive*, September 14, 2007.

171 "an arrangement where one service ..." David Deptula, "Toward Restruc-turing National Security," *Strategic Studies Quarterly*, Air University, October 27, 2007.

172 Among other pungent critiques of the concept ("Assumes a level of unachievable predictability") Mattis pointed out: James N. Mattis, "USJF-COMM Commanders Guidance with Respect to Effects Based Opera-tions," *The U.S. Army War College Quarterly Parameters*, Autumn 2008, p. 20.

174 "our guys are below the general civilian population as far as risk for PTSD": "Combat Stress in Remotely Piloted/UAS Operations," Twenty-First-Century Defense Initiative, Brookings Institute, February 3, 2013.

174 The scale was impressive ... even if the end result was a tsunami: John M. Doyle, "Actionable Intelligence: Getting Accurate Info to Decision

Makers Quickly," Institute for Defense and Government Advancement, June 21, 2013.

175 "I cannot see a situation": Stew Magnuson, "Swimming in Sensors, Drowning in Data," *National Defense*, January 2010.

176 DCGS-A attracts a great deal of well-merited abuse: Robert Draper, "Boondoggle Goes Boom, a Demented Tale of How the Army Actually Does Business," *New Republic*, June 19, 2013.

176 Much of its appeal derives from its ease of use: Telephone interview with CEO of surveillance industry contractor, April 7, 2014.

176 "Palantir works because it's a commercial system, constantly refined": Interview with former Pentagon official, Washington, DC, April 6, 2014.

176 Palantir has expanded its market: Richard Waters, "Counter-terrorism Tools Used to Spot Fraud," *Financial Times*, December 13, 2012.

177 it is indeed "a great system": Email from marine officer then deployed in Afghanistan, March 23, 2013.

177 "They developed and fielded it in a hurry": Interview, Pentagon City, VA, October 3, 2013.

177 Reaper is extremely expensive: Winslow Wheeler, "Revisiting the Reaper Revolution," *Time*'s Battleland defense blog, February 22, 2012. http://nation.time.com/2012/02/27/1-the-reaper-revolution-revisited/; Craig Whitlock, "When Drones Fall from the Sky," *Washington Post*, June 20, 2014.

178 In fact, it carries essentially the same sensors: U.S. Central Command, "Summary of Interview with Captain [name redacted] on April 19, 2011," Report of investigation into friendly fire incident, Upper Sangin, Helmand, April 6, 2011, p. 203.

178 Association of Unmanned Vehicle Systems International: Andrea Stone, "Drone Lobbying Ramps Up Among Industry Manufacturers, Developers," *Huffington Post*, May 25, 2012.

179 Cessna operation yielded at least 6,500 captives: Winslow Wheeler, "Finding the Right Targets," *Time*'s Battleland defense blog, February 29, 2012. http://nation.time.com/2012/02/29/3-finding-the-right-targets/.

179 "Northrop took billions and billions of dollars off us, and gave us a piece of junk": Interview with senior Pentagon acquisition official, Pentagon City, VA, February 7, 2013.

179 A best-selling 2009 book on drones: Peter Singer, *Wired for War, The Robotics Revolution and Conflict in the 21st Century* (New York: Penguin, 2009), p. 230.

180 "Junk is right": Interview, Arlington, VA, November 6, 2013.

180 Global Hawk stays on the ground: Aram Roston, "The Battle over Global Hawk," *Defense News*, July 15, 2013.

181 By 2012, even the air force had had enough: Richard Sia and Alexander Cohen, "The Huge Drone That Could Not Be Grounded," Center for Public Integrity, September 24, 2013. http://www.publicintegrity.org /2013/07/16/12969/huge-drone-could-not-be-grounded.

181 In recognition of his stellar performance: The Hill Staff, "Top Lobbyists 2013," *The Hill*, October 30, 2013.

181 On February 24, 2014, Defense Secretary Chuck Hagel announced a series of stringent cuts: U.S. Department of Defense, Press Operations, "Remarks by Secretary Hagel and General Dempsey on the fiscal year 2015 budget preview in the Pentagon Briefing Room." http://www.defense.gov/Tran scripts/Transcript.aspx?TranscriptID=5377.

182 a "revolutionary airborne surveillance system": Ellen Nakashima and Craig Whitlock, "With Gorgon Stare, 'We Can See Everything,'" *Washington Post*, January 2, 2011.

182 "Instead of looking at a truck or a house . . .": Richard Whittle, "Newest Afghanistan Surveillance System," InvestorsHub, January 1, 2011. http:// investorshub.advfn.com/boards/read_msg.aspx?message_id=58320282.

182 That October, the U.S. Geospatial Intelligence Foundation: Sierra Nevada Corporation, "SNC-led Gorgon Stare Team Wins US GeoInt Foundation 2011 Industry Award," Press Release, October 18, 2011.

183 "very powerful in the [Afghan] battle space": Lieutenant General Larry James, "The Service Chiefs Speak," 2012 U.S. GeoInt Symposium, GeoInt TV. http://geointv.com/archive/geoint-2012-panel-the-intelligence-chiefs/.

183 "The combatant commanders love it": Caitlin Lee, "Gorgon Stare Wide Area Sensor Proving Effective in Afghanistan," *Jane's Defense Weekly*, May 1, 2013.

183 Earlier, *Air Force Times*: Michael Hoffman, "New Reaper Sensors Offer a Bigger Picture," *Air Force Times*, February 16, 2011.

183 Civil libertarians, no less impressed: Glenn Greenwald, "Domestic Drones and Their Unique Dangers," *theguardian.com*. Accessed March 29, 2013.

183 "rewind the tapes": Richard Whittle, "Newest Afghanistan Surveillance System" InvestorsHub, January 1, 2011. http://investorshub.advfn.com /boards/read_msg.aspx?message_id=58320282.

183 Gorgon Stare didn't work: Department of the Air Force, 203 West D Avenue, Suite 609, Eglin Air Force Base, Florida, "Memorandum to USAFWC/ CC from 53 WG/CC, Subject: MQ9 Gorgon Stare Fielding Requirements," December 31, 2010.

185 "moderate-resolution": Senate Committee on Armed Services, National Defense Authorization Act for Fiscal Year 2010, p. 84. http://www.dtic .mil/congressional_budget/pdfs/FY2010_pdfs/SASC_111-35.pdf.

186  For example, in 2004 they hired Dawn Gibbons: Jeff German and J. Patrick Coolican, "More Questions Raised About Gibbons," *Las Vegas Sun*, March 31, 2007.

186  A 2010 Congressional Ethics Office report: Eric Lichtblau and David C. Kirkpatrick, "Panel Clears 7 Lawmakers in Lobbying Scandal," *New York Times*, February 27, 2010.

187  Following his retirement, Meermans embarked on a second career: Richard Whittle, "Predator's Big Safari," op. cit., p. 11.

187  Given Meermans' subsequent third career as vice president for strategic planning: Linkedin profile page, "Mike Meermans, VP for Strategic Planning at Sierra Nevada Corporation." https://www.linkedin.com/pub/mike-meermans/7/349/ab7. Accessed July 26, 2014.

187  "so close they share rubbers": Aram Roston, "The Colonel and His Labyrinth," Vocativ, www.vocativ.com. http://www.vocativ.com/usa/nat-sec/colonel-labyrinth/. Accessed October 30, 2013.

187  The pilot . . . was blind in one eye: Aram Roston: "A Secret Mission, a One-Eyed Pilot, and a Fiery Crash in Colombia, Vocativ, www.vocativ.com. Accessed December 16, 2013.

## 11 | Death by a Number

189  Petraeus told reporters that special forces operations in Afghanistan were "at absolutely the highest operational tempo": Viola Gienger, "Petraeus Says Afghan Raids on Rebels Exceed Iraq," *Bloomberg News*, September 3, 2010.

190  "Petraeus knew he was only going to be there a short time": Interview with former ISAF adviser, Washington, DC, April 13, 2014.

190  The renewed emphasis on high-value targeting in Afghanistan: Gareth Porter, "How McChrystal and Petraeus Built an Indiscriminate Killing Machine," *Truthout*, September 26, 2011.

191  Apart from his Taliban leadership status: Gienger, op. cit.

191  which in this period was Task Force 373: Nick Davies, "Afghan War Logs, Task Force 373, Special Ops Hunting Top Taliban," *The Guardian*, July 25, 2010.

191  "mowing the grass": Interview with former U.S. civilian adviser, Afghanistan, Washington, DC, December 9, 2012.

191  "targets to eliminate": U.S. Army Counterinsurgency Field Manual FM3-24, ch. 5, p. 106.

191  specialties such as leader, facilitator: Felix Kuehn and Alex Strick van Linschoten, "A Knock on the Door: 22 Months of ISAF Press Releases," Afghanistan Analysts Network, Kabul, October 12, 2011.

192  NSA recorded every single conversation and stored them for five years:

Wikileaks, "Statement on the Mass Recording of Afghan Phone Calls by NSA," May 23, 2014.

192 turning a blind eye: Gareth Porter, "How McChrystal and Petraeus Built an Indiscriminate 'Killing Machine,'" *Truthout*, September 26, 2013.

192 in 2009 they launched a campaign to destroy the system: Frances Robinson, "Fewer Cell Towers Shut Down in Afghanistan," *Wall Street Journal*, February 28, 2013.

193 IMSI Catcher: For a good explanation of the technology, see Amicus Brief filed by Electronic Privacy Information Center in *New Jersey v. Earls*, December 20, 2012, p. 17. http://epic.org/amicus/location/earls/EPIC -Supplemental-Amicus-Brief.pdf.

194 A little after 9:00 a.m., as the first two vehicles moved out of one of these narrow passes: The story of the Takhar attack is taken from journalist Kate Clark's incisive account: Kate Clark, "The Takhar Attack," AAN Thematic Report, Afghanistan Analysts Network, Kabul, May 2011, pp. 20–24. http://www.afghanistan-analysts.org/wpcontent/uploads /downloads/2012/10/20110511KClark_Takhar-attack_final.pdf.

195 That same day, ISAF issued a press release: ISAF News, "Coalition Forces Conduct Precision Strike Against Senior IMU Member in Takhar Province," ISAF Joint Command, Afghanistan 2010-09-CA-027, September 2, 2010.

195 "I can confirm that a very senior official": Christopher Bodeen, "NATO Airstrike Killed Civilians According to Afghan President," *Christian Science Monitor*, September 3, 2010.

195 "for a better future": WGBH Boston, "Kill Capture," PBS *Frontline*, May 10, 2011.

195 The dead, campaign volunteers all: Kate Clark, op. cit., p. 17.

196 Clark was perfectly aware that the high-tech assassins had murdered the wrong man: Telephone interview with Clark, Kabul, March 6, 2014.

196 "They hung me from the ceiling": Kate Clark, op. cit., p. 15.

197 "We're aware of the allegations": ISAF press release, op. cit.

198 "We had days and days of what's called 'the unblinking eye'": WGBH Boston, op. cit.

198 "He basically ordered the Special Forces to be frank with me": Telephone interview with Kate Clark, March 6, 2014.

199 "targeting the telephones": Clark, op. cit., p. 13.

199 getting himself expelled from Afghanistan: Alastair Leithead, "'Great Game' or Just Misunderstanding?" BBC News, January 5, 2008.

199 "I am well known": Clark, "Takhar Attack," op. cit., p. 17.

200 "gray area insurgent": Michael Semple, "Caught in the Crossfire," Foreign Policy.com, May 16, 2011.

200 "I did come to the conclusion": Telephone interview with Michael Semple, March 19, 2014.

200 "On September 2, coalition forces did kill the targeted individual, Mohammed Amin": Quil Lawrence, "Afghan Raids Common but What if Targets Are Wrong?" NPR *Morning Edition*, May 12, 2011.

201 A-10 pilots had refused orders to bomb the same target: Andrew Cockburn, "Tunnel Vision," *Harper's*, January 2014.

202 many Afghans "have a few Taliban commander numbers saved in their mobile phone contacts": Telephone interview with Michael Semple, March 19, 2014.

202 The whole complex effort: Pamphlet #4, "Doctrinal Implications of Operational Net Assessment," February 24, 2004.

203 Marine Major General Richard Mills evoked a bucolic note: U.S. Marine Corps History Division: Oral History Interview–Field Report: Interviewee Major General Richard P. Mills, Institute for the Study of War, May 2, 2011, p. 8.

203 In August 2008, the United States had obligingly bombed a family memorial service in Azizabad: Robert Dreyfus, "Mass Casualty Attacks in Afghanistan," *The Nation*, September 19, 2013.

203 In an infamous February 2010 incident in Gardez: Jeremy Scahill, *Dirty Wars* (New York: Nationbooks, 2013), pp. 334–43.

203 The May 2012 B-1 strike in Paktia Province: Interview with Colonel Robert Brown, USAF, November 22, 2013.

203 "The bottom line is we have been played like pawns": Email, March 23, 2014.

204 One measure of the cost to the overall U.S. war effort: Gareth Porter, "Doubling of SOF Night Raids Backfired in Kandahar," Inter Press Service, September 15, 2010.

204 In a series of media interviews in August 2010: Ibid.

204 Leaving aside the number of innocent civilians represented in those figures: Felix Kuehn and Alex Strick van Linschoten, "A Knock on the Door: 22 Months of ISAF Press Releases," Afghanistan Analysts Network, Kabul, October 12, 2011.

205 seventeen commanders had been killed: Antonio Gustozzi and Christopher Reuter, "The Insurgents of the Afghan North," Afghanistan Analysts Network, Kabul, April 2011, p. 29.

205 Squadron Leader Keith Dear: Keith Patrick Dear, "Beheading the Hydra: Does Killing Terrorist or Insurgent Leaders Work?" RAF Department of Defense Studies, August 2011, p. 22.

205 They were also younger: Ibid., p. 22.

206 "We want to die anyway": WGBH Boston, "Kill Capture," op. cit.

206 A marine officer who served two tours in the lethally dangerous

neighborhood of Sangin: Interview with marine officer, Jacksonville, NC, December 2, 2012.

207 making the Taliban *even more cruel*: Alex Strick van Linschoten, "Entropy and Insurgent Radicalisation: An ISAF Goal?" A Different Place (blog), December 7, 2011. http://www.alexstrick.com/2011/12/entropy -and-insurgent-radicalisation-an-isaf-goal/.

207 Three of the victims were children: Rod Nordland and Habib Zahori, "Killing of Afghan Journalist and Family Members Stuns Media Peers," *New York Times*, March 26, 2014.

209 "It just shows you": Email, March 14, 2014.

209 The Taliban, said Lavoy, were making significant gains: U.S. State Department Cable, "Allies find briefing on Afghanistan NIE 'Gloomy' but focus on recommendations to improve situation," Secret—NOFORN, December 5, 2008: Wikileaks, Public Library of U.S. Diplomacy. http://www .wikileaks.org/plusd/cables/08USNATO453_a.html.

209 "I simply doubt our ability": Email from Matthew Hoh, April 3, 2014.

210 "I have yet to see one of those out here": Email, April 9, 2014.

## 12 | Drones, Baby, Drones!

211 The Richard M. Helms Award dinner: CIA Officers Memorial Foundation: "Richard M. Helms Award Dinner 2011," *Compass* (no. 1), undated.

211 Joining them were senior executives of various defense corporations: Recollection of attendees at dinner.

211 "the CIA gets what it wants": Daniel Klaidman, *Kill or Capture: The War on Terror and the Soul of the Obama Presidency* (New York: Houghton Mifflin–Harcourt, 2012), p. 121.

212 At just under $15 billion: Barton Gellman and Greg Miller, "'Black Budget' Summary Details U.S. Spy Networks' Successes, Failures, and Objectives," *Washington Post*, August 29, 2013.

212 "those bastards": Communication from the late Colonel Richard M. Hallock, who had many discussions with Helms on this topic when the latter was ambassador to Iran.

213 "all-consuming ambition": Interview with former CIA official Ray McGovern (the supervisor in question), Arlington, VA, January 9, 2014.

213 On one occasion, notorious within the community: Aram Roston, "Obama's Counterterror Czar Gave Bogus Intel to Bush White House," *C4ISR Journal*, October 1, 2012.

214 Exiting government service in 2005: Aram Roston, "Intel Firm Paid CIA Nominee Well as He Left for White House," *Defense News*, February 4, 2013.

214 "finishing Brennan's sentences": Daniel Klaidman, op. cit., p. 23.

214 "You know, our president has his brutal side": Interview with former CIA official, Washington, DC, April 13, 2011.

215 After paying due tribute to previous honorees: Interview with attendee at dinner, April 6, 2011.

215 As is the custom in Pashtun culture: Kathy Gannon, "Timing of U.S. Drone Strike Questioned," AP Exclusive, August 2, 2011.

216 Although the ominous buzz of drones was always in the air: Akbar Ahmed, *The Thistle and the Drone* (New York: HarperCollins, 2013), p. 85.

216 However, the land in question: Gannon, op. cit.

216 In Lahore, a burly American named Raymond Davis: Mark Mazzetti, *The Way of the Knife* (New York: Penguin, 2013), p. 264.

217 The man they selected to kill: Ahmed, op. cit., p. 82.

217 "The CIA was angry": Gannon, op. cit.

217 After all, it was an established point of drone-strike doctrine: Jo Becker and Scott Shane, "Secret 'Kill List' Proves a Test of Obama's Principles and Will," *New York Times*, May 29, 2012.

217 Finally, sometime after 10:00 a.m.: International Human Rights and Conflict Resolution Clinic at Stanford Law School and Global Justice Clinic at NYU School of Law, "Living Under Drones; Death, Injury and Trauma to Civilians from U.S. Drone Practices in Pakistan" (2012), p. 59. http://livingunderdrones.org/report/.

218 "The smell was awful.": Ben Emmerson, UNSRCT Drone Inquiry, "Interview with witness #3," Case Study #1: Datta Khel, March 14, 2014. http://vimeo.com/79102292.

218 The country's foreign office called it: Manzoor Ali, "Pakistan Furious as U.S. Drone Strike Kills Civilians," *Express Tribune*, March 18, 2011.

218 "in a manner consistent...": Sebastian Abbott, "New Light on Drone War's Death Toll," *AP Impact*, February 26, 2012.

218 "These guys were terrorists": Tom Wright and Rehmat Mehsud, "Pakistan Slams U.S. Drone Strike," *Wall Street Journal*, March 18, 2011.

219 A separate probe by the Associated Press: Abbott, op. cit.

219 Although the positions held by the dead men were now of course vacant: Stanford and NYU Law Schools, op. cit., p. 60.

219 When presented with the tool of a Hellfire-armed Predator: Steve Simon and Dan Benjamin, *Age of Sacred Terror* (New York: Random House, 2002), p. 345.

220 Soon, visiting dignitaries: Mazzetti, op. cit., p. 6.

220 In 2004, when the CIA sought Pakistani permission to launch drone strikes: Mazzetti, op. cit., p. 103ff.

221 Nor was the tally of high-value targets impressive: Bill Roggio, "Senior al-Qaeda and Taliban leaders killed in US airstrikes in Pakistan," *Long

*War Journal*, 2004–2013. http://www.longwarjournal.org/pakistan -strikes-hvts.php#ixzz2yiEkZAY0.

221 "completely done by the Pakistani military": *New York Times,* October 30, 2006.

221 "It is something that we have done": "Bajaur Operation Not under Any Pressure: FO," Dawn.com, October 31, 2006.

221 police barracks: Ahmed, op. cit., p. 81.

221 "Is Cofer some sort of vampire?": Interview with former senior CIA official, Washington, DC, March 27, 2014.

222 "I've had a lot of run-ins with the CIA": Interview with former State Department official, Washington, DC, April 25, 2014.

223 By 2011 the Counterterrorism Center accounted for 10 percent: Greg Miller and Julie Tate, "CIA Shifts Focus to Killing Targets," *Washington Post,* September 1, 2011.

223 "We're not thinking about bloodthirsty butchers": Interview with former CIA official, Washington, DC, April 16, 2014.

224 "They were coming at us": Eric Schmitt and Thom Shanker, *Counterstrike* (New York: Times Books, 2012), p. 101.

225 Interestingly, these bellicose remarks were guided by Richard Clarke: Klaidman, op. cit., p. 18.

225 "We did nothing": Columbia School of Law, Human Rights Clinic and Center for Civilians in Conflict, *The Civilian Impact of Drones— Unexamined Costs, Unanswered Questions,* p. 21.

225 Afterward, when Hayden and Kappes explained the concept of a signature strike: Daniel Klaidman, "Drones: The Silent Killers," *Newsweek,* May 28, 2012.

226 According to a rare outside observer: David Rhode, "The Drone War," *Reuters* magazine, January 26, 2012.

226 "We do not come out of our villages": NYU and Stanford Schools of Law, op. cit., p. 96.

227 The sole survivor of Obama's first strike: Ibid., p. 74ff.

228 "We got played all the time": Interview with former CIA official, Washington, DC, April 16, 2014.

228 Naturally, the Pakistani government was happy: Ahmed, op. cit., p. 73.

229 As related in Joby Warrick's gripping account: Joby Warrick, *The Triple Agent: The al-Qaeda Mole Who Infiltrated the CIA* (New York: Doubleday, 2011).

229 In reality the driver of the car: Ibid., p. 86.

230 In fact, given reports that the rival Mehsud and Wazir tribes: Azhar Masood, "Pakistani Tribesmen Settle Scores Through US Drones," *Arab News,* May 24, 2011.

230 ISI . . . were supplying the targeting information: Patrick Cockburn,

"Revenger's Tragedy: The Forgotten Conflict in Pakistan," *Independent*, May 10, 2010.

231 Ahmed Wali Karzai: Wikileaks, "Ahmed Wali Karzai Seeking to Define Himself as US Partner," February 25, 2010. https://wikileaks.org/cable /2010/02/10KABUL693.html.

232 "very precise precision strikes": David Jackson, "Obama Defends Drone Strikes," State Department Cable, *USA Today*, January 31, 2012.

232 Defense Secretary Leon Panetta echoed the sentiment: U.S. Department of Defense, Press Operations, "Remarks by Secretary Panetta at the Center for a New American Security," November 20, 2012.

232 John Brennan insisted: Scott Shane, "C.I.A. Is Disputed on Civilian Toll in Drone Strikes," *New York Times*, August 11, 2011.

232 "Drones were a cheap, politically painless way of dealing with that": Interview with Cameron Munter, ambassador to Pakistan from 2010 to 2012, Washington, DC, April 24, 2012.

232 John Brennan did like to put a "strategic" gloss on the undertaking: Interview with former White House official, Washington, DC, April 22, 2014.

232 Despite Brennan's theorizing about table legs: Jonathan Landay, "Obama's Drone War Kills 'Others,' Not Just al-Qaida Leaders," *McClatchy Newspapers*, April 9, 2013.

233 By 2012, for example, the CIA had clearance: Greg Miller, "White House approves broader Yemen Drone Campaign," *Washington Post*, April 25, 2012.

233 So near neighbors might not know: NYU and Stanford Schools of Law, op. cit., p. 5.

233 "The drone campaign only makes sense": Interview, Washington, DC, April 12, 2014.

234 "truly disturbing": Bureau of Investigative Journalism, "Reported U.S. covert actions 2001–2011," *Yemen Times*, March 29, 2012.

234 Edmund Hull: Wikileaks, U.S. State Department Cable, "Ambassador's 4/10 Meeting with Amnesty." https://wikileaks.org/cable/2004/04 /04SANAA860.html.

235 He has also laid claims: *Yemen Times*, April 13, 2008.

236 Saleh, who was distrustful of banks: Interview with Sana'a former government official, January 2011.

236 When he had first seized power in a 1978 coup: The winning ticket was claimed by the late Selma al-Radi, whose knowledge of Yemen was unmatched.

236 Well-informed political sources in Sana'a: Interview with Sana'a former government official, January 2011.

237 "They were supposed to have used forks": Interview with Sana'a former government official, January 2011.

237 CIA built a special base in Saudi Arabia: *Foxnews.com*, "Obama Administration Building New Drone Bases in Horn of Africa, Saudi Arabia," September 21, 2011. http://www.foxnews.com/politics/2011/09/21/obama -administration-building-new-drone-bases-in-horn-africa-saudi /#ixzz38jrJi5Gw.

237 Jaber was also a business partnership of a Saleh relative: Interview Sana'a former government official, January 2011.

238 "How could this happen?" Klaidman, *Kill Capture*, op. cit., p. 255.

238 Brennan, meanwhile, was "pissed": Adam Enthous, "U.S. Doubts Intelligence That Led to Yemen Strike," *Wall Street Journal*, December 29, 2011.

238 This mistargeted killing had more far-reaching consequences: Jeb Bone, "Drone Wars, Attacks Fuel Anger in Yemen," *Global Post*, October 10, 2011. http://www.globalpost.com/dispatch/news/regions/middle-east /111007/drone-warsyemen-unrest-protests-aqap-al-qaeda.

239 "no one has asked us": Ghaith Abdul-Ahad, "Shabwa: Blood Feuds and Hospitality in al-Qaida's Yemen Outpost," *The Guardian*, August 23, 2010.

239 "slapdash pastiche": The Editorial Board, "A Thin Rationale for Drone Killings," *New York Times*, June 23, 2014.

239 Israeli Supreme Court: *The Public Committee Against Torture in Israel* v. *The Government of Israel*, HCJ 769/02, December 13, 2006.

239 However, as revealed by Anat Kamm: Noa Yachot, "Timeline—The Anat Kamm Affair," *+972 Magazine*, October 29, 2011.

240 "The regime decided to hand over this territory": Interview with Abdul-Ghani al-Iryani, "Yemenis Celebrate as Saleh Flees," *Democracy Now*, June 6, 2011.

240 Al-Qaeda member Hamid al-Radmi, for example: Human Rights Watch, "Between a Drone and Al-Qaeda, Pt. 2, Wessab, Strike on Alleged Local AQAP Leader," October 22, 2013, p. 7. http://www.hrw.org/node/119909 /section/7.

240 Adnan al-Qadhi, a colonel: Ibid.

240 "They could have picked him up any time": Telephone interview, January 25, 2014.

240 Inevitably, collateral victims accumulated: Human Rights Watch, op. cit.

241 This document stated clearly and unequivocally: Office of the Press Secretary, "Fact Sheet: U.S. Policy Standards and Procedures for the Use of Force in Counterterrorism Operations Outside the United States and Areas of Active Hostilities," White House, May 23, 2014. http://www .whitehouse.gov/the-press-office/2013/05/23/fact-sheet-us-policy -standards-and-procedures-use-force-counterterrorism.

241 Over fifteen days in the summer of 2013: Eric Schmidt, "Embassies Open but Yemen Stays on Terror Watch," *New York Times*, August 11, 2013.

242 "Turns out I'm really good at killing people": John Heilemann and Mark Halperin, *Double Down: Game Change 2012* (New York: Penguin Press, 2013), p. 55.

242 In April 2014, Western media took notice: Barbara Starr, "Unsettling Video Shows Large al-Qaeda Meeting in Yemen," CNN, April 16, 2014.

242 Reports from Sana'a indicated: Adam Baron, "U.S. Drone Strikes Came Despite Yemen's Hopes to Limit Them," *McClatchy New Service*, April 21, 2014.

### 13 | One Big Robot

244 "We want to be everywhere, know everything": Melanie D. G. Kaplan "JSOC Commander Outlines Intel Demands," *Trajectory Magazine*, U.S. Geospatial Intelligence Foundation, April 17, 2014. http://trajectorymaga zine.com/got-geoint/item/1721-jsoc-commander-outlines-intel-demands .html (video of speech embedded).

245 Operating in at least 134 countries: Admiral William H. McRaven, Posture Statement to the House Armed Services Committee, February 27, 2014.

245 From a mere $2.3 billion in 2001: U.S. Special Operations Command, "FY 2015, Budget Highlights," pp. 5–6. http://www.socom.mil/News/Docu ments/USSOCOM_FY_2013_Budget_Highlights.pdf.

245 and was looking for $9.9 billion: Andrew Feickert, "U.S. Special Opera- tions Forces, Background and Issues for Congress," Congressional Research Service, May 8, 2014.

245 "They have professional lighting engineers for the displays": Interview with House Appropriations Committee staffer, Washington, DC, March 28, 2014.

245 "When SEAL Team 6 operators are sent on 'training' missions to Alaska": Rowan Scarborough, "Obama Runs Special Forces into the Ground," *Washington Times*, March 11, 2014.

245 Nevertheless, there was little sign: Matt Cox, "Congress Wants More Con- trol of Special Ops Iron Man Suit," *Defense Technology*, April 29, 2014. http://defensetech.org/2014/04/29/congress-wants-more-control-of -special-ops-iron-man-suit/.

246 with a slick, expensive gamelike video: Sidney Freedberg Jr., "SOCOM Wants YOU to Help Build High-tech 'Iron Man' Armor," *Breaking Defense*, October 21, 2013. http://breakingdefense.com/2013/10/socom -wants-you-to-help-build-high-tech-iron-man-armor/.

246 Among other items on a Special Operations wish list: Mark Thompson, "Check Out This New Wish List for U.S. Special Ops," *Time*, April 28, 2014.

246 Conducted in conjunction with the CIA: Dana Priest, "Covert Action in Colombia," *Washington Post*, December 31, 2013.

246 Mono Jojoy, for example: Ariel Avila, "Who Is Mauricio, the Man Directing Farc's Negotiations?" *Semana* (Bogotá), August 28, 2012.

247 Paul Reyes, a senior leader killed: Garry Leech, "The Significance of the Deaths of the FARC Leaders," *Colombia Journal*, March 10, 2008. http://colombiajournal.org/the-significance-of-the-deaths-of-the-farc -leaders-2.htm.

247 "They've had two ceasefires in recent years and made them stick": Telephone interview, May 6, 2014.

247 In May 2014, in seeming rejection of long-standing U.S. policy: Sara Schaefer Muñoz and Juan Forero, "Colombia Agrees with Rebels to Jointly Fight Trafficking," *Wall Street Journal*, May 16, 2014.

247 Notwithstanding the claimed victory in Colombia: Janet Hook, "Americans Want to Pull Back from World Affairs, Poll Finds," *Wall Street Journal*, April 30, 2014.

248 Three days after this speech: Patrick Galey, Jack Serle, and Alice K. Ross, "Drone Strikes in Yemen: Bloodiest US and Yemeni Attacks in Two Years Kill at Least 40 People," Bureau of Investigative Journalism, April 22, 2014.

248 "Dear America": Tweet from Farea al-Muslimi, May 3, 2014. https://twitter .com/almuslimi/status/462465907085029376.

248 "tsunami": Tweet from Farea al-Muslimi, April 21, 2014. https://twitter .com/almuslimi/status/458376151556423680.

248 a detailed Human Rights Watch on-the-ground investigation: Human Rights Watch, "A Wedding That Became a Funeral," February 19, 2014. http://www.hrw.org/reports/2014/02/19/wedding-became-funeral.

248 Officials shown the drone-feed video: Kimberly Dozier, "Report: U.S. Drone Strike May Have Killed Up to a Dozen Civilians in Yemen," Associated Press, February 20, 2014.

249 However, in an implicit reminder: Michael Isikoff, "U.S. Investigates Yemenis' Charge That Drone Strike Turned Wedding into a Funeral," NBCnews.com, January 7, 2014.

249 Meanwhile a convenient leak suggested: Ken Dilanian, "Debate Grows over Proposal for CIA to Turn Over Drones to Pentagon," *Los Angeles Times*, May 11, 2014.

250 Fifteen years earlier: George W. Bush: "A Period of Consequences," speech delivered at The Citadel, Charleston, SC, September 23, 1999.

250 In 2012, Barack Obama, in a speech at the Pentagon: President Barack H. Obama, "Defense Strategic Guidance Briefing from the Pentagon," Press Operations, U.S. Department of Defense, January 5, 2012.

251 "devastating blows": Dominique Pastre, "Biden Says Terror Leaders' Deaths Significant Blow to Al Qaeda," Foxnews.com, April 19, 2010.

251 At the end of the Bush tenure: Nick Turse, "America's Secret War in 134 Countries, Huffington Post, January 16, 2014.

251 Djibouti indeed was the centerpiece: Eric Schmidt, "U.S. Signs New Lease to Keep Strategic Military Installation in the Horn of Africa," *New York Times*, May 5, 2014.

251 The camp, home to the JSOC drones: Nick Turse, "The Next Generation of Shadow Wars: America's Military-Industrial Complex Is Expanding," *Salon*, April 14, 2014.

251 Even less visibly, the U.S. Air Force was maintaining: Joe Trevithick, "The Pentagon Plans for More Drones in More Places," Medium.com/War-Is-Boring, April 14, 2014.

252 As of 2014 the air force planned to have 346 of these: Inside Defense.com, "Air Force to Acquire Fleet of 346 Reapers by FY-21, 55 Fewer Than Planned," March 6, 2014.

252 of which more than 80 would likely be under CIA control: Aram Roston, "Targeted Killing: CIA's Fleet of 80+ UAVs Unlikely to Be Transferred to Military," *Defense News*, May 15, 2013.

252 a new acronym entered military jargon: Air-Sea Battle Office, "Air Sea Battle, Service Collaboration to Address Anti-Access & Area Denial Issues," Department of Defense, May 2013. http://www.defense.gov/pubs /ASB-ConceptImplementation-Summary-May-2013.pdf.

253 Thanks to Predator and Reaper: The Federal Procurement Data System has provided the following report on the top 100 defense contractors in 2013: FY https://www.fpds.gov/downloads/top_requests/Top_100_Con tractors_Report_Fiscal_Year_2013.xls. Accessed July 30, 2014.

253 For the twelve Reapers the air force planned to buy: InsideDefense.com, March 6, 2014.

253 Boeing's F/A-18 "Growler" electronic warfare plane: Fiscal Year (FY) 2013 President's Budget Submission: Navy Justification Book, Vol. 1: Aircraft Procurement, Navy Budget Activities 1–4, pp. 1–15.

253 while Lockheed was happily extracting $106 million for the C-130J trans-port plane: U.S. Department of Defense, "Selected Acquisition Report (SAR) Summary Tables As of December 31, 2013."

254 So in 2013 the U.S. Navy: Government Accountability Office, "Navy Strategy for Unmanned Carrier-Based Aircraft System Defers Key Oversight Mechanisms," GAO-13-833, September 26, 2013.

254 That feat was ultimately accomplished: "X-47 Makes Successful Launch," *Defense News*, May 14, 2013.

255 Already, a single Global Hawk drone: GlobalSecurity.org, "Satellite Bandwidth." http://www.globalsecurity.org/space/systems/bandwidth .htm.

256 In 2009, Shia insurgents in Iraq: Barry Watts, "The Maturing Revolution

in Military Affairs," Center for Strategic and Budgetary Assessments (2011), p. 17.

256 GPS signals . . . equivalent of a car headlight: Paul Marks, "TV and Radio Signals Take Over when GPS Goes Wrong," *New Scientist* blog, June 29, 2012.

256 As an Iranian engineer explained: Scott Peterson, "Exclusive: Iran Hijacked US Drone, Says Iranian Engineer," *Christian Science Monitor*, December 15, 2011.

256 Despite energetic attempts by U.S. officials: David Axe, "Did Iran Capture a US drone Intact?" DangerRoom, *Wired*, December 4, 2011.

257 Todd Humphreys: Cyrus Fariver, "Professor Fools $80M Superyacht's GPS Receiver on the High Seas," *ars technica*, July 30, 2013.

257 Nevertheless, the supposed imminence: Daniel Suarez: "The Kill Decision Shouldn't Belong to a Robot," *TED Global*, June 2013.

257 In November 2012, Human Rights Watch: "Advancing the Debate on Killer Robots," Human Rights Watch, May 2014.

257 "an absolute must": Stew Magnuson, "Military 'Swimming in Sensors and Drowning in Data,'" *National Defense*, January 2010.

257 The Office of Naval Research has even funded: Sebastian Anthony, "U.S. Military Begins Research into Moral, Ethical Robots," *Extreme Technology*, May 9, 2014.

257 An experiment involving two small drones: Peter Finn, "A Future for Drones: Automated Killing," *Washington Post*, September 19, 2011.

258 According to an al-Qaeda tip sheet, "Revealed: al-Qaeda's 22 Tips for Dodging Drones," *Daily Telegraph*, February 22, 2013.

258 But it has become clearer: Hubert L. Dreyfus, *What Computers Still Can't Do* (Boston: MIT Press, 1992); Tao Ruspoli, "Being in the World," Mangusta Films, 2011. http://beingintheworldmovie.com/.

259 "We kept decapitating the leadership of these groups": James Kitfield, "Flynn's Last Interview: Iconoclast Departs DIA With a Warning," Breaking Defense, August 7, 2014. http://breakingdefense.com/2014/08/flynns-last-interview-intel-iconoclast-departs-dia-with-a-warning. Accessed August 9, 2014.

259 Among the recipients: Bryan Bender, "Air War in ISIS Fight Gets Guidance from Cape," *Boston Globe*, September 26, 2014.

259 As David Deptula promised: Aaron Mehta, "Experts: As Operation Continues, ISR Demand to Grow in Syria," *Defense News*, September 29, 2014.

259 Wall Street analysts hailed the prospect: Tony Newmayer, "The War on ISIS Already Has a Winner: The Defense Industry," *Fortune*, September 13, 2014.

**Afterword to the 2016 Edition**

261 Buddy-lasing: David Axe, "Drones Take Over America's War on Isis," *The Daily Beast,* June 17, 2015.

262 "The level of centralized execution": Personal communication, published http://harpers.org/blog/2015/03/war-by-remote/. Accessed July 8, 2015.

262 Obama: https://www.whitehouse.gov/blog/2014/08/18/president-obama -provides-update-latest-iraq-and-ferguson-missouri. Accessed July 9, 2015.

262 Cheater: David Axe, "Drones Take Over America's War on Isis," *The Daily Beast,* June 17, 2015.

263 "More than 10,000" http://america.aljazeera.com/articles/2015/6/3/us -coalition-haskilled-10000-isil-fighters.html. Accessed June 25, 2015.

263 "6,000 kills" Julian Barnes, "U.S., Iraq, Prepare Offensive to Retake Mosul from Islamic State," *The Wall Street Journal,* January 22, 2015.

263 Saudis avoid hitting Al Qaeda: http://harpers.org/blog/2015/06/before -the-war/. Accessed July 9, 2015.

263 Micro-UAVs: Inside the Air Force, June 26, 2015.

263 Sea Mob: Department of Defense, FY-2016 Budget Request, Vol 3, p.496.

263 CICADA: http://phys.org/news/2015-05-cicadas-military-swarm-mini -drones.html. Accessed July 8, 2015.

# ACKNOWLEDGMENTS

This book has been made possible by the insights and advice of many people. To name them all would be impossible, and, in the case of some, unwise. However, I must express heartfelt thanks to my agent, Anna Stein, for her unfailing encouragement and support, and to my editor, Serena Jones, who grasped the idea of this book immediately and thereafter provided a deft editorial touch and sound advice. Ellen Rosenbush and James Marcus at *Harper's* magazine kindly allowed their Washington editor to disappear for several months. Noga Malkin and Michael Smallberg provided invaluable research at the shortest notice. Danijel Zezelj has my gratitude and admiration not only for the brilliance of his illustrations but the speed with which they were produced. Most of all, I thank Leslie Cockburn, once again my surest guide, supporter, and friend.

# INDEX